IMAGES
*of America*

# PONTE VEDRA BEACH

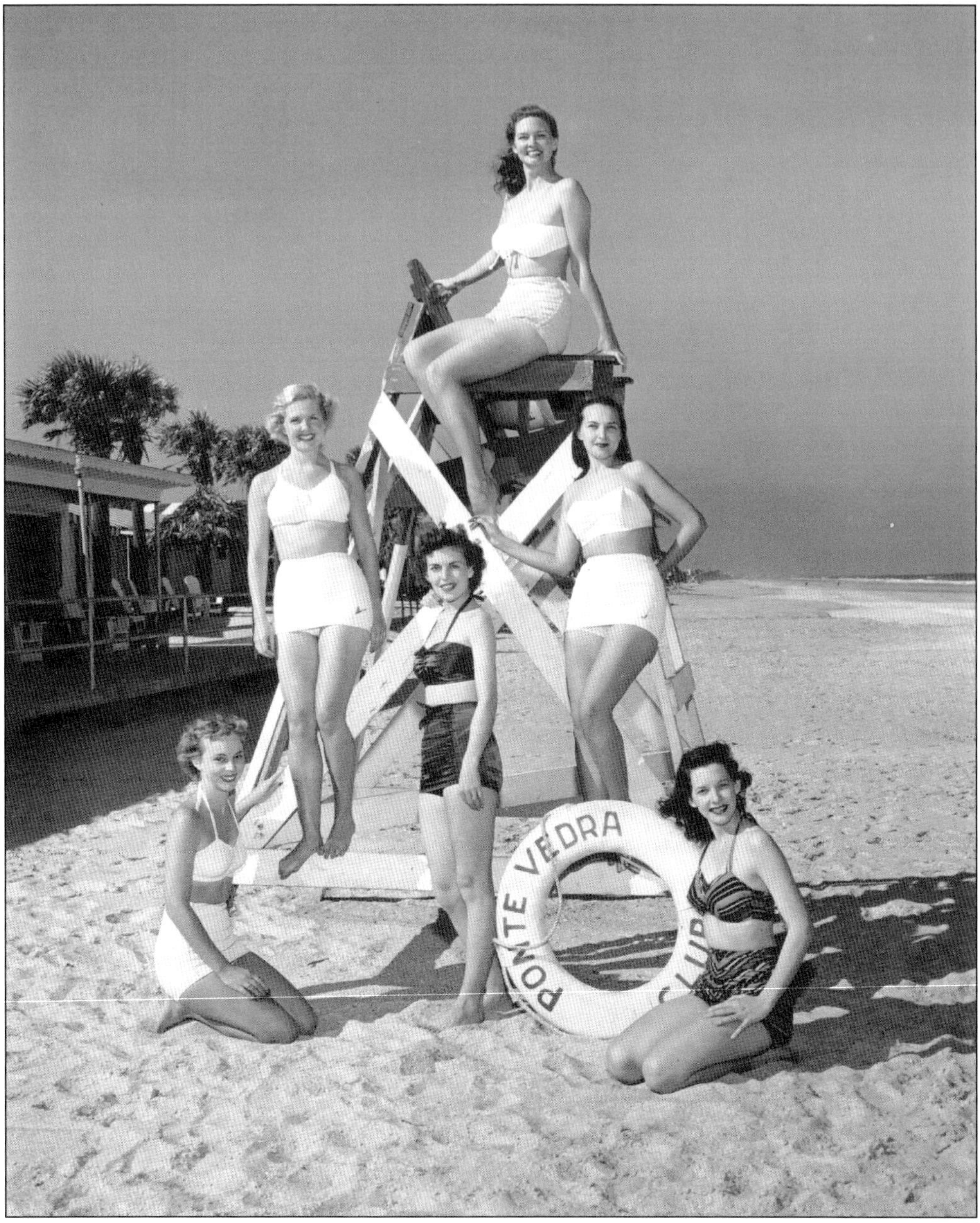


Bathing beauties pose for a glamour shot at the Ponte Vedra Club in 1950. The seaside town of Ponte Vedra Beach developed around the upscale club resort on the Atlantic Ocean in the northeast corner of St. Johns County, Florida. When it opened in the late 1920s, the resort began attracting visitors from around the country, who came to enjoy its wide white beaches, golf courses, tennis courts, and social soirées. Delighted by the warm, sunny climate and beautiful landscape, dotted with palm trees and flowers, many decided to stay and make Ponte Vedra Beach their home. (Beaches Museum & History Park.)

**ON THE COVER:** Men and women dance on the patio of the Surf Club at the Ponte Vedra Club in the late 1940s. The photograph was taken by longtime Jacksonville Beach photographer Virgil Deane. (Beaches Museum & History Park.)

IMAGES
*of America*

# PONTE VEDRA BEACH

Maggie FitzRoy and
Beaches Museum & History Park

ISBN 978-0-7385-9182-7

Published by Arcadia Publishing
Charleston, South Carolina

Printed in the United States of America

Library of Congress Control Number: 2011943541

For all general information, please contact Arcadia Publishing:
Telephone 843-853-2070
Fax 843-853-0044
E-mail sales@arcadiapublishing.com
For customer service and orders:
Toll-Free 1-888-313-2665

Visit us on the Internet at www.arcadiapublishing.com

*This book is dedicated to the memory of Virgil Deane and other talented photographers who captured the history of the Ponte Vedra Beach area.*

# Contents

# ACKNOWLEDGMENTS

The Beaches Area Historical Society houses thousands of historical photographs in the archives of its Beaches Museum & History Park at 381 Beach Boulevard in Jacksonville Beach, Florida. Many of these photographs document the fascinating history of the town of Ponte Vedra Beach, and this book would not have been possible without them.

With the help of a dedicated group of volunteers, historical society archivist Taryn Rodriguez-Boette organizes, files, and digitally scans images that are donated to the museum from a variety of sources. Volunteer Phyllis Haeseler spent countless hours filing and scanning the original images for this book, along with the help of volunteers Jane Alexander, Kathy Mays, Linda Oberdorfer, Mary Ann Kapke, and Ron Lunde. Maggie FitzRoy has lived in Ponte Vedra Beach since 1991. She is a journalist, a photojournalist, and an editor and has been writing about and photographing the Ponte Vedra Beach and Jacksonville Beaches area since 1998.

Many of the photographs were the work of a popular and successful photographer named Virgil Deane, who for several decades operated his business from an office in Jacksonville Beach.

Deane, who moved to the area in the mid-20th century, took pictures of many people, places, and events in the Jacksonville Beaches area, including Ponte Vedra Beach. His widow donated thousands of photographs and negatives from his 46-year career to the historical society after his death in 1999.

Many of the images in this book from the 1940s on are the work of Deane, and this visual history of Ponte Vedra Beach benefits greatly from his work. But countless other unidentified photographers also contributed to this book, which would not have been possible if they had not been on the scene with their cameras.

In addition, local historians have worked hard to research and record the history of Ponte Vedra Beach, and their work contributed greatly to the text. They include Maurice Robinson, author of *Ponte Vedra Beach, a History*; Neil McGuinness, author of *The Beaches, A History and Tour*; and Elaine Koehl, author of *The Ponte Vedra Club, the First 55 Years*.

All images that appear in this book are courtesy of the Beaches Museum & History Park.

# INTRODUCTION

Ponte Vedra Beach's history is colorful, action packed, and multifaceted. It is a place that many types of people have called home, all valuing the land for different reasons.

For thousands of years, Timucua Indians fished in its waters and hunted in the woods and swamps. Living in round huts with palm-thatched roofs, they planted maize, squash, and beans, and celebrated life with festivals and dances.

In April 1513, when Spanish explorer Juan Ponce de León discovered the land he called Pascua de Florida ("Feast of Flowers"), he and his crew first came ashore on a beach that historians believe was in the area of present-day Ponte Vedra Beach.

Spanish missionaries soon followed, as did soldiers and farmers. From 1565, when they founded the city of St. Augustine, the Spanish also began settling the Ponte Vedra Beach area to the north. They built missions along the coast to convert the Timucua Indians to Christianity and raised cattle in the land they called Diego Plains, now known as Palm Valley.

When Florida was transferred to England, English-speaking settlers moved in from 1763 to 1783, transforming the area into large plantations specializing in indigo and rice, where hundreds of enslaved Africans labored in the sun.

After Florida was returned to Spain, the plantations were carved into small farms and ranches. Then, in the early 1900s, years after Florida became part of the United States, minerals were discovered in the sand on the area's beaches, and the beaches were transformed into a mining operation. Titanium and other minerals mined there became important for making weapons in World War I. The small town that sprang up around a few houses, a commissary, and a post office was named Mineral City.

After the war, mining operations waned, so developers began creating a wealthy community around a golf course, an inn, and a few oceanfront homes. They called it Ponte Vedra Beach.

Just west in Palm Valley, some residents who lived in and around the woods and marshes near the Intracoastal Waterway found a way beyond farming and fishing to make a living after Prohibition began in 1921. They set up homemade stills to make whiskey, constantly striving to hide their activities from the local law.

In the mid-1930s, the area began attracting well-to-do people from around the country, who came to live on or near the beach and join the growing Ponte Vedra Club, known for its inn, golf course, and tennis courts.

World War II temporarily halted the growing community's development. But Ponte Vedra Beach was the scene of a visit by four German saboteurs during that time. In 1942, the Nazi invaders snuck ashore from a submarine off the coast and buried explosives in the sand on an empty beach. They planned to dig them up later and use them to blow up important sites around the country. Dressed in bathing suits, the four men blended into the beach scene for a short time. They were later caught after a member of the mission turned himself in to authorities. The FBI dug up their explosives, and they were found guilty in court and executed.

After the war, the area grew rapidly. Sawgrass Country Club was created, as was Sawgrass Tournament Club, Marsh Landing, and many other communities.

The PGA Tour moved its national golf headquarters to Ponte Vedra Beach, and the ATP Tour moved its national tennis headquarters there.

Thousands of people visit Ponte Vedra Beach every year for The Players Championship, held at the TPC Sawgrass Stadium Course. And many visitors who come for golf or the beach decide they want to live in the beautiful town of about 35,000 residents.

Today, the unincorporated oceanfront community in northeast Florida with the zip code 32082 is a pristine, upscale community of manicured neighborhoods and gated communities, valued for its beaches, golf courses, tennis courses, great schools, and beauty.

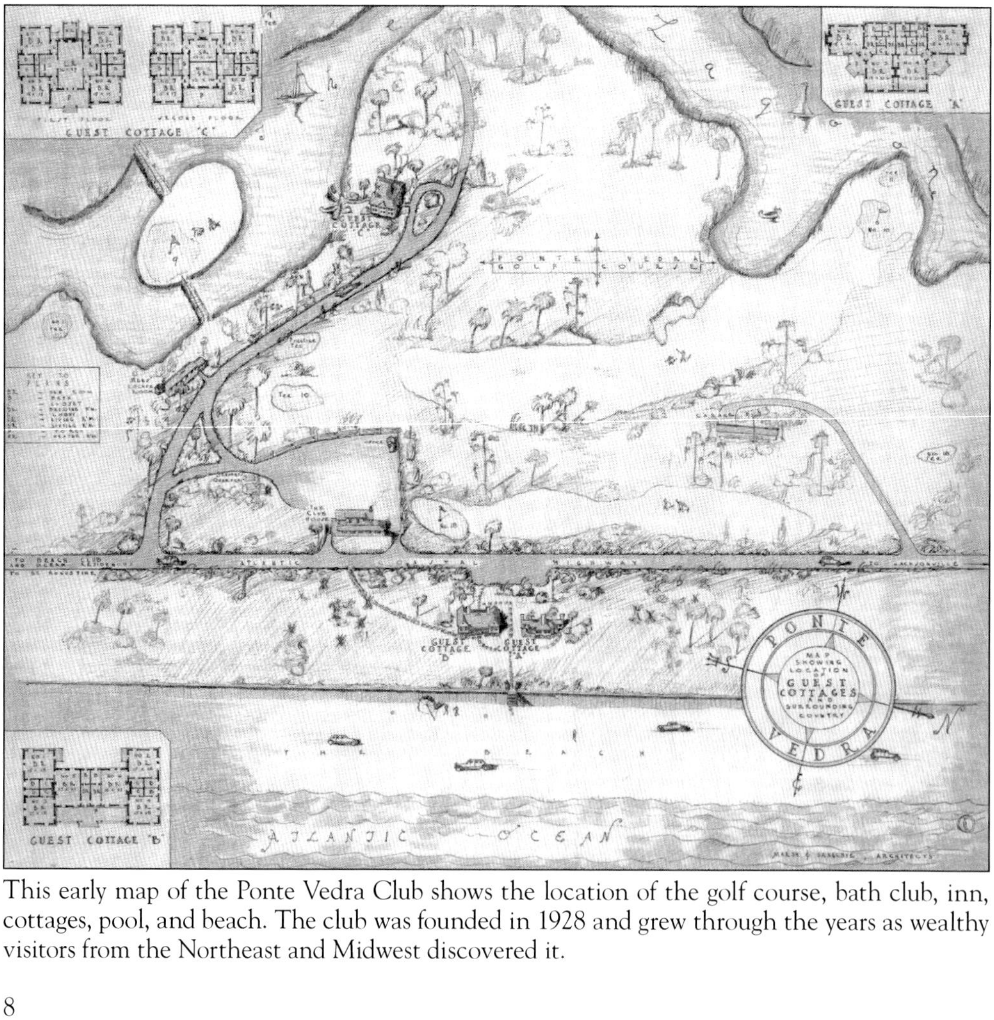


This early map of the Ponte Vedra Club shows the location of the golf course, bath club, inn, cottages, pool, and beach. The club was founded in 1928 and grew through the years as wealthy visitors from the Northeast and Midwest discovered it.

# *One*

# Mineral City

Few people lived in the area that would become Ponte Vedra Beach at the beginning of the 20th century.

To the north, the Duval County town of Pablo Beach, which would later become Jacksonville Beach, was attracting tourists, who flocked to its grand oceanfront resorts by train. Tourists also visited the city of St. Augustine to the south, which was founded in 1565 and well established. The northeast corner of St. Johns County, however, which lay along the Atlantic coast and stretched west to the Intracoastal Waterway, was mostly filled with a lot of empty beaches and sand dunes, wild woods, and alligators.

Then, in 1912, mining engineers George Anson Pritchard and Henry Holland Buckman discovered a rich vein of rare and valuable minerals in the sand on the beaches. They set up a mining operation on the beach using mules to haul sand over the dunes to a mill, where workers separated out the minerals.

The titanium, rutile, and zircon they extracted were needed to make weapons during World War I, and the Sand Plant grew, especially after Pritchard and Buckman formed a partnership with the National Lead Company of Pittsburgh.

They named the small town that grew around the mining plant Mineral City, and Pritchard became its first postmaster. His son Allen was the first child born there in 1920. The Pritchard and Buckman families and the workers and their families were the town's only residents. They bought their groceries at the town's commissary. Since there were no roads, people had to travel along the beach at low tide.

After the war, the minerals were used in a variety of products, including steel, paint, linoleum, dyes, porcelain, and automobile tires and sparkplugs. In the early 1920s, the National Lead Company created a nine-hole golf course for its employees, as well as a log cabin clubhouse that also served as an inn.

Through that decade, the market for the minerals slowly declined, so in 1928 the mining company hired the Telfair Stockton Company, a major Jacksonville land developer, to sell oceanside real estate around the golf course and inn.

In order to attract wealthy visitors and residents, the town needed a new name. Someone saw the name of a town in Spain called Pontevedra mentioned in a newspaper and suggested it to area leaders. So, in 1928, Mineral City became Ponte Vedra Beach.

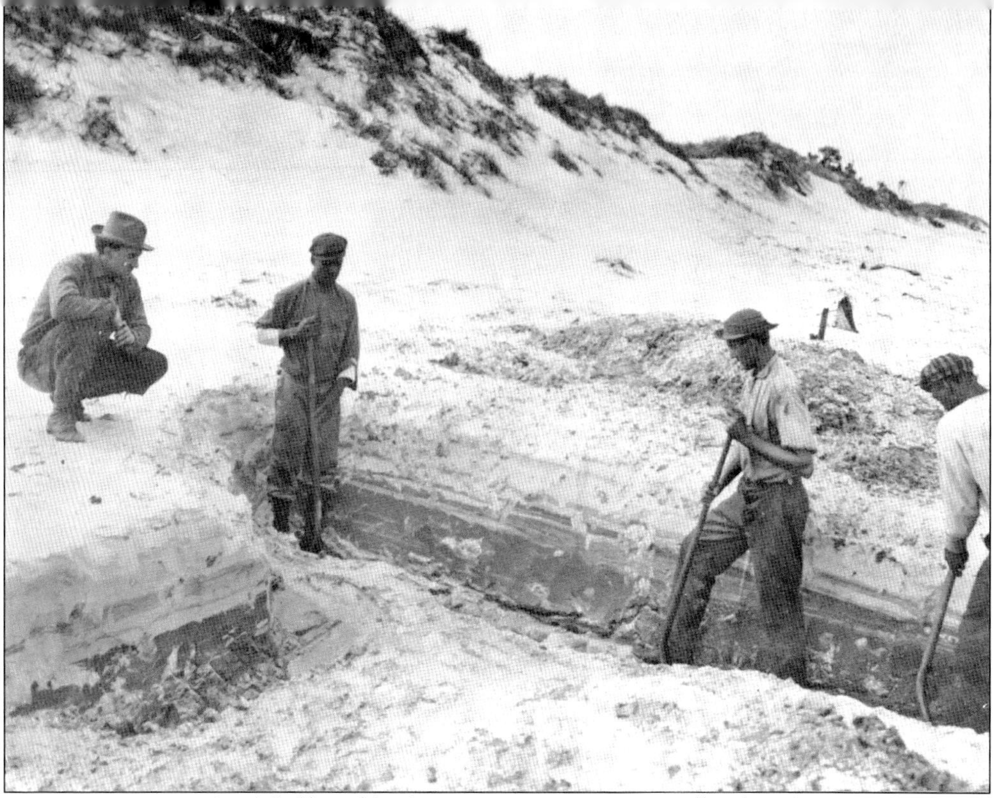

George Anson Pritchard (left) and his business partner Henry Holland Buckman dig a test pit on the beach in Mineral City (later named Ponte Vedra Beach) in 1914. The men, both mining engineers, discovered that the area's beaches contained many valuable minerals that could be used in a variety of industrial products. With that knowledge, they purchased beach land and set up the Buckman and Pritchard Sand Plant mining operation on the beach, just over the dunes.

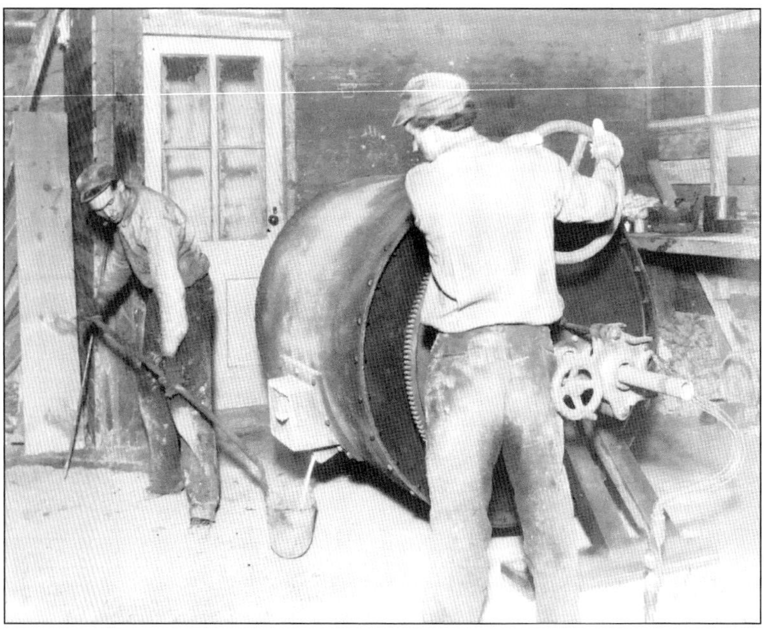

Mining engineers Buckman (left) and Pritchard work inside their Sand Plant processing center in 1914 in Mineral City. The men invented a method using gravity to separate valuable minerals out of the area's beach sand. With the help of a crew of workers and mules, they mined ilmenite (also called titanium), rutile, and zircon.

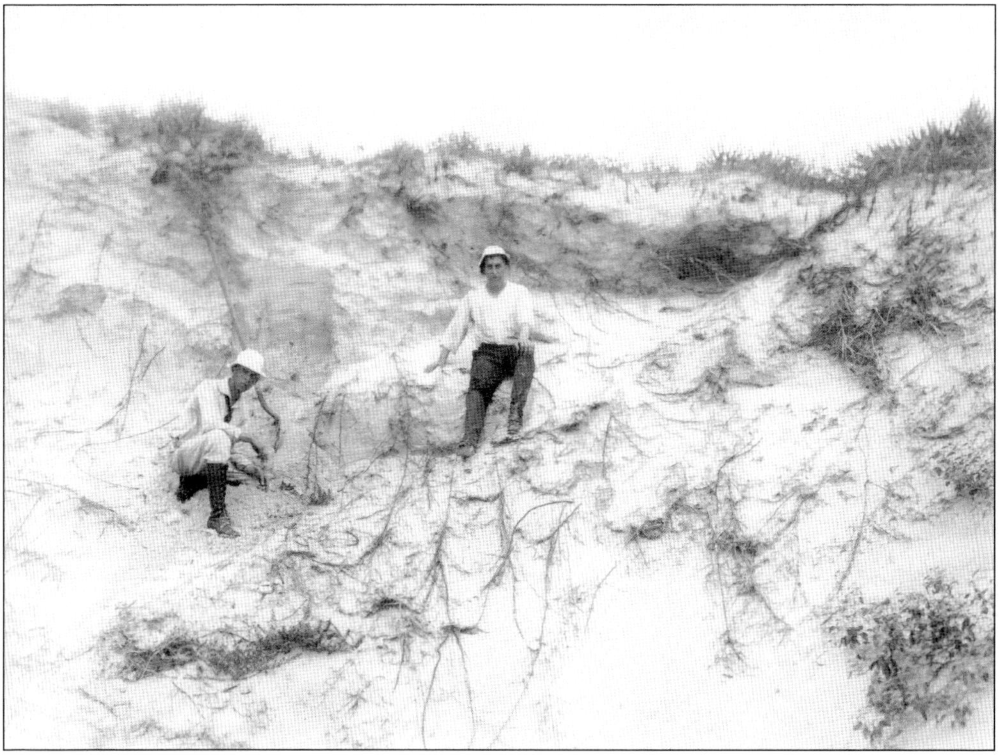

Buckman (left) and Pritchard rest on a dune in Mineral City in 1915 while prospecting for minerals in the area. At the time, that area of northeast St. Johns County was mostly wilderness, a landscape of wide-open beaches, sand dunes, palmettos, marshes, and woodlands.

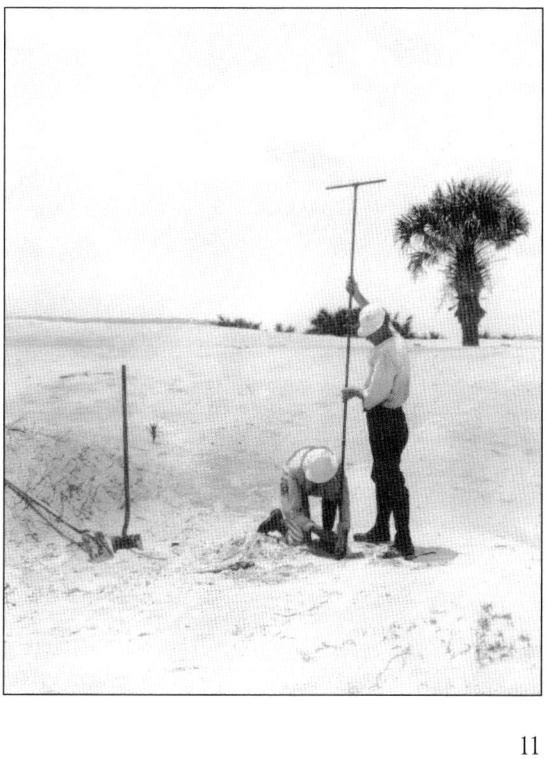

Kneeling, mining engineer Buckman prospects for minerals on a beach in Mineral City with business partner Pritchard in 1915. Pritchard was a self-trained engineer who met Buckman and went into business with him in 1911 in Indiana. Buckman was from a wealthy Jacksonville, Florida, family. After graduating from Harvard College, he studied industrial engineering in Germany.

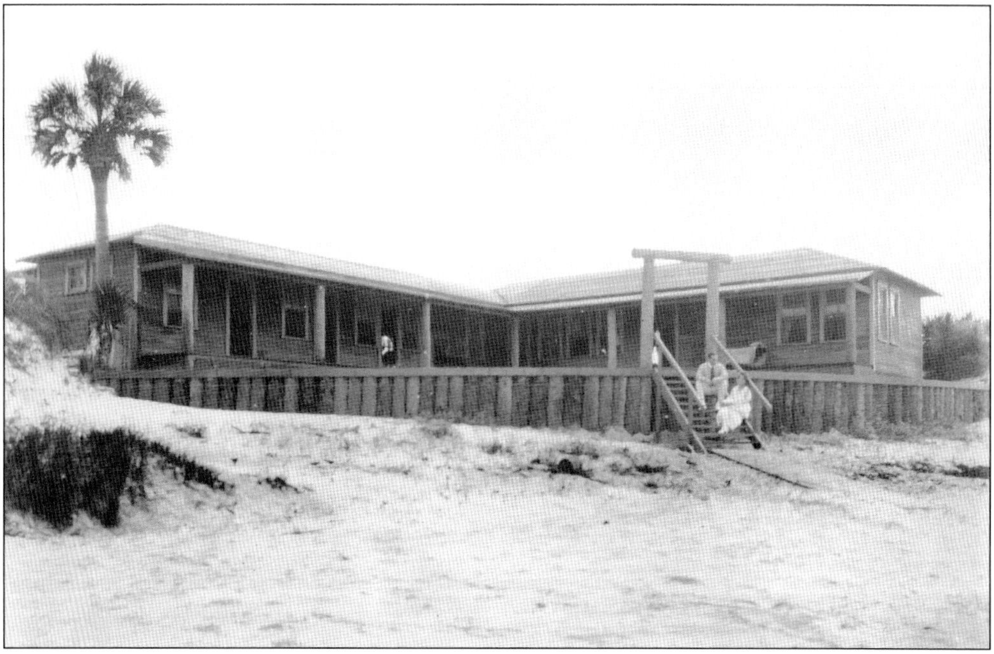

Mining engineer George Pritchard and his wife, Nelle, sit on the steps of their oceanfront home Bonnie Dune in 1917. Their home was one of the first to be built in the town of Mineral City, close to where Pritchard and Buckman operated Mineral Sand Plant. It was located about 150 feet north of the present-day Ponte Vedra Inn and Club.

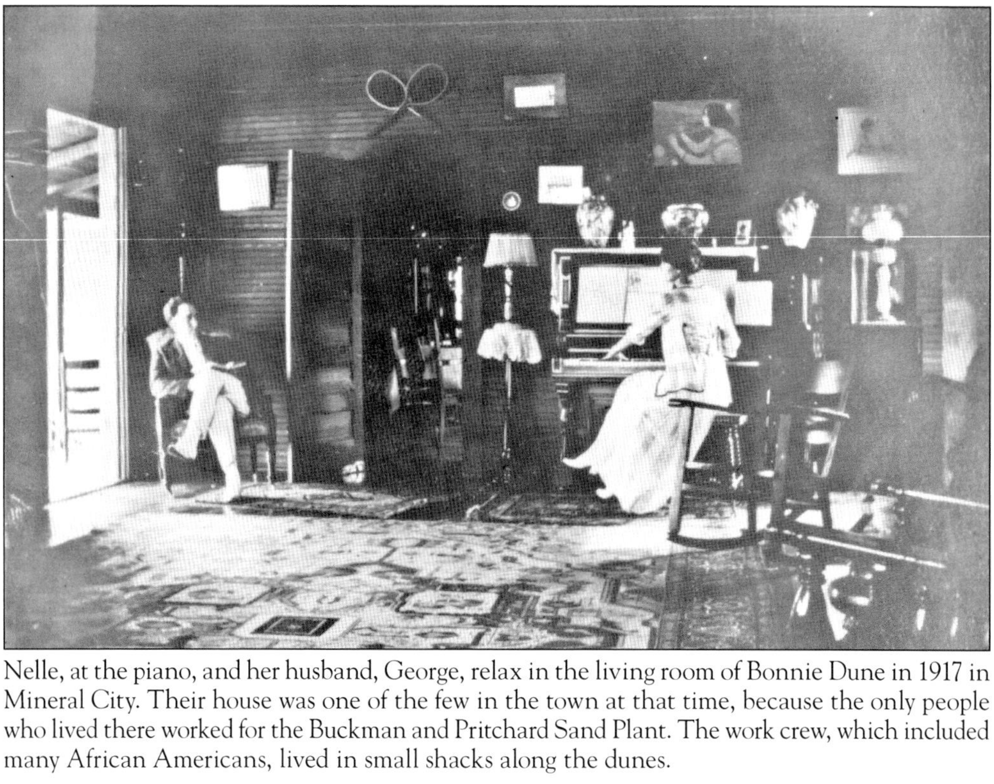

Nelle, at the piano, and her husband, George, relax in the living room of Bonnie Dune in 1917 in Mineral City. Their house was one of the few in the town at that time, because the only people who lived there worked for the Buckman and Pritchard Sand Plant. The work crew, which included many African Americans, lived in small shacks along the dunes.

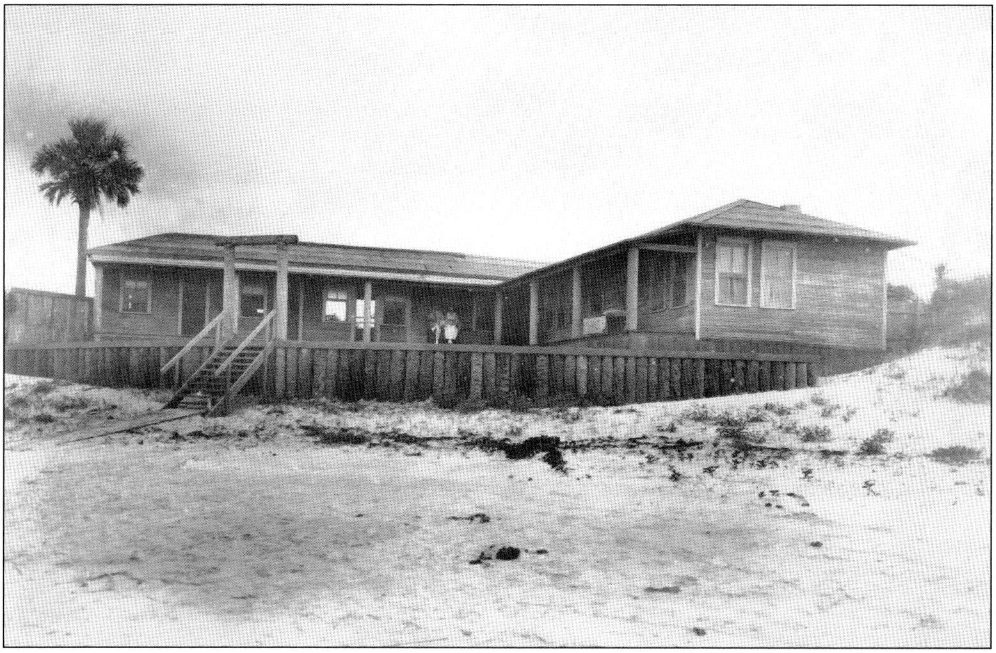

When George and Nelle built their home Bonnie Dune, they became the first family to live in Mineral City. When George and Buckman began prospecting for minerals in the beach sand in that area, they roomed at a boardinghouse in the town of Pablo Beach, later named Jacksonville Beach, over the St. Johns County/Duval County line.

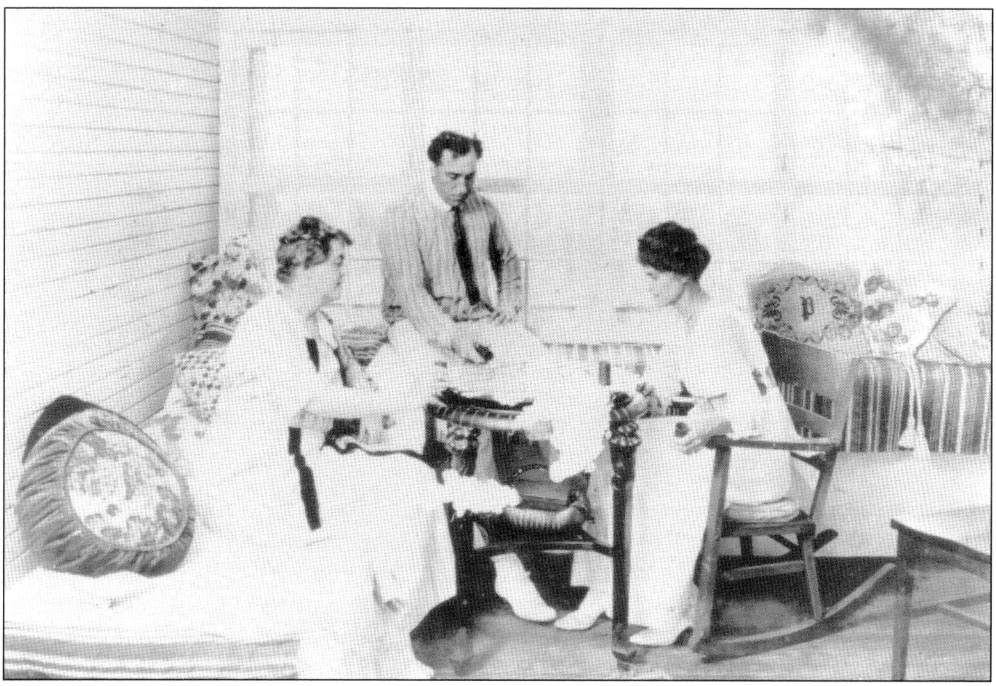

Nelle (right), her husband, George, and her sister Clare Wales Belt play a board game on the sun porch of Bonnie Dune in 1918. Mineral City residents lived in an isolated area, where the only road in and out was the beach at low tide and the only store was the Sand Plant commissary.

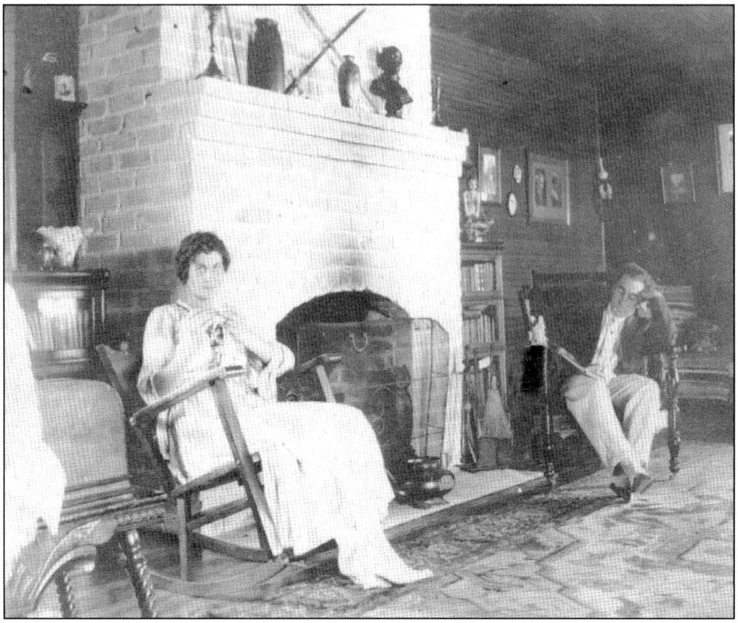

Nelle and George Pritchard pose for a photograph in their Mineral City home Bonnie Dune in 1919. Their son Allen was the first child born in Mineral City in 1920. Allen's older sister Patricia was born in New York, and when Allen and Patricia were growing up, they were among the few children living in the area. Patricia later lived in Ponte Vedra Beach as an adult and enjoyed talking about her childhood days.

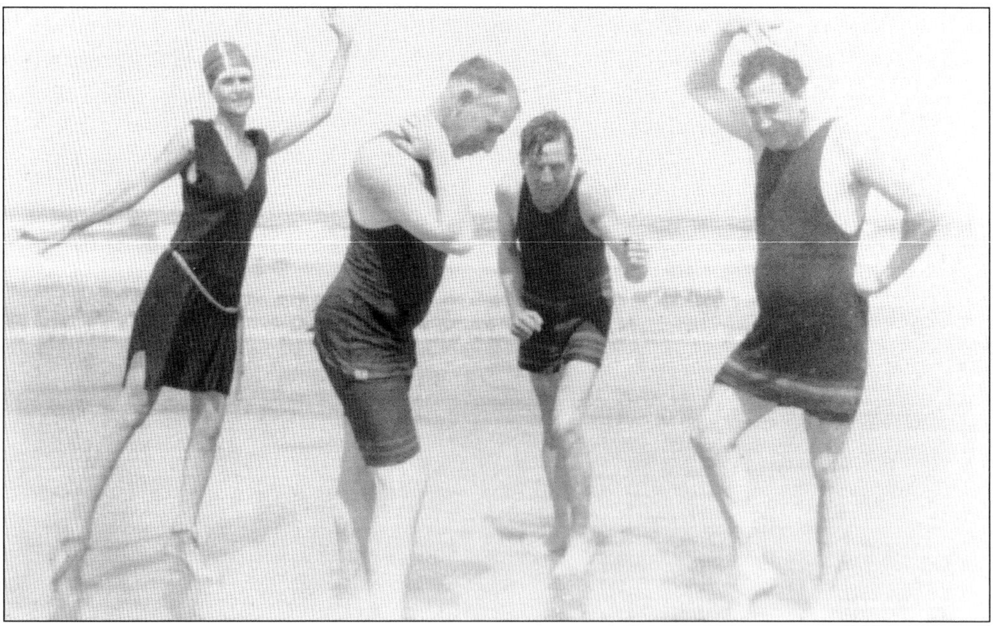

From left to right, Nelle Pritchard, John Straughn, Walter Phillips, and George Pritchard clown around in their bathing suits at the edge of the ocean in Mineral City in 1919. Since the Sand Plant workers were the only residents in the area, they had the beach to themselves. Photographs of the time indicate they enjoyed the beach as a place to have fun in the sun, as well as a place to work.

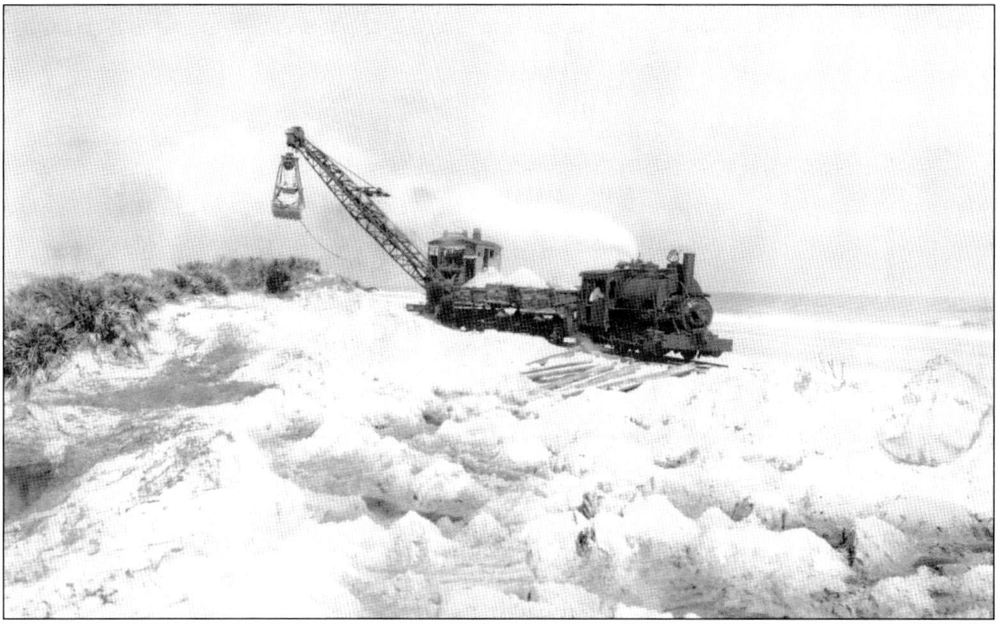

A train sits on a track that runs through dunes by the Buckman and Pritchard Sand Plant in Mineral City in 1919. The company used the railroad track to transport the minerals processed from the beach sand. A logging company that operated in the area had previously built the track between Pablo Beach and Palm Valley. When George Pritchard and Henry Buckman moved there, the track had been abandoned.

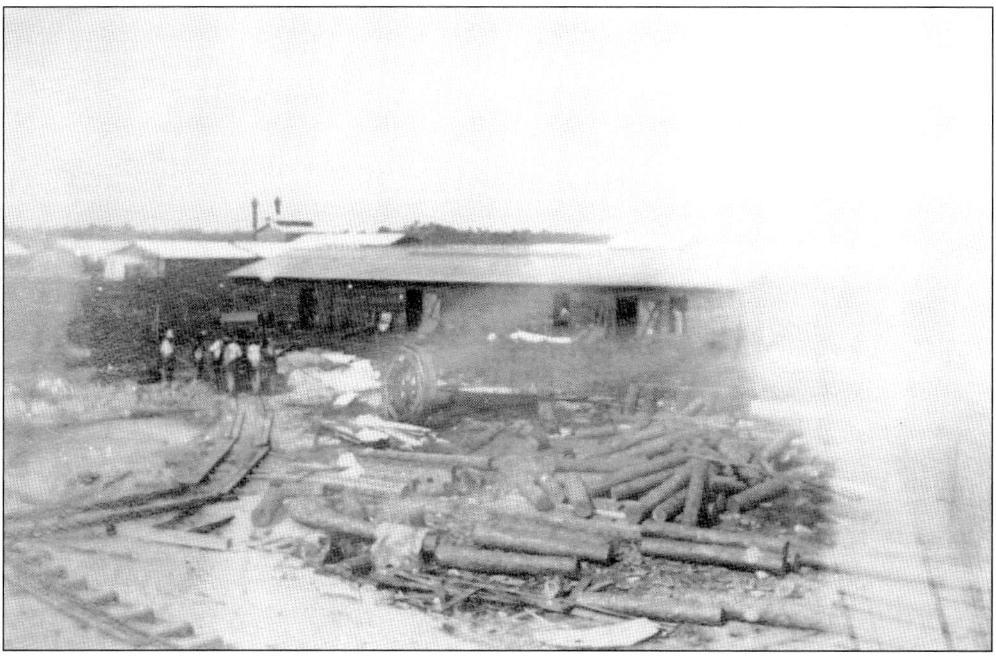

The Buckman and Pritchard Sand Plant was located at the northern end of St. Johns County because the engineers discovered that area of land had the greatest concentration of the types of minerals they were searching for. They purchased 18 miles of beach between Pablo Beach to the north and St. Augustine to the south.

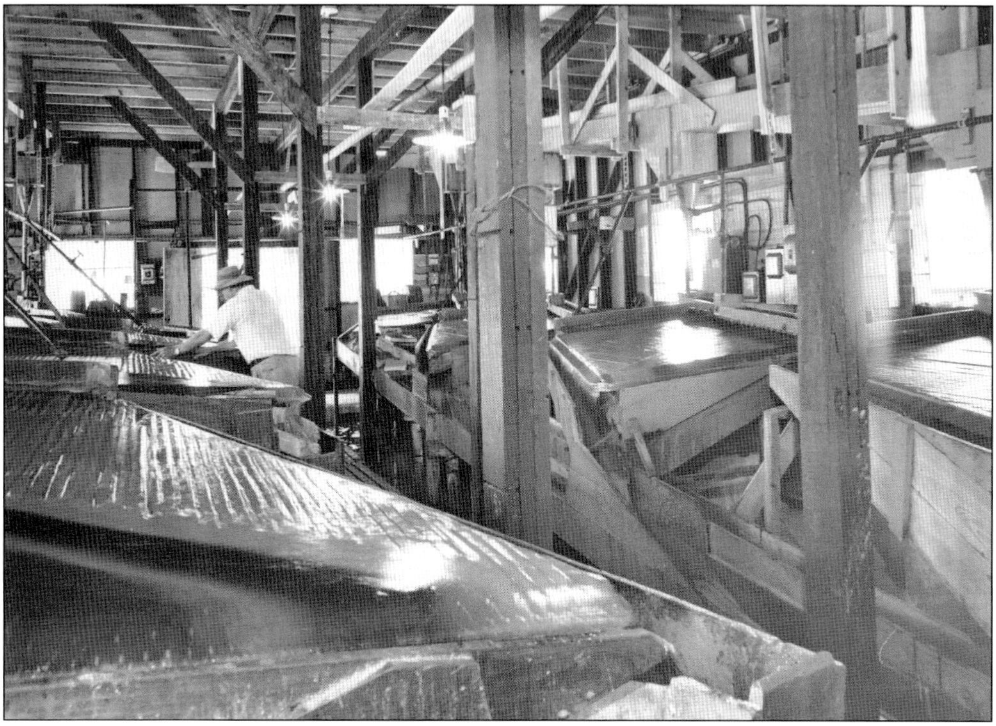

The Mineral City Sand Plant was located just west of the dunes. Workers mined the minerals directly on the beach with the use of mules. Workers loaded sand onto slip pans that the mules pulled along the beach. To expand, plant owners Buckman and Pritchard later went into a partnership with a company based in Pittsburgh called the National Lead Company.

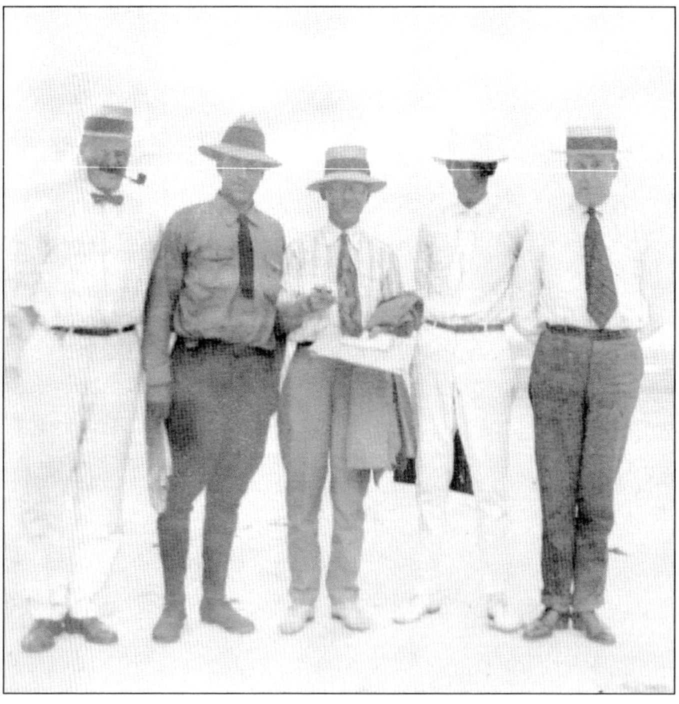

Five unidentified Buckman and Pritchard Sand Plant employees pose for a photograph during the early days in Mineral City. Despite the isolated location of the plant in a town with no roads and few homes, the mining operation was photographically well documented.

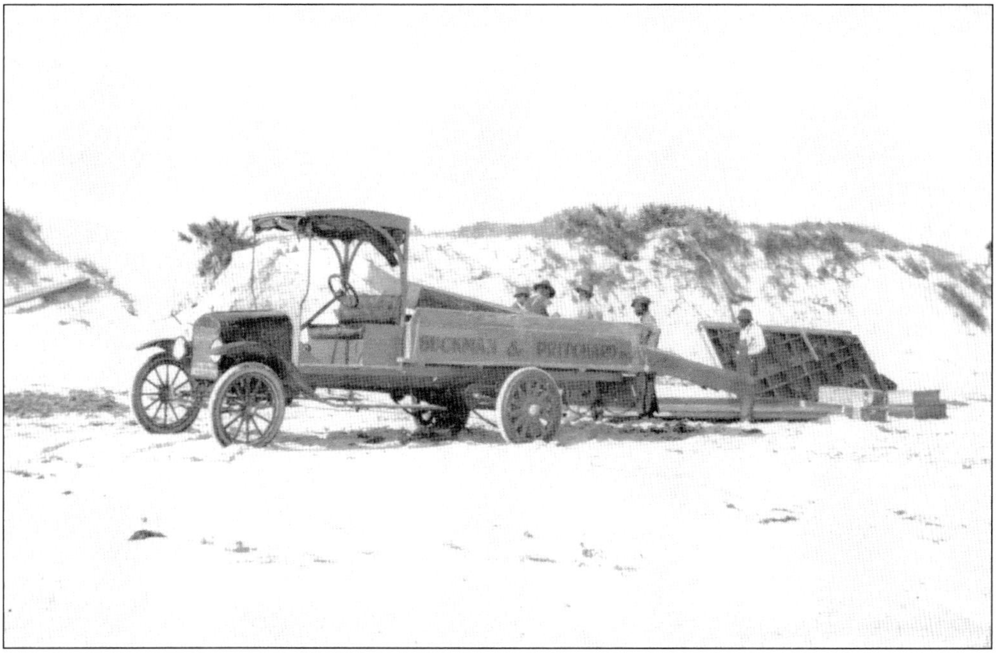

A Buckman and Pritchard mining operation truck sits on a beach in Mineral City. No roads existed at the time in that area, so cars and trucks had to travel along the beach at low tide. At first, mules were used almost exclusively to haul sand, but as the operation grew, the company also used trucks. While the trucks were useful, they never completely replaced the mules.

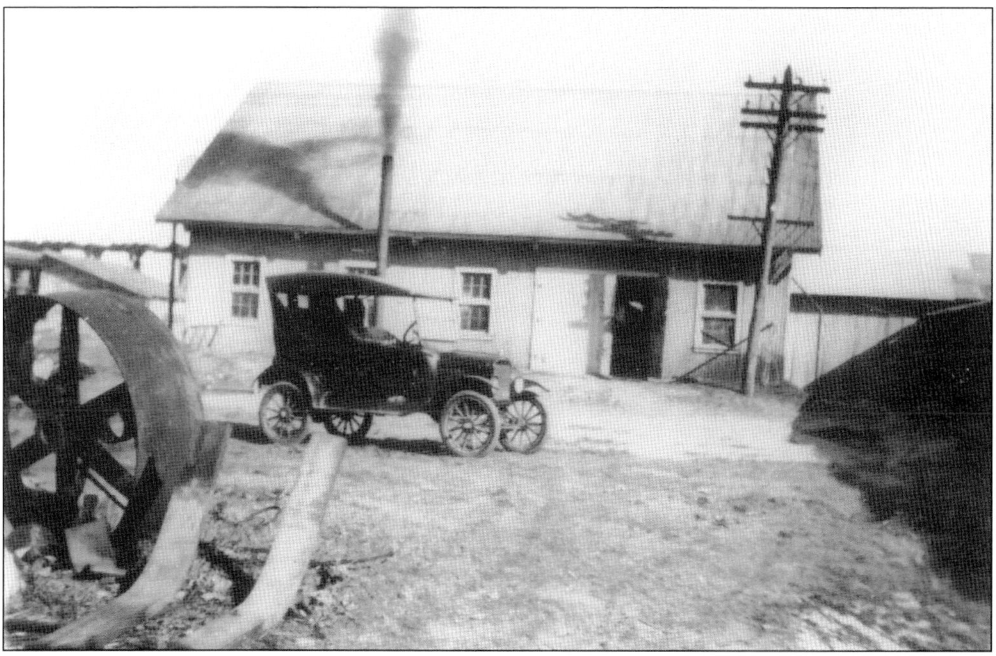

A Model T is parked in front of the Sand Plant in Mineral City. There were not many cars in town at the time because there were no roads. Buckman and Pritchard sold their minerals to a large alloy company and its subsidiaries, which held patents giving them the exclusive right to manufacture some products using titanium, including steel.

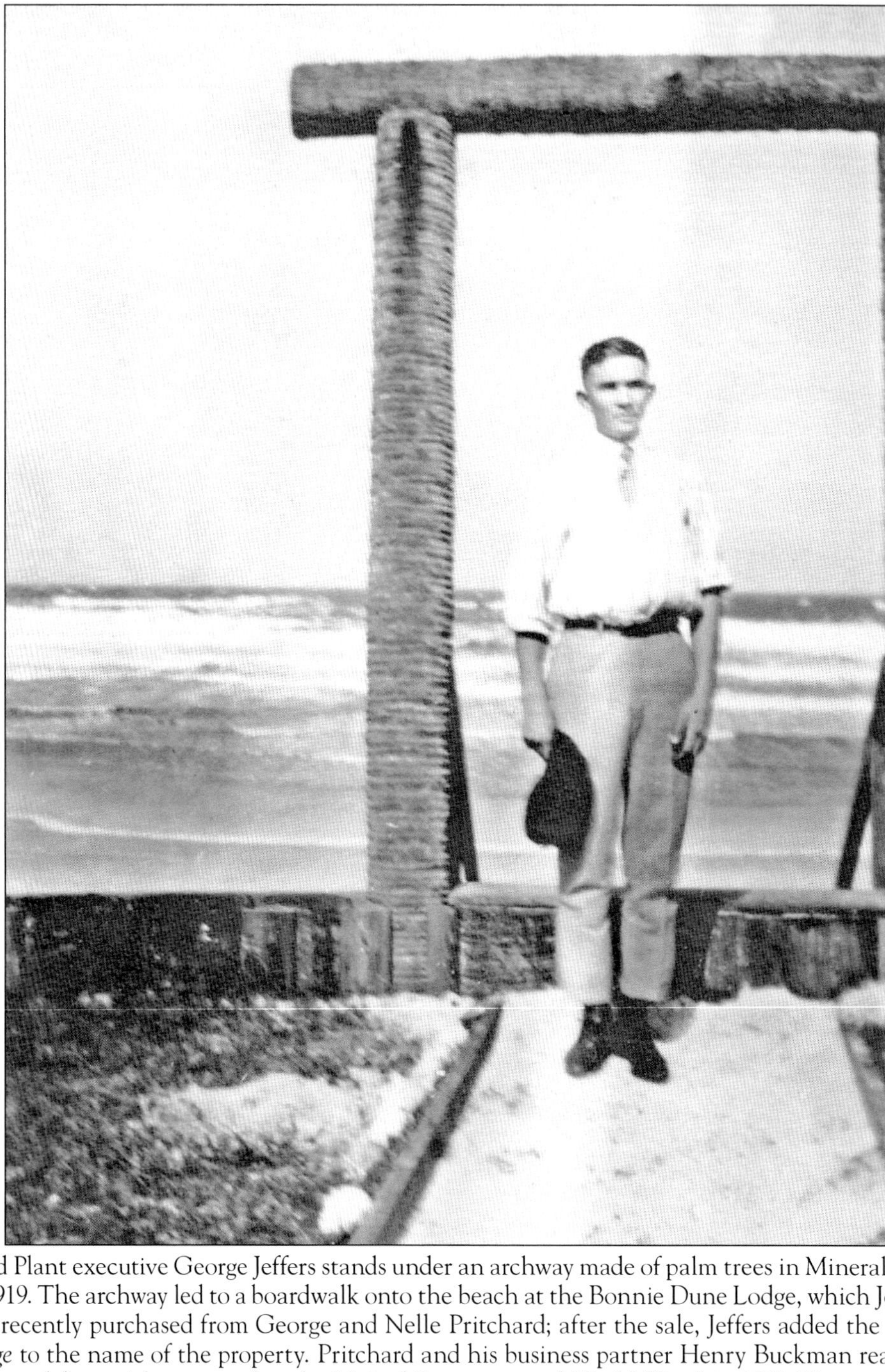

Sand Plant executive George Jeffers stands under an archway made of palm trees in Mineral City in 1919. The archway led to a boardwalk onto the beach at the Bonnie Dune Lodge, which Jeffers had recently purchased from George and Nelle Pritchard; after the sale, Jeffers added the word *Lodge* to the name of the property. Pritchard and his business partner Henry Buckman realized increased financial success after the United States entered World War I in 1917. The minerals they were extracting from the beach were rare and valuable and could be used to make weapons. Titanium is made from the minerals ilmenite and rutile, and at that time, the only other principal source in the world was in Brazil, under the control of Germany. Zircon, another mineral in the sands, also became valuable after the Germans invented zirconium steel, used in making armor-plated missiles and airplanes.

Mining executive George Jeffers poses with a snakeskin while standing at the entrance to a boardwalk that led to the beach at his Mineral City home Bonnie Dune Lodge. While the story of that snakeskin is lost to history, the area was a wilderness filled with snakes and alligators and other creatures that residents would have likely often encountered.

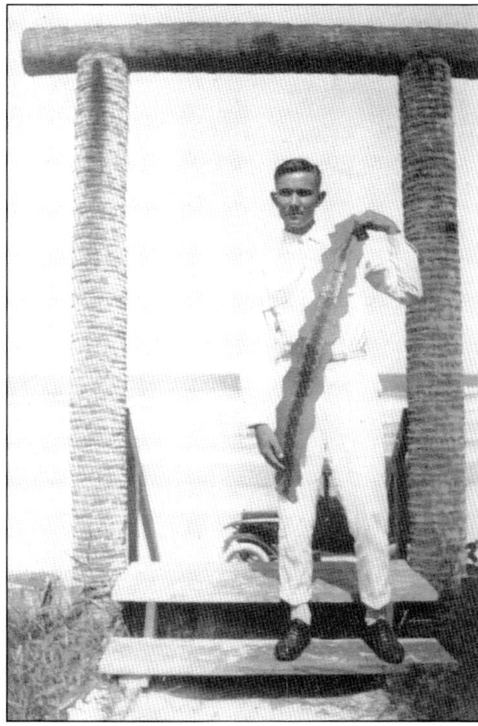

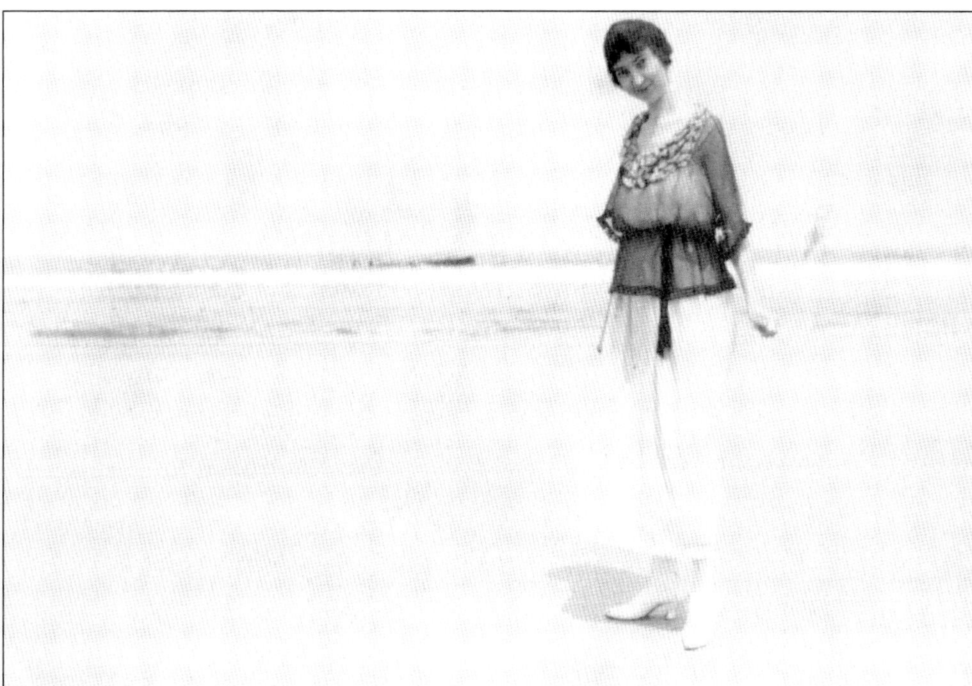

A young woman identified as Miss Regal poses on the beach in Mineral City in 1919. She seems to be proud of her dress, modeling it on a wide-open beach. While Pablo Beach, the town to the north, had a grand resort and oceanfront establishments, Mineral City had nothing like that at the time. There were few places where a young woman could show off a new ensemble.

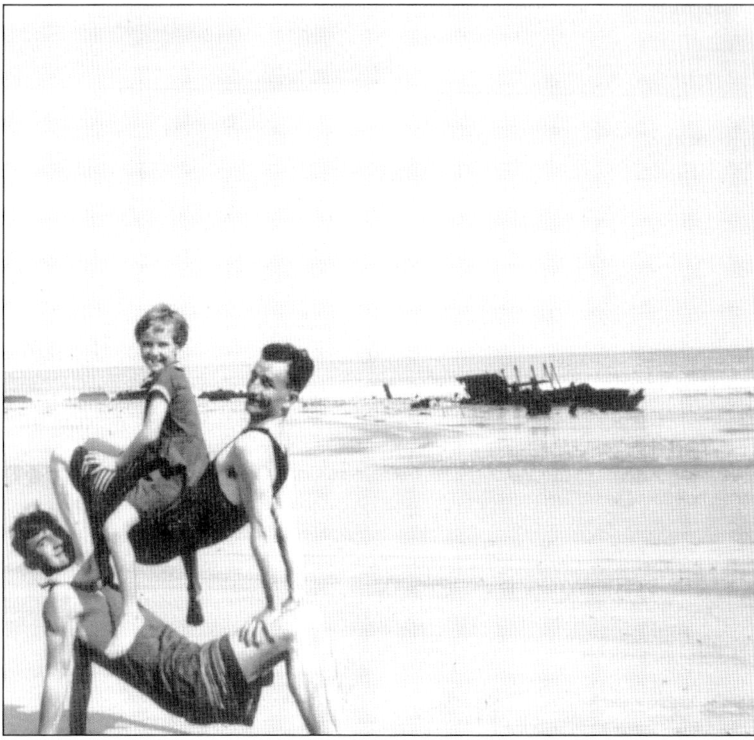

A man and two children clown around on a beach in Mineral City in 1919. They are identified as Mr. Dow, Dorothy Jeffers, and George Jeffers Jr. A shipwrecked vessel, the *Hugh de Payne*, can be seen off the coast behind them. It ran ashore in a gale near the Bonnie Dune Lodge.

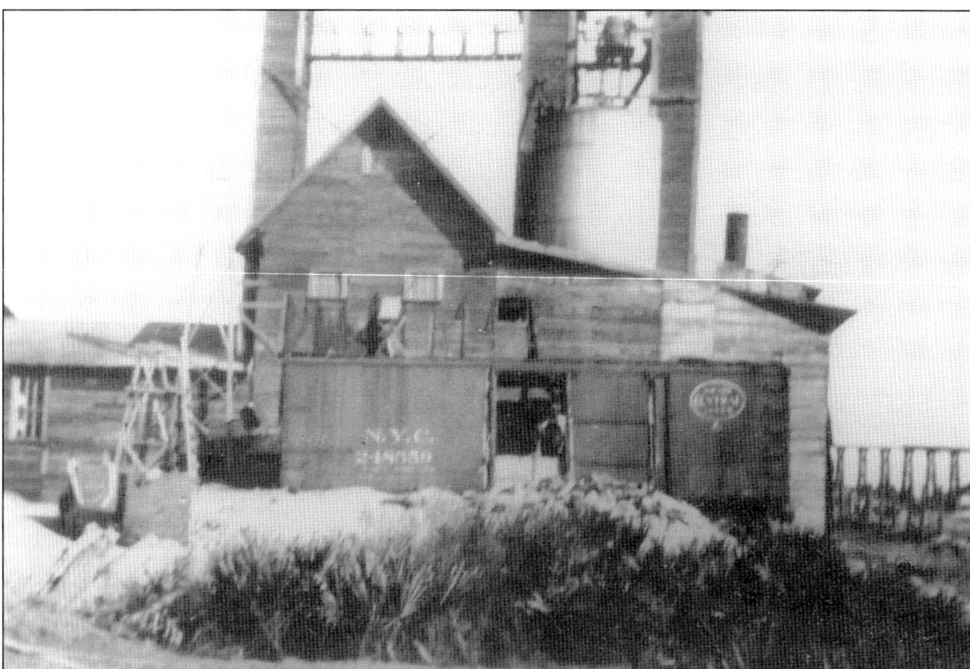

In 1922, the Buckman and Pritchard Sand Plant had grown due to the demand for minerals. After World War I ended, the minerals mined there were needed for making steel, paint, linoleum, automobile tires, and various types of dyes. American railroads needed steel made with ilmenite, and zircon was used in porcelain, transmission wire insulation, and automobile sparkplugs.

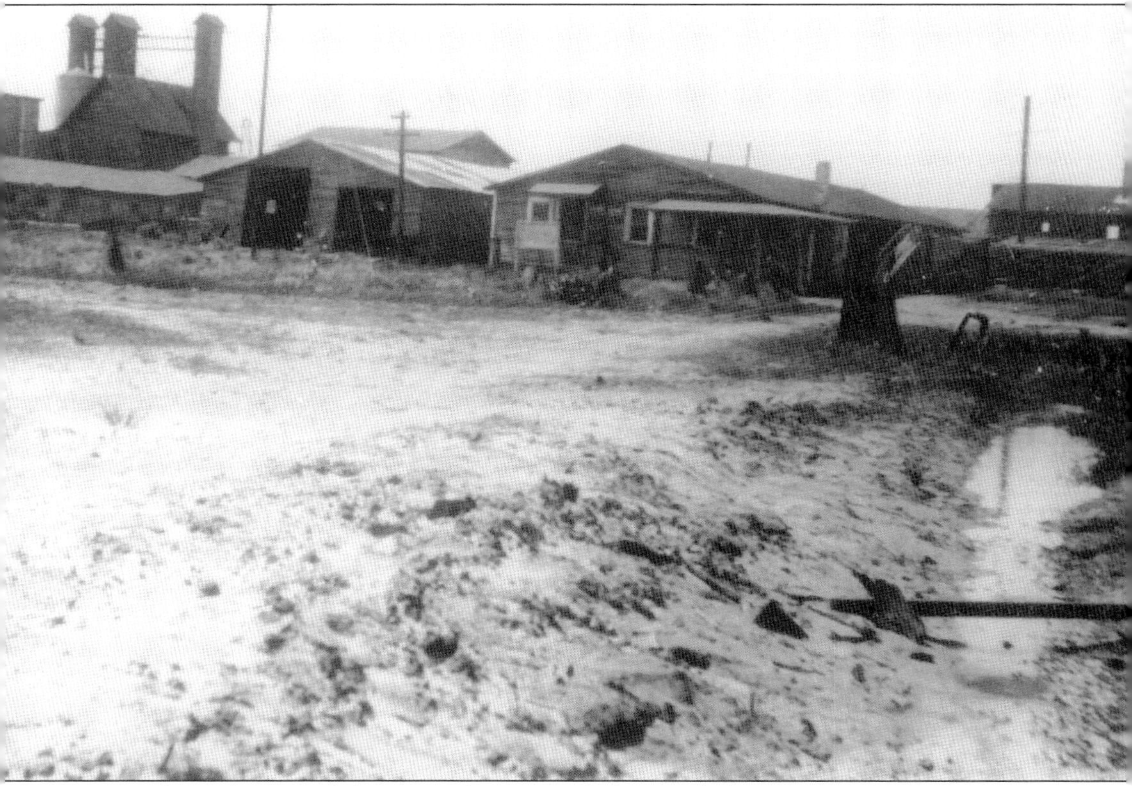

A 1922 wide-angle view of the Mineral City Sand Plant includes employee housing. When Buckman and Pritchard merged their company with the National Lead Company, they obtained the financial support to expand the business. Foremen lived in small houses, and workers lived in shacks along the dunes. Pritchard was appointed the first postmaster of Mineral City, which got its name from a contest held among workers. The story goes that the worker who came up with the winning name won $50. Later, when the town was transformed into an oceanfront destination for wealthy visitors looking for relaxation and recreation, the name was changed to Ponte Vedra Beach.

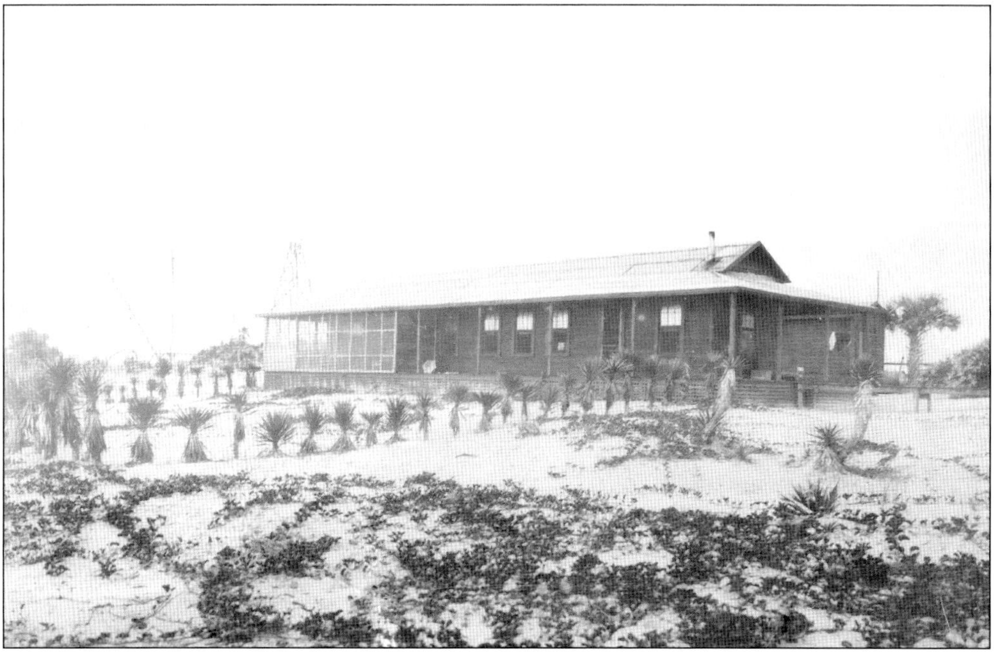

The Mineral City Commissary was the only store in town, located at the Sand Plant. As such, it was the only place that families could buy groceries and other needed goods. There were stores in Pablo Beach to the north and St. Augustine to the south, but they were miles away and could only be reached by traveling along the beach at low tide.

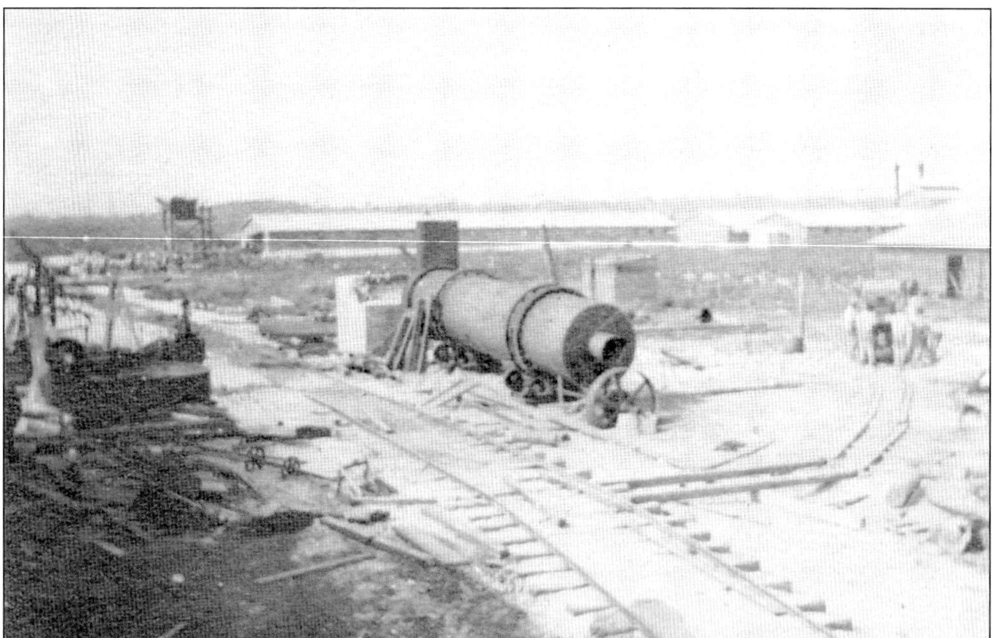

This photograph offers a wide-angle view of the Sand Plant and train track in 1922. After minerals were extracted from beach sand, they were shipped north along the track to Pablo Beach and, from there, to other destinations via railroad. In the early years, the mining company had shipped the minerals by mule to Pablo Beach.

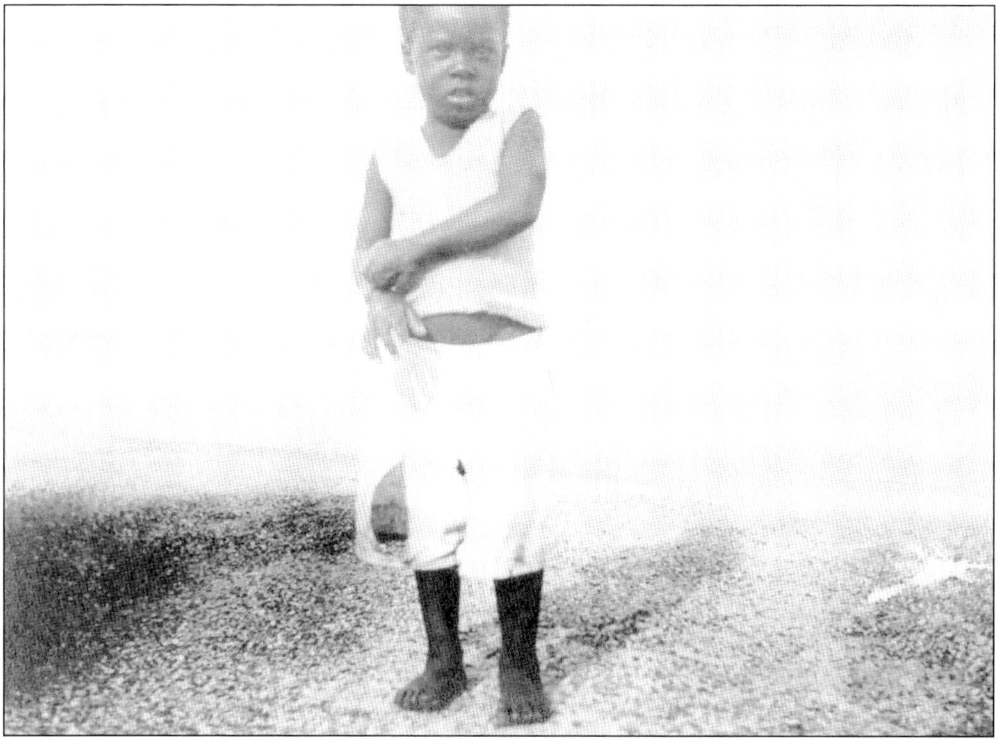

A young boy identified as Louis Williams poses for a picture in 1922 in Mineral City. He was most likely the child of a worker at the Sand Plant. Many of the workers were African Americans who lived in shacks in the area.

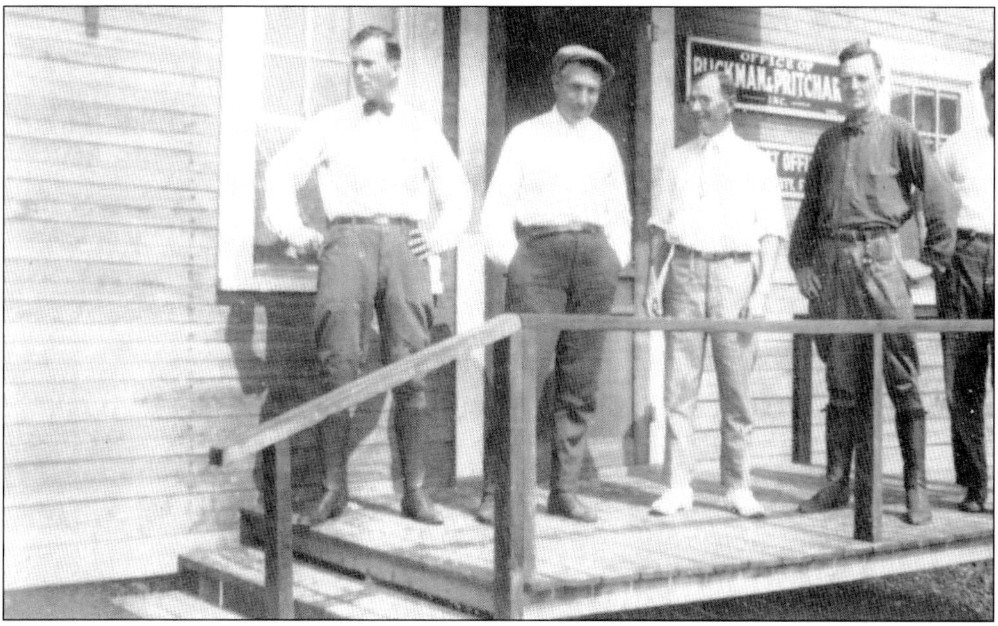

Sand Plant employees pose for a photograph on a porch in front of the Buckman and Pritchard office in 1922. They are, from left to right, Walter Phillips, John Straughn, George Jeffers, and two unidentified workers.

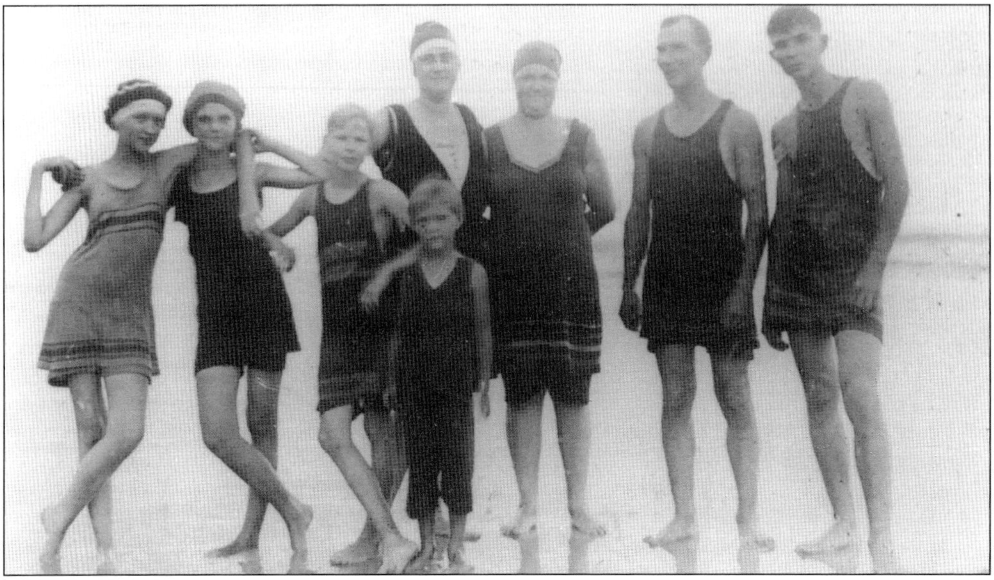

Eight Mineral City beachgoers pose for a group shot in 1922. The woman on the far left is identified as Marion Jeffers, wife of Sand Plant executive George Jeffers. Bathing suits at that time were modest compared to modern standards, but based on scenes in photographs of the time, swimming in the ocean was just as much fun.

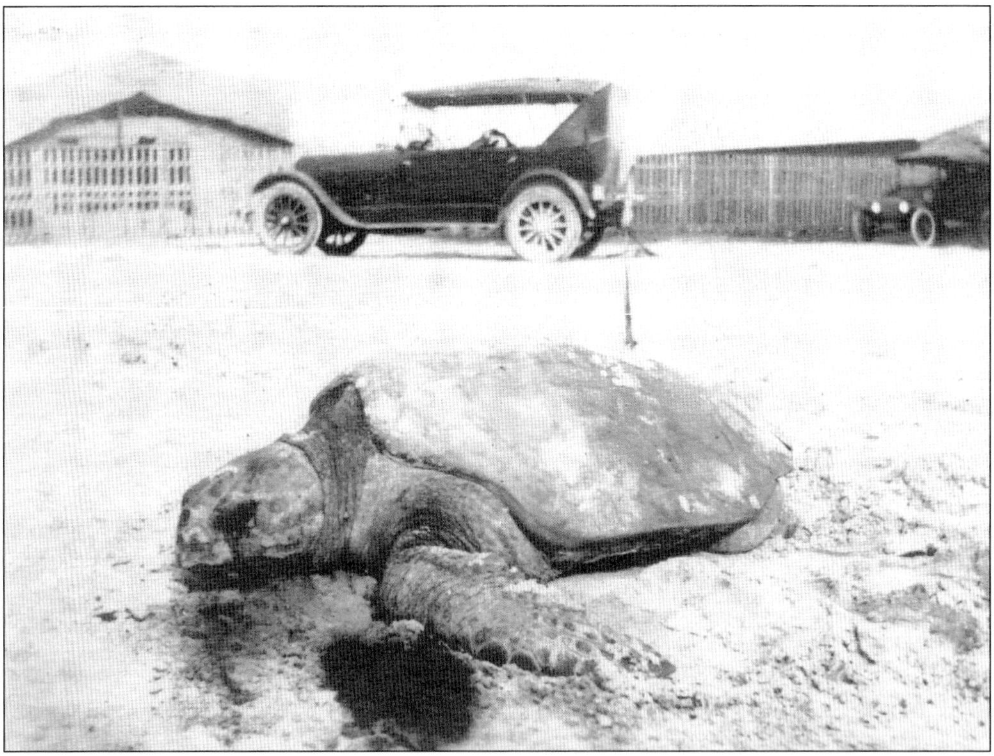

A photographer captured a shot of a loggerhead sea turtle in front of a Model T car in 1922 at the Sand Plant in Mineral City. Workers probably put the turtle there after it washed up on the beach, although the story of why it was there was not documented.

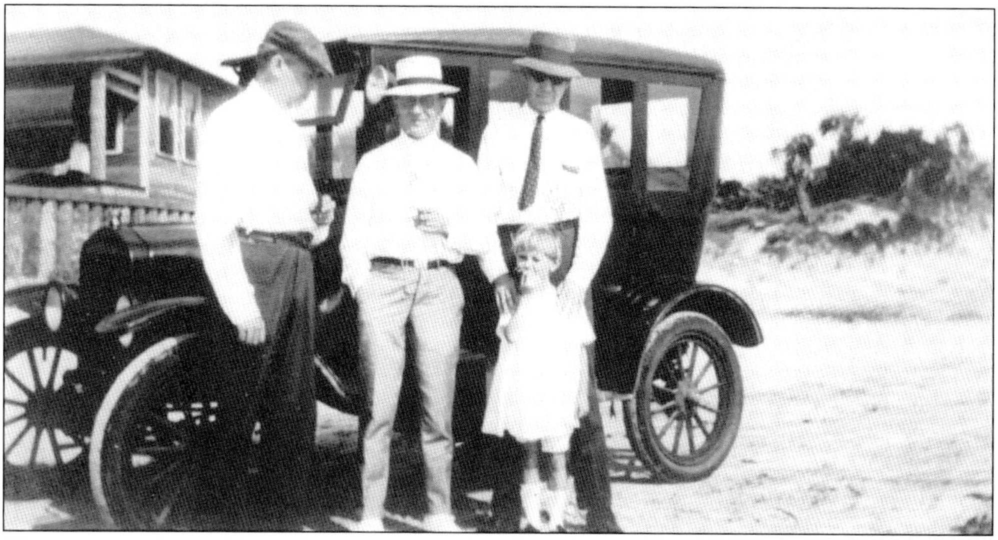

Three men and a child pose by a car on the beach in front of the Bonnie Dune Lodge in 1922. At that time, cars in Mineral City traveled the beach at low tide to get to neighboring towns.

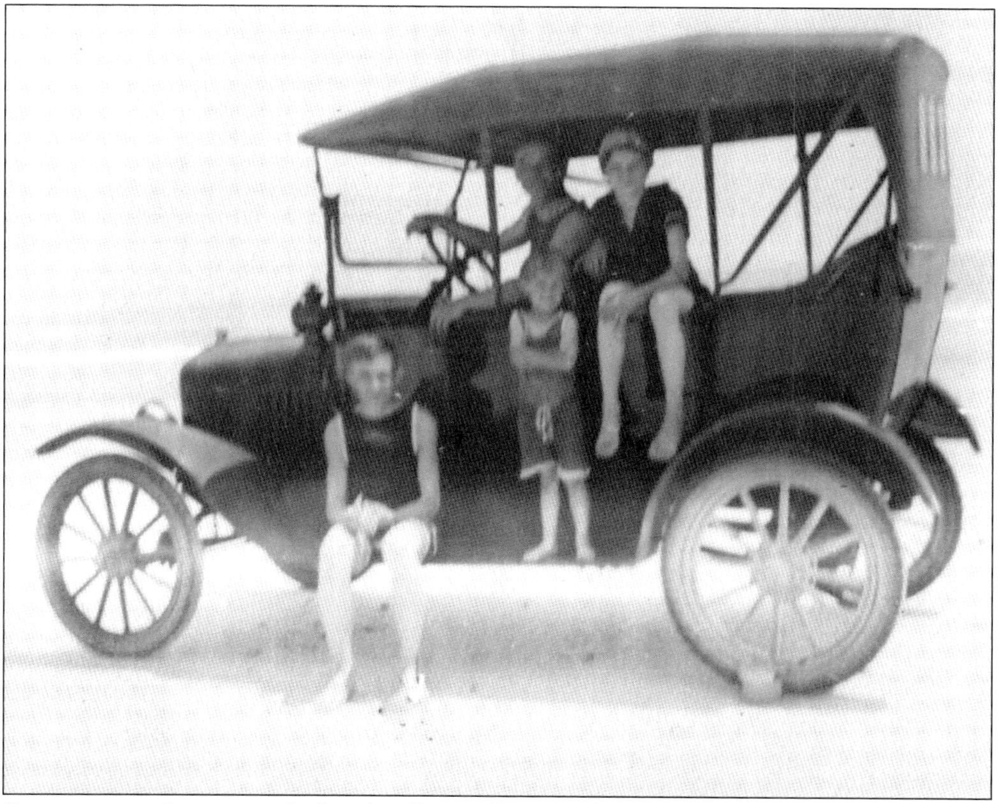

Swimmers pose by a car on the beach at Bonnie Dune Lodge in Mineral City in 1922. There were few cars in town at the time and few people as well. They probably all knew each other well in the small community that was essentially a mining town on the beach.

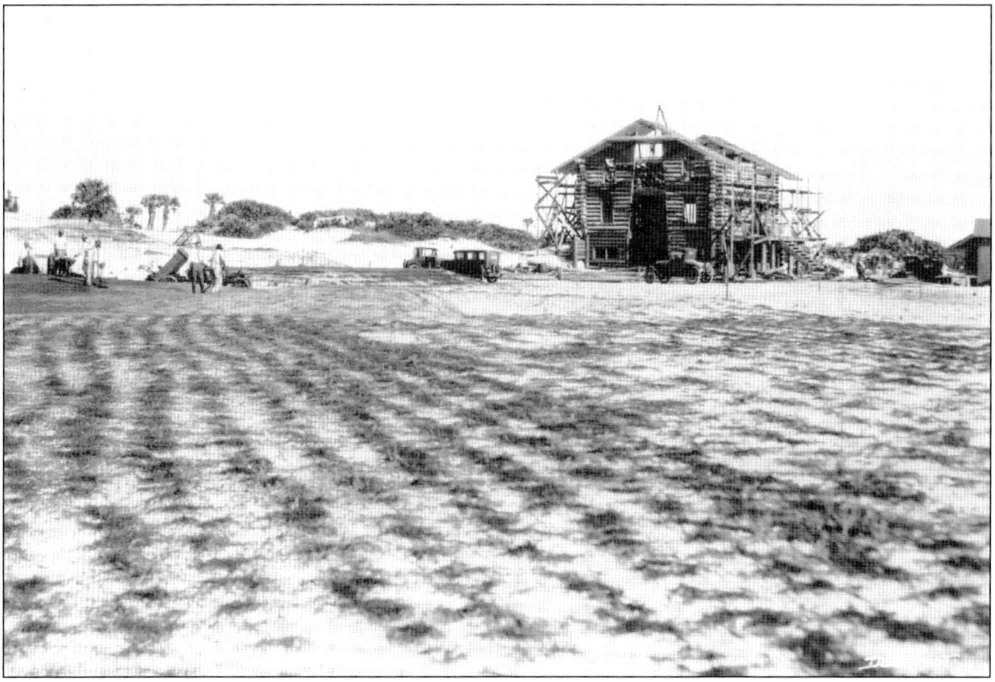

The National Lead Company built a nine-hole golf course for its mining employees so they had something to do in their spare time. This photograph shows the golf course's log cabin clubhouse under construction in 1926. It was later used as a clubhouse for Ponte Vedra Club members.

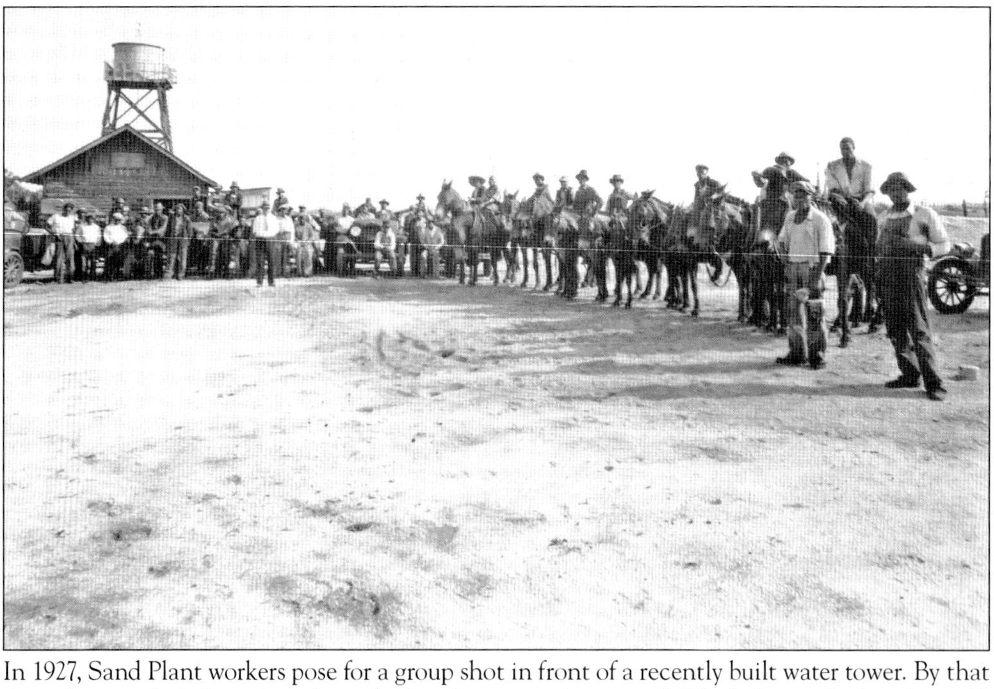

In 1927, Sand Plant workers pose for a group shot in front of a recently built water tower. By that time, the era of mining minerals on the beach was nearing an end. The holes on the beach would soon be filled in, and the railroad tracks would be removed so the area could be turned into an upscale resort and community.

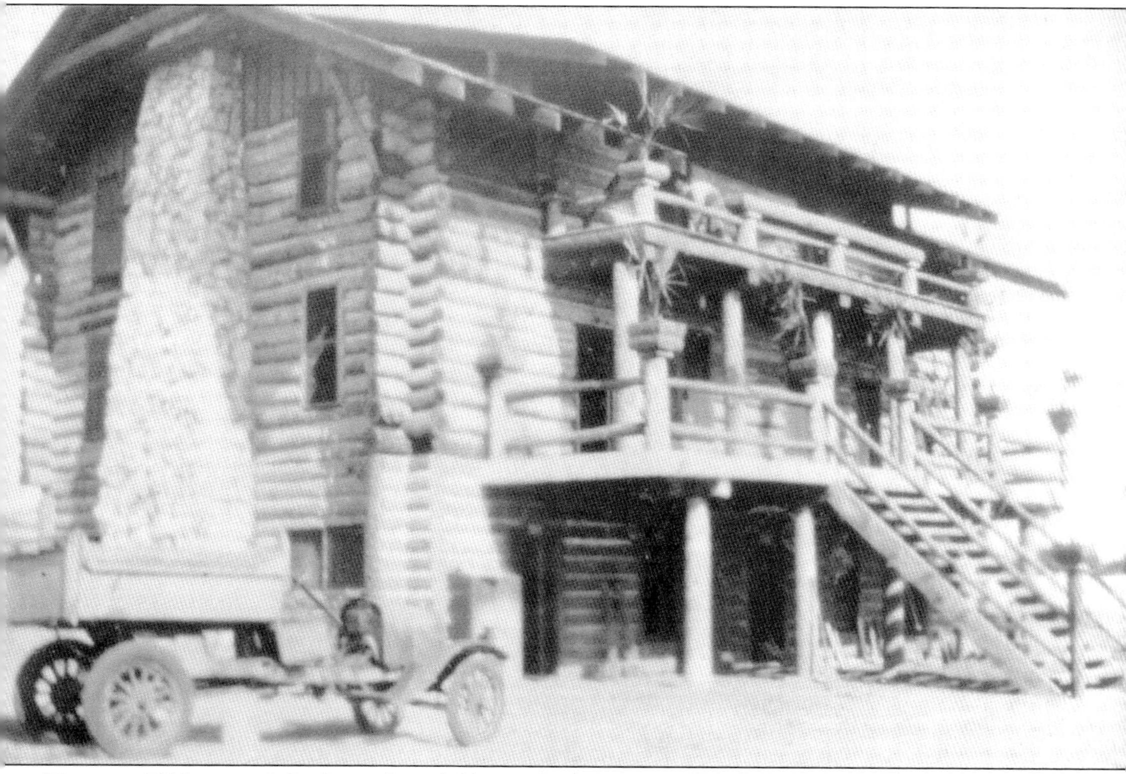

This is a 1928 view of the log cabin clubhouse built on a small golf course in Mineral City for mining employees. At the time, it was called the Jacksonville Beach Golf Links Club House after the more populated town to the north called Jacksonville Beach, formerly Pablo Beach. The name of Mineral City was changed that year to Ponte Vedra Beach to fit the new image that developers wanted to project. The National Lead Company shut down the mining operations and started promoting the area as a resort destination, using its seaside golf course and clubhouse as an attraction.

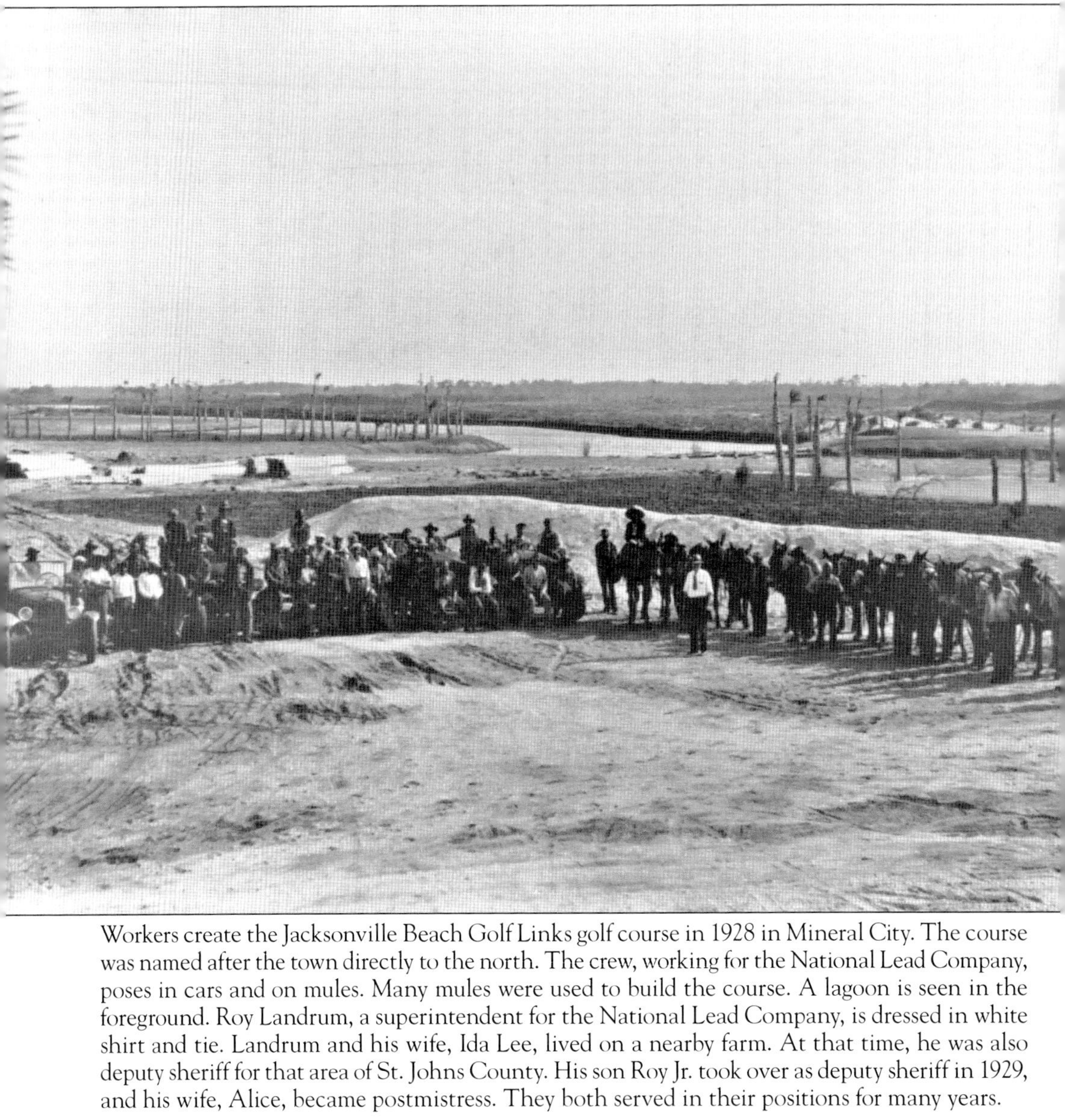

Workers create the Jacksonville Beach Golf Links golf course in 1928 in Mineral City. The course was named after the town directly to the north. The crew, working for the National Lead Company, poses in cars and on mules. Many mules were used to build the course. A lagoon is seen in the foreground. Roy Landrum, a superintendent for the National Lead Company, is dressed in white shirt and tie. Landrum and his wife, Ida Lee, lived on a nearby farm. At that time, he was also deputy sheriff for that area of St. Johns County. His son Roy Jr. took over as deputy sheriff in 1929, and his wife, Alice, became postmistress. They both served in their positions for many years.

# *Two*

# The Ponte Vedra Club

Ponte Vedra Beach was created around the Ponte Vedra Club, now the Ponte Vedra Inn and Club.

In 1928, when the National Lead Company asked the Telfair Stockton Company to develop the area, Telfair Stockton's son Jim was charged with planning, designing, and managing the club resort around an existing small golf course and log cabin inn.

It opened in 1937 with 30 guest rooms in the inn, as well as cottages, and immediately began attracting wealthy people from the Eastern Seaboard and the Midwest. Jim, a 1916 Princeton graduate, personally sent a letter to all members of his class to invite them to the new northeast Florida community by the sea. Many came to play golf and tennis, swim in the ocean and sunbathe on the beach, and dance at the club's new Bath Club. Some stayed for weeks or months; others came to stay, buying lots along the beach and building oceanfront homes.

The nine-hole golf course was improved, and the road between Jacksonville Beach and St. Augustine was completed.

During World War II, the National Lead Company sold all of its land to the Ponte Vedra Corporation.

During that time, many more people discovered the Ponte Vedra Club. Recruits trained at the US Naval Air Force officer's training school at the Naval Air Station in Jacksonville recommended the inn to their parents and girlfriends when they came to visit. When the servicemen got married, many spent their honeymoons at the inn.

The resort grew and so did the staff. The golf course was redesigned in 1947 and then was enlarged to 27 holes in 1961. In 1977, another nine holes were added, creating the Lagoon Course, a companion to the original 18-hole course, now the Ocean Course.

For tennis players, the Racquet Club grew from the single court built next to the inn in 1937. Courts were added over the years, as was a pro shop, clinics, and tournaments.

Pool swimming was also always popular at the resort, and swim teams were formed that produced many champion swimmers.

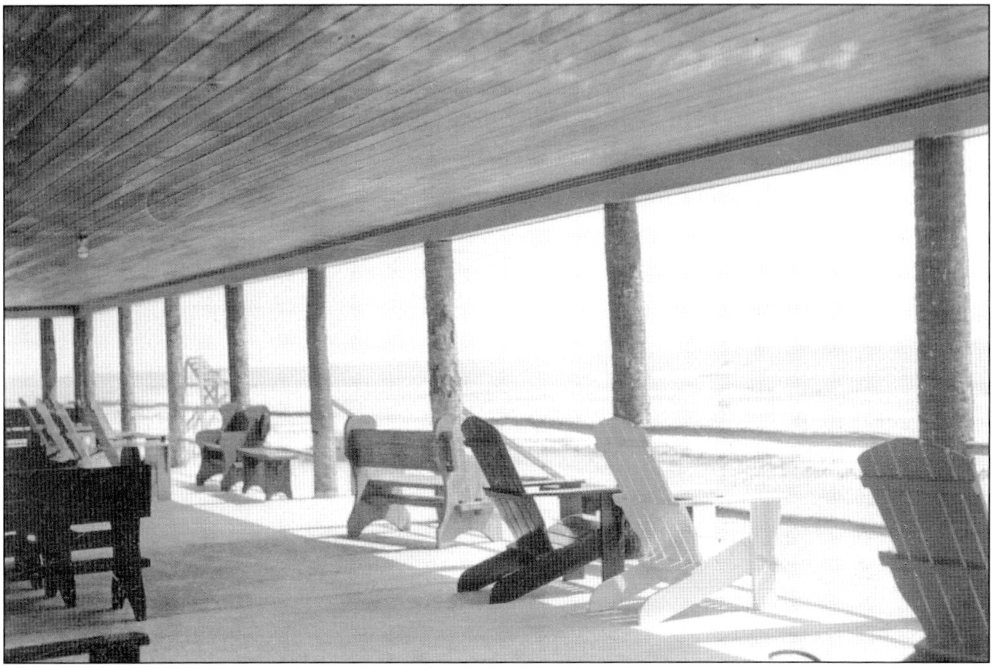

This is a 1935 view of the breezeway at the Ponte Vedra Club's Bath Club, later called the Surf Club. Chairs along the breezeway face the ocean where visitors could relax and take in the view.

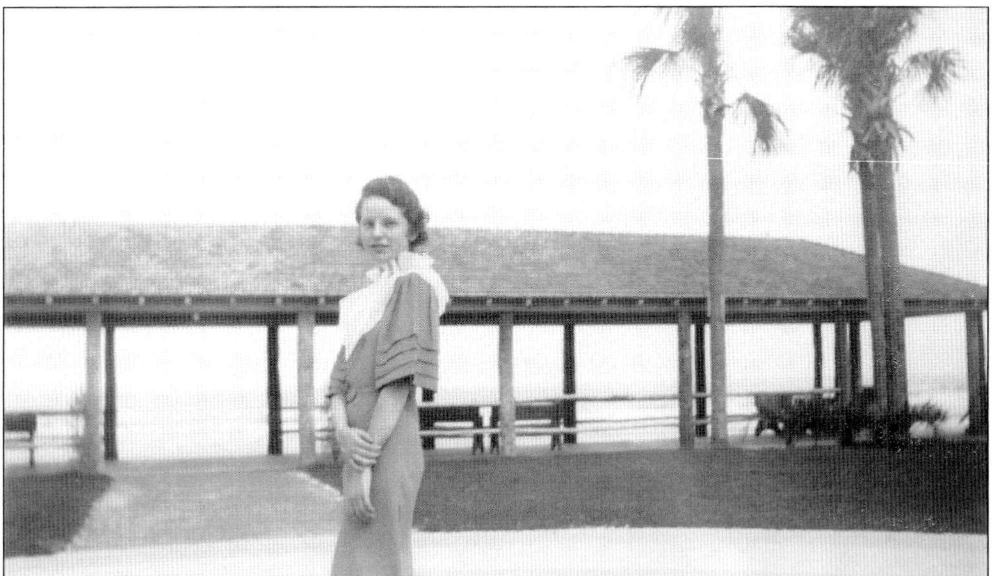

A young woman identified as Betty Davis was photographed in front of the dance floor at the Ponte Vedra Club Bath Club in 1937. The club was a popular place for visitors and club members to socialize.

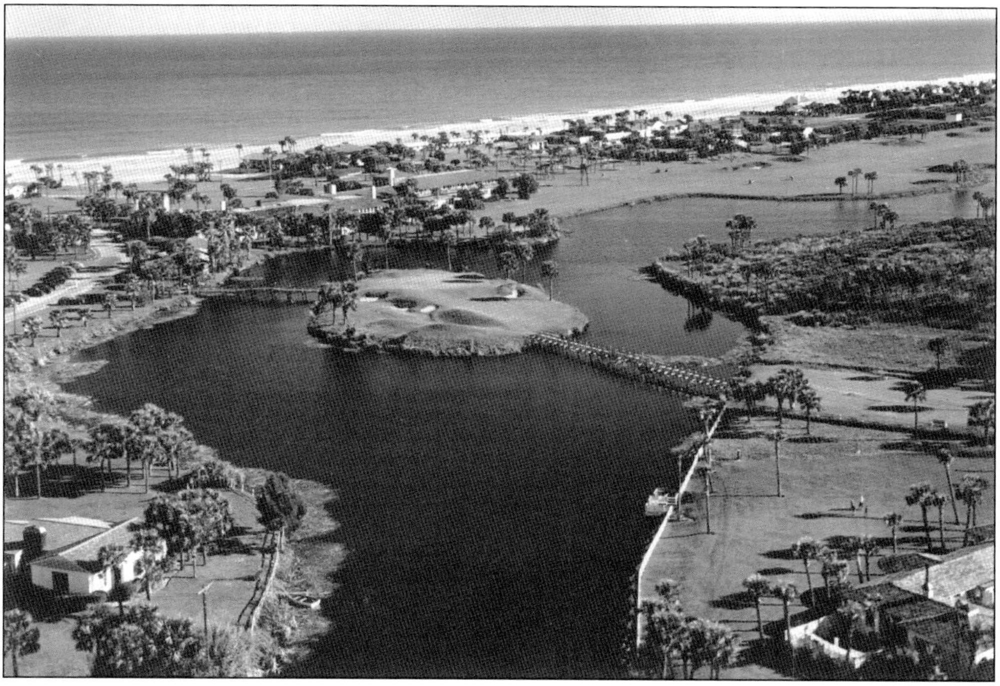

An aerial image captured sometime in the 1940s shows the Ponte Vedra Club, golf course, and Atlantic Ocean. The club grew in popularity during that decade, up until World War II, and then continued after the war.

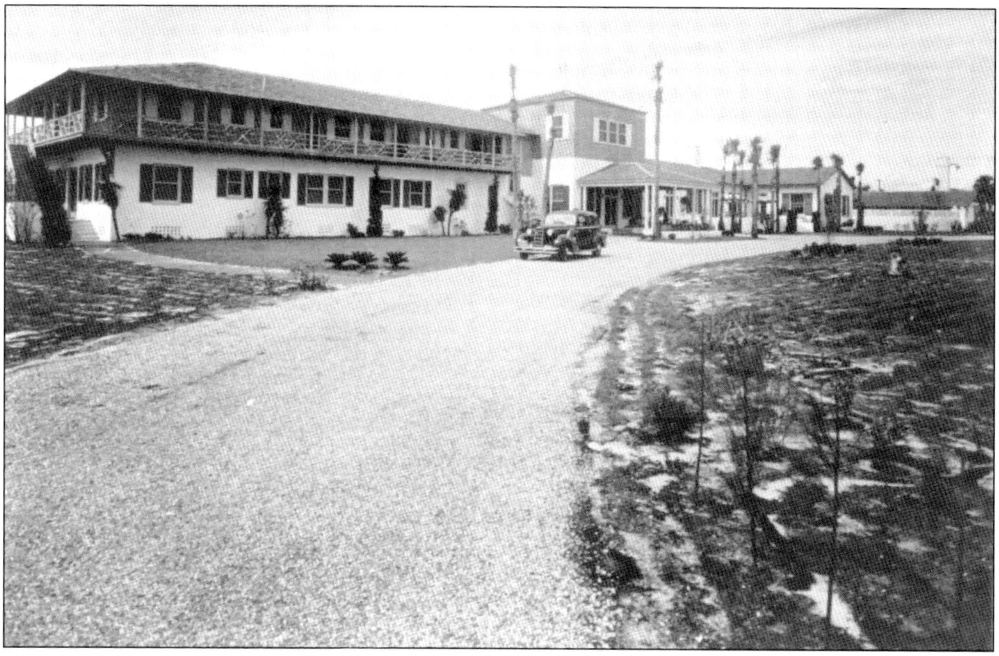

This photograph shows the Ponte Vedra Club in 1940. The club began in October 1928 when National Lead Company executives decided to convert its thousands of acres of oceanfront property into a seaside destination for wealthy visitors from around the country. The company hired the Telfair Stockton Company, a major land developer in Jacksonville, to plan it.

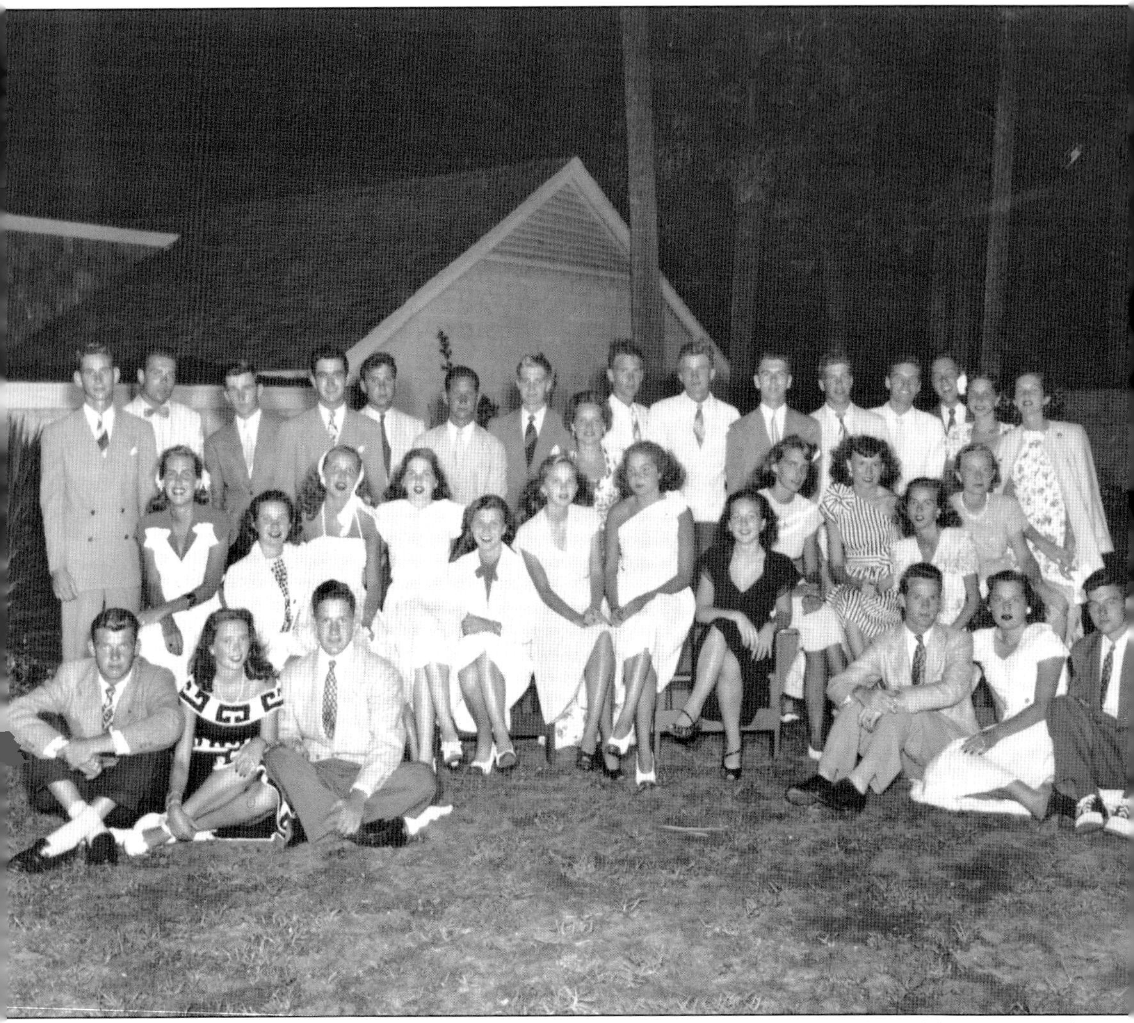

A group of young adults poses for a group photograph at the Ponte Vedra Club in 1947. The club grew in popularity after World War II, in part because some military servicemen who were stationed in nearby Jacksonville discovered it and made it a point to return during peacetime. In addition, Telfair Stockton's son Jim was in charge of managing the resort. As a Princeton graduate of the class of 1916, Jim Stockton had many friends and acquaintances that he thought would enjoy the club, so he wrote letters inviting all of them to visit. They came and spread the word to other friends from many other states. Many visitors did not want to go home, so some purchased lots along the ocean and built homes. As members of the club, they enjoyed its social scene year-round.

A family poses for a picture by a beachfront patio at the Ponte Vedra Club in August 1947. The club was growing in popularity during that time. The club's inn was built in 1937, replacing the log cabin clubhouse that had served as an inn until then.

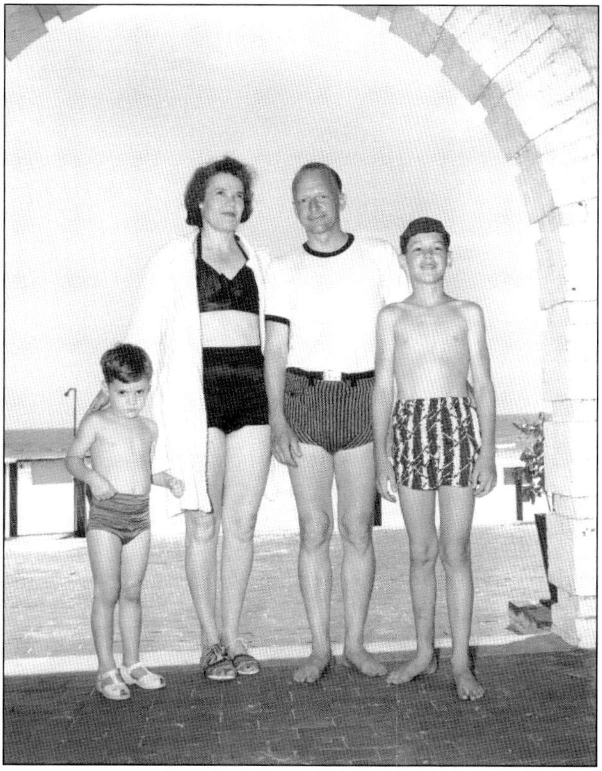

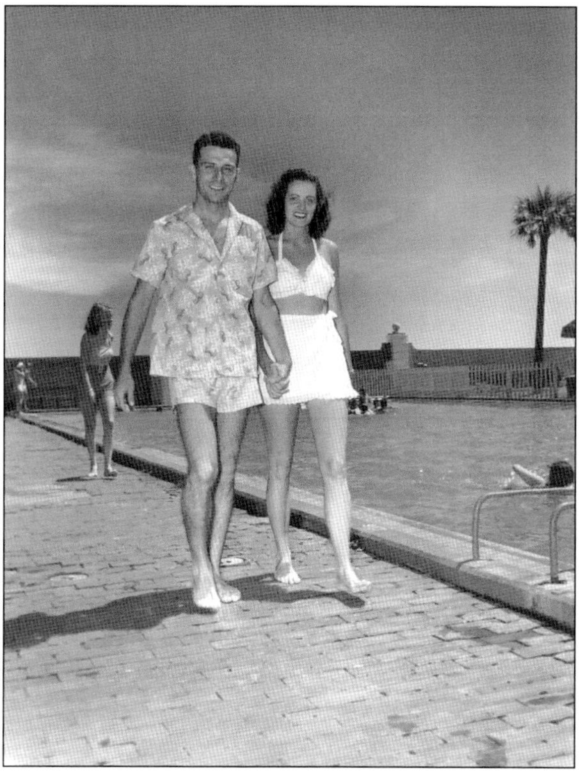

A young couple strolls by a pool at the Ponte Vedra Club in September 1947. During that year, the resort was expanding, with guests coming from many northern states, including New Jersey, Rhode Island, and Connecticut. They came to enjoy the balmy climate, and the oceanfront pool was a popular recreational option.

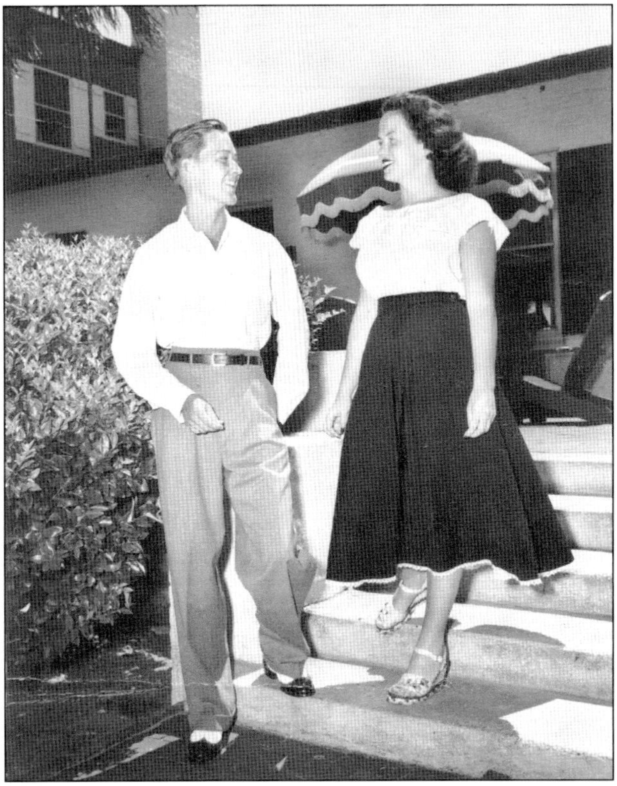

A young couple is dressed up to enjoy the social scene at the Ponte Vedra Club in 1948. The club was a place where wealthy families could meet other wealthy families, and many people captured memories of special events by having their pictures taken.

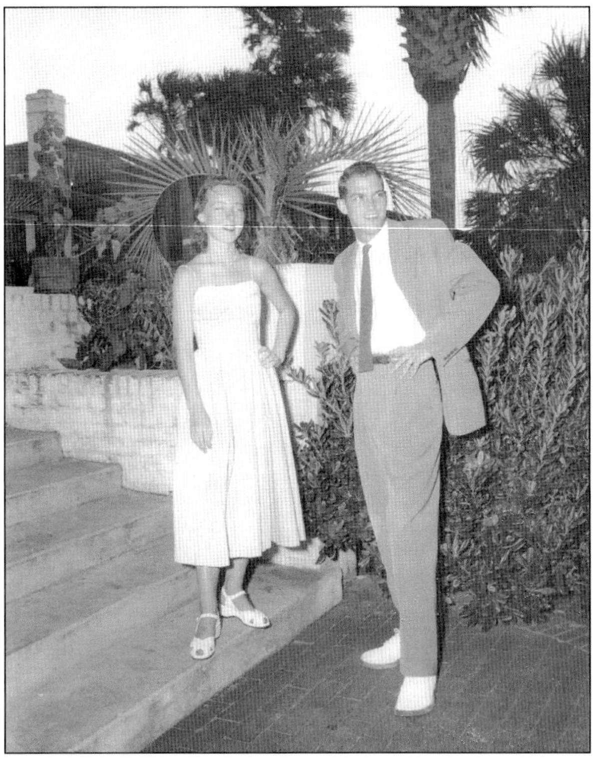

A young couple on their honeymoon pauses to have their picture taken at the Ponte Vedra Club in 1948. Many servicemen who discovered the resort while stationed in Jacksonville during World War II decided to spend their honeymoons there after the war.

A young couple relaxes at the Ponte Vedra Club in 1948. The resort's rates at the time were considered high compared to other resorts, although they were low compared to today's rates. In the late 1930s, it cost $5 per day for a single-occupancy rate in a guest cottage.

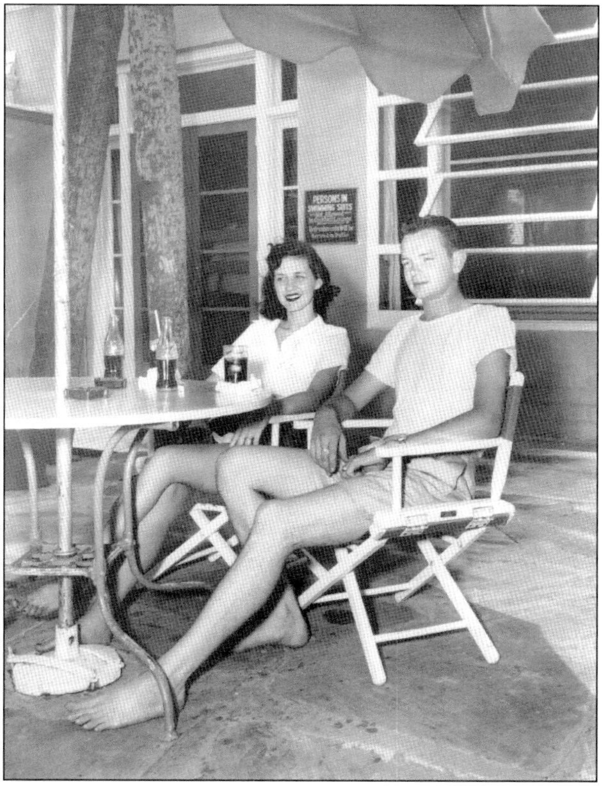

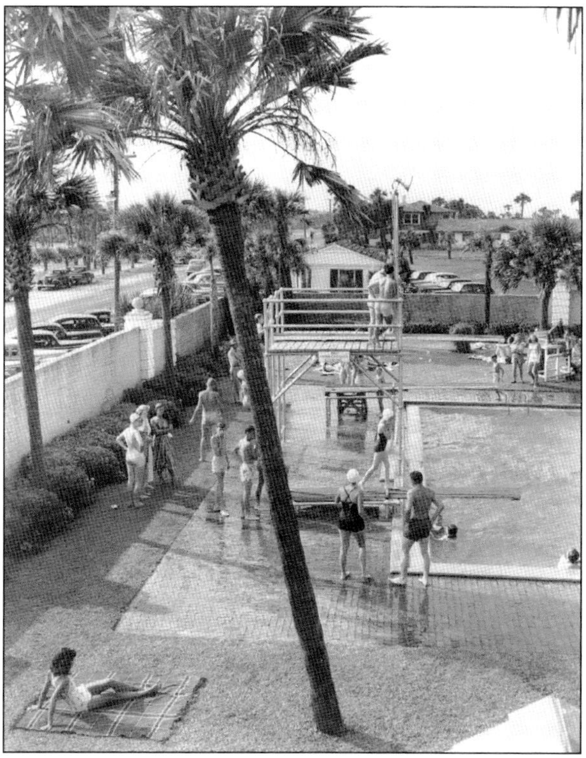

This photograph offers a glimpse of what the Ponte Vedra Club pool looked like in the 1940s. Pool scenes were often depicted in postcards of the time, showing people having fun in the sun.

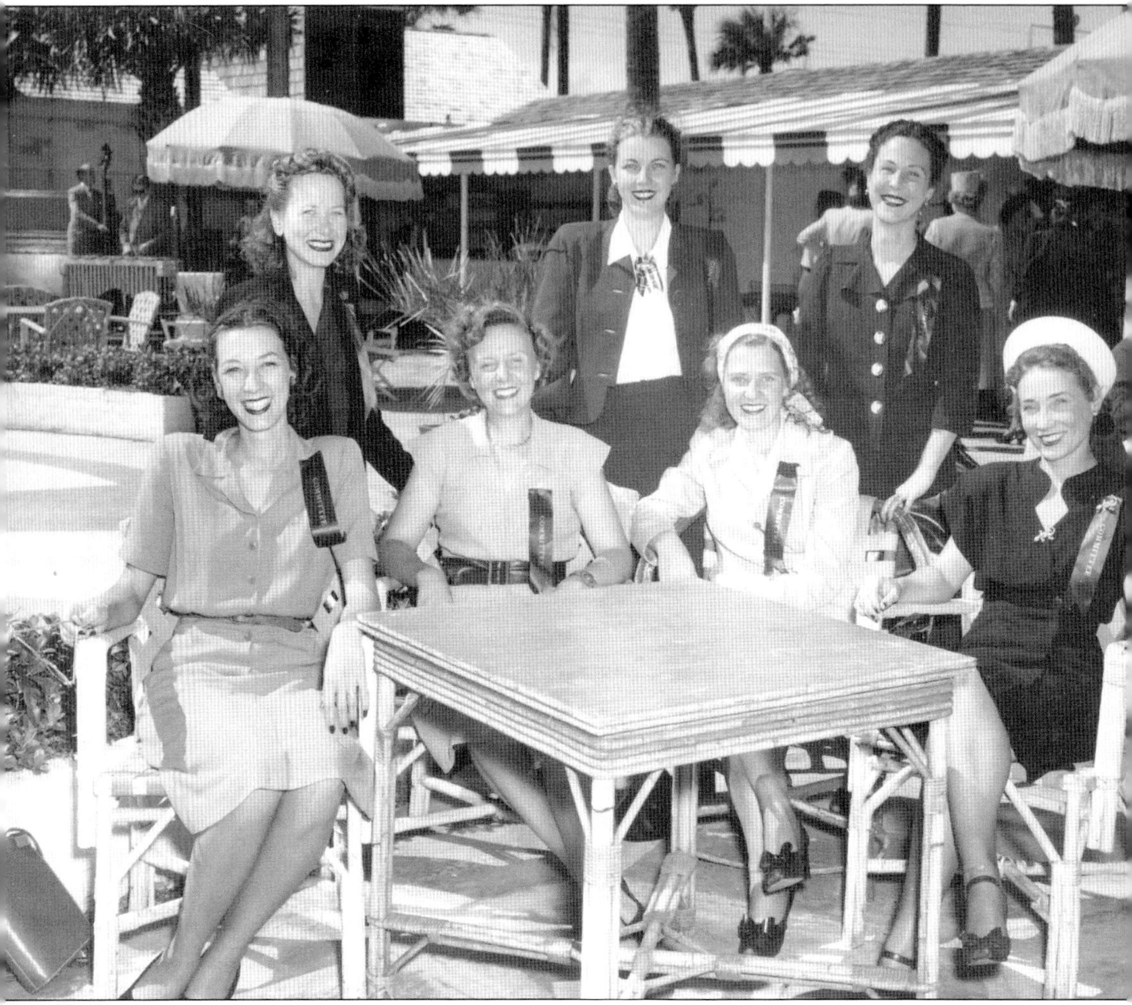

The Ponte Vedra Club was as popular with residents of the town as it was with guests from out of town, as seen in this 1949 image captured by popular area photographer Virgil Deane, who had a studio in Jacksonville Beach. In this picture, Junior Women's Club committee members pose for Deane at the Surf Club. From left to right are Madeline Wilkerson Borum, Olive Hulett, Edna Mauro, Vi Cobb, Harriet Paten, Jean McCormick, and Harriet Shore. Deane photographed many people at the club through several decades, documenting and preserving that piece of Ponte Vedra Beach history while providing a valuable service to guests and members. His widow later left thousands of his images and negatives to the Beaches Area Historical Society, founded by Jean McCormick.

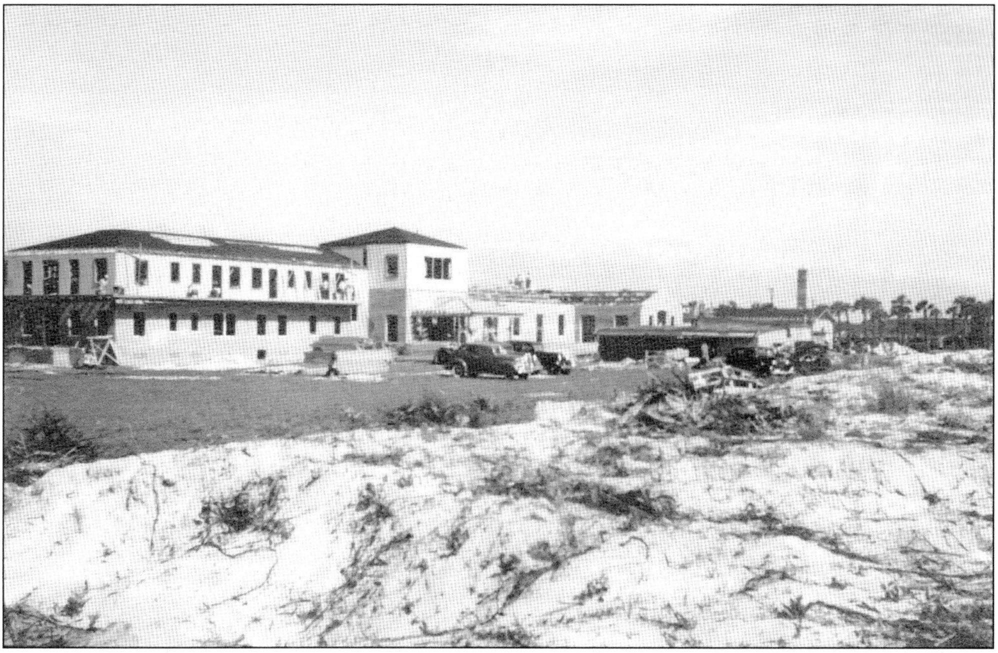

This photograph documents construction at the Ponte Vedra Club in the 1940s, when the club was expanding and attracting an increasing number of guests and members.

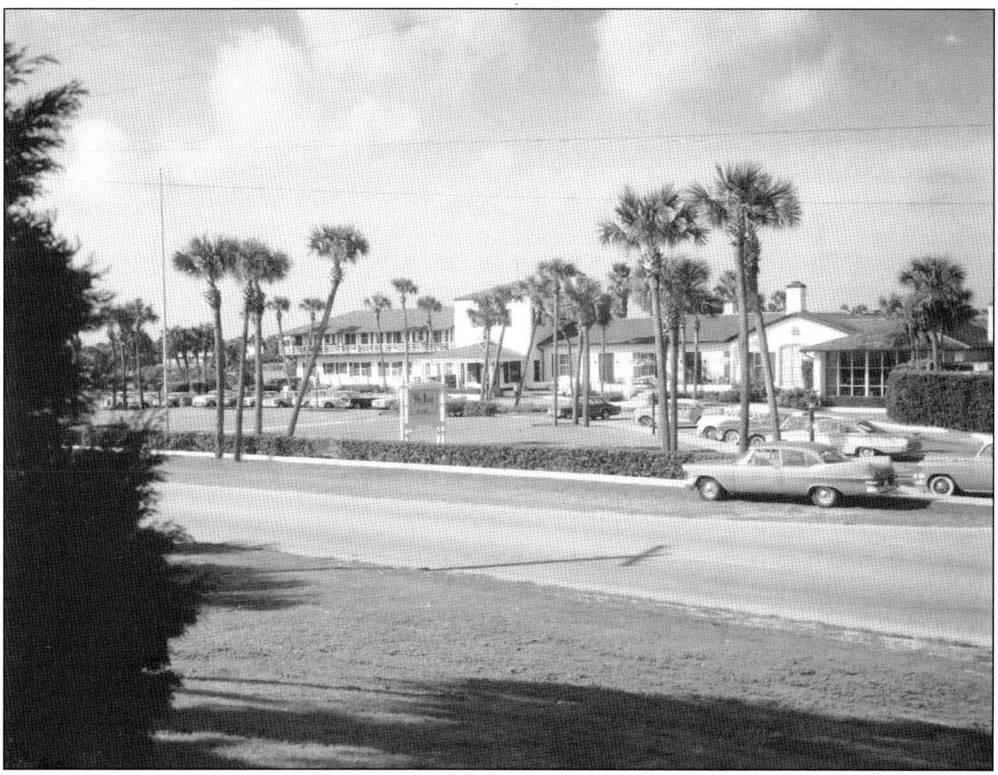

This image depicts the Ponte Vedra Club in the 1950s. Then, as now, the resort aimed at providing guests and members a taste of the best in life.

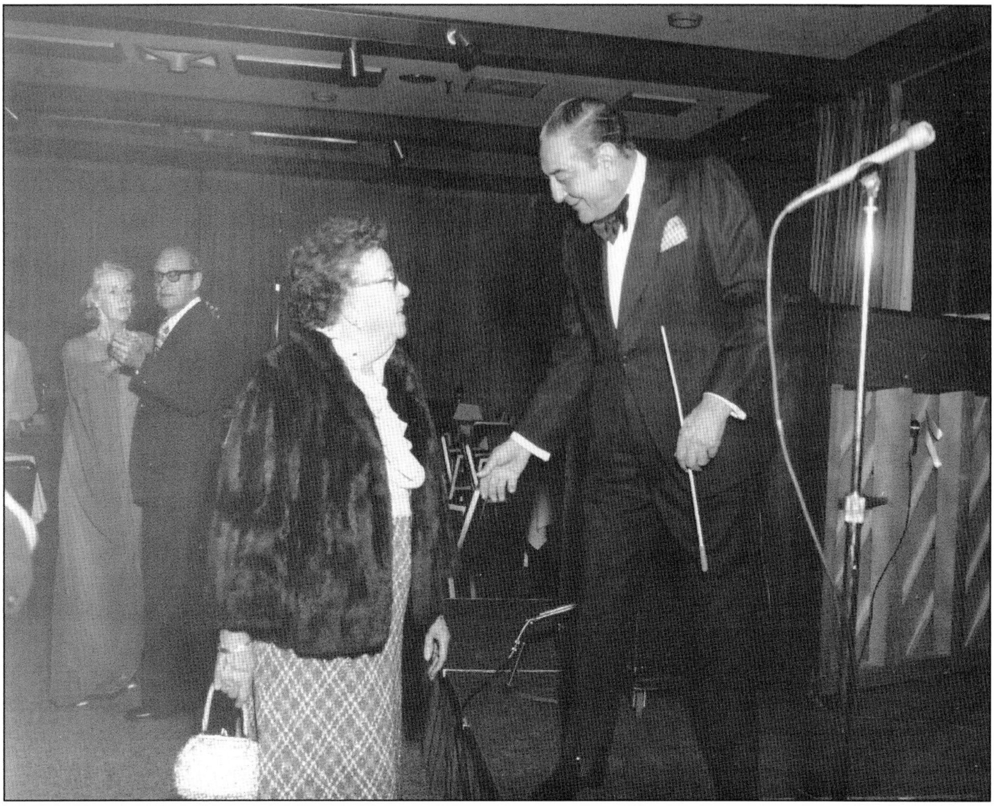

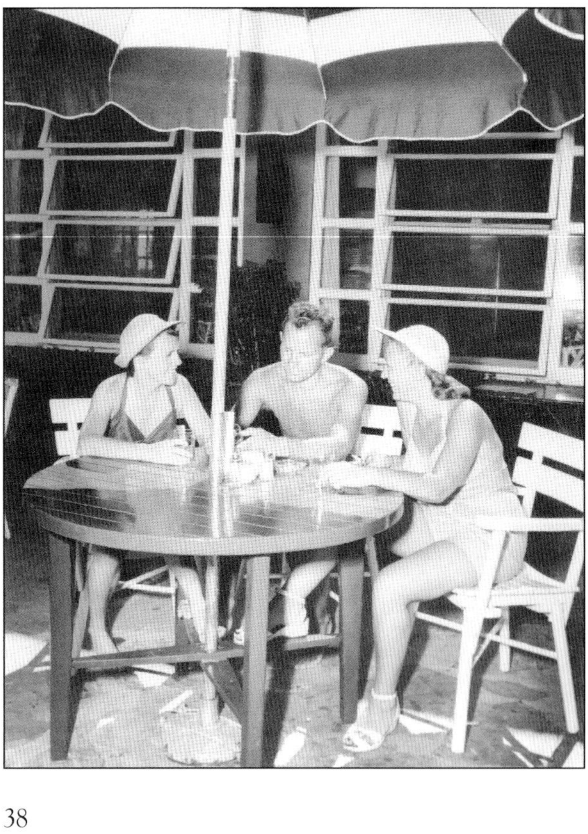

Famous bandleader Guy Lombardo visited the Ponte Vedra Club in the 1950s. Famous for creating "the sweetest music this side of heaven," according to the news stories of the time, Lombardo was one of many famous people to have visited the resort through the years.

A small group relaxes under an umbrella at the Ponte Vedra Club in 1950. If on vacation, they probably purchased a copy of the picture as a memento.

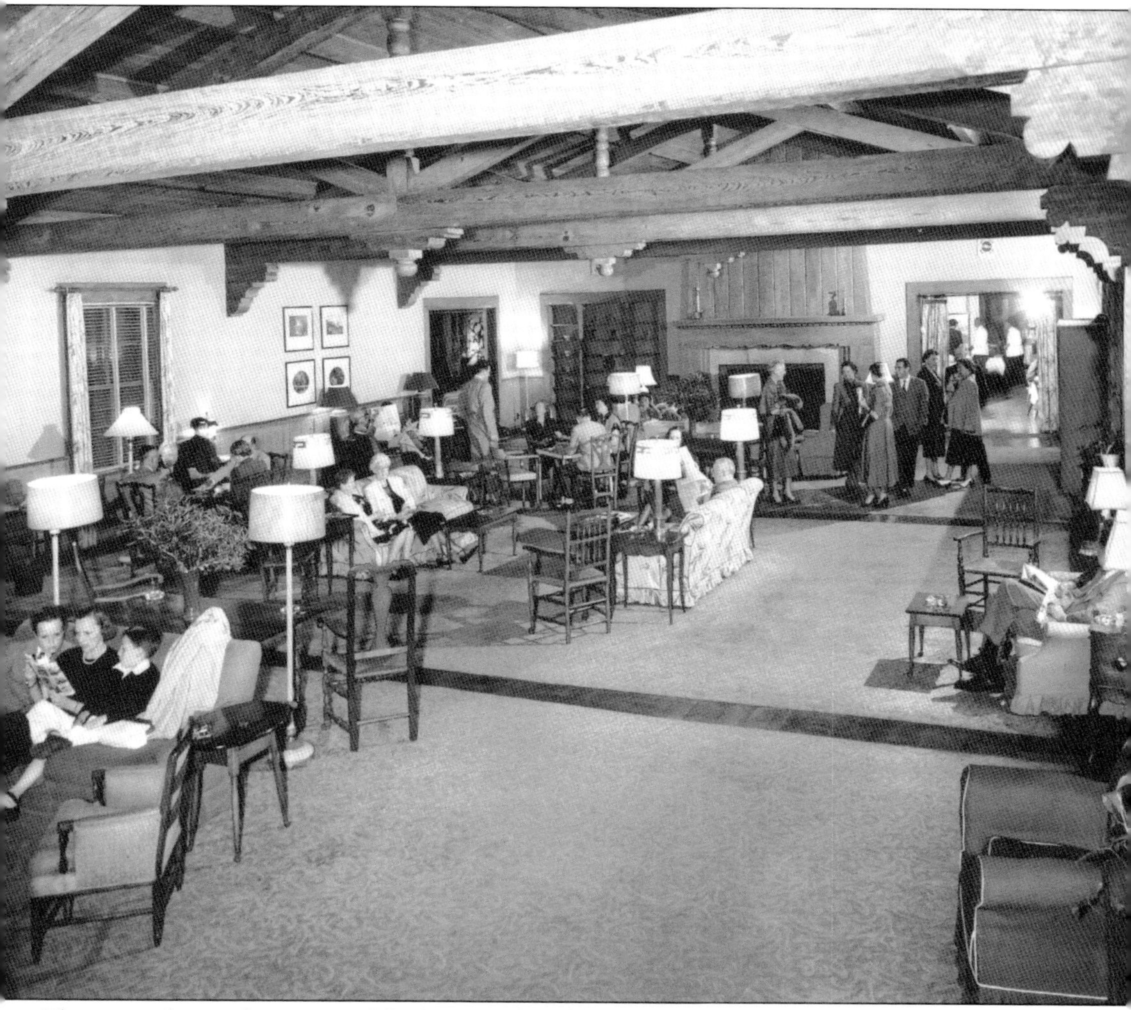

This image depicts the interior of the Ponte Vedra Club Great Lounge in the 1950s. The lounge has been preserved over the years as the club has expanded around it. It features magnolia planking, cypress beams, large fireplaces, and quiet corners to read and socialize. After World War II, the resort also began attracting Southern bankers and businessmen, and today, people come from all around the country and the world to enjoy its luxury and attractions.

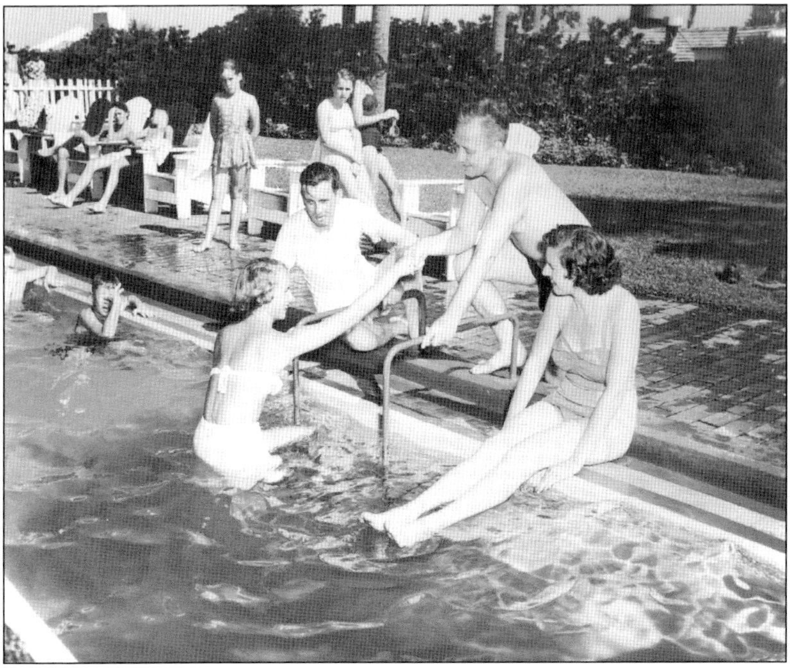

Swimmers cool off on a summer day in 1950 at the Ponte Vedra Club pool. Since the popular pool was located next to the beach, swimmers could go back and forth between the pool and the ocean.

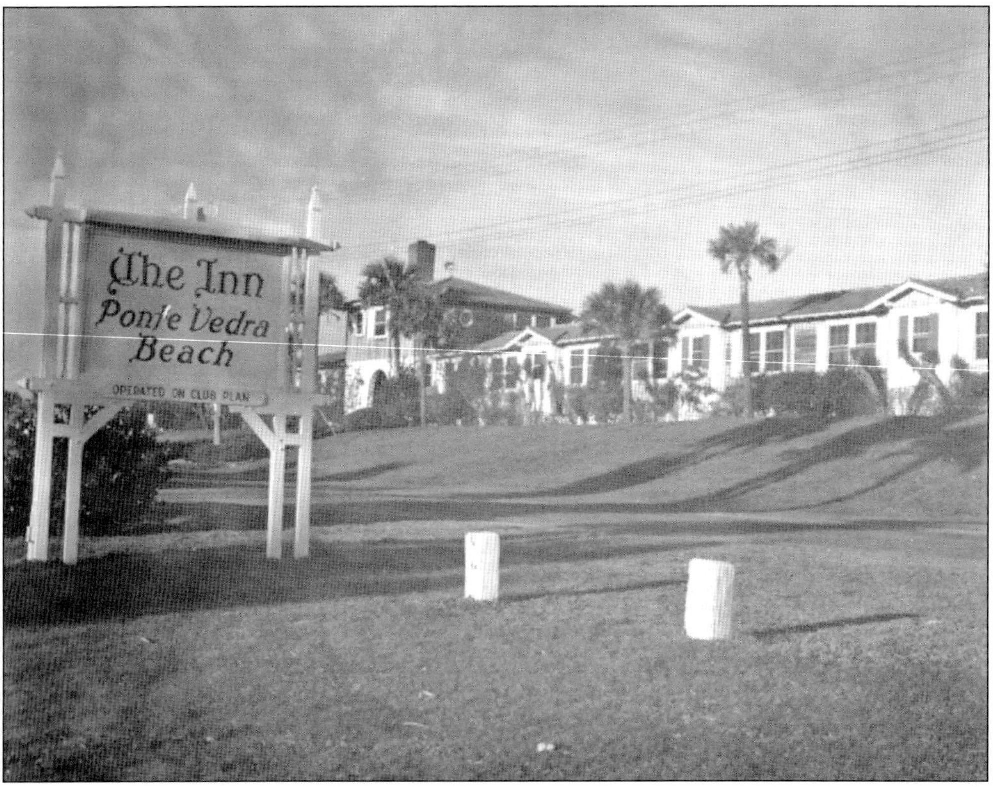


This image shows how the inn at the Ponte Vedra Club looked in the 1950s. When the club first opened, guests stayed in the original log cabin clubhouse, which had 12 rooms. After the inn opened in 1937, the log cabin was used as an employee residence until 1966.

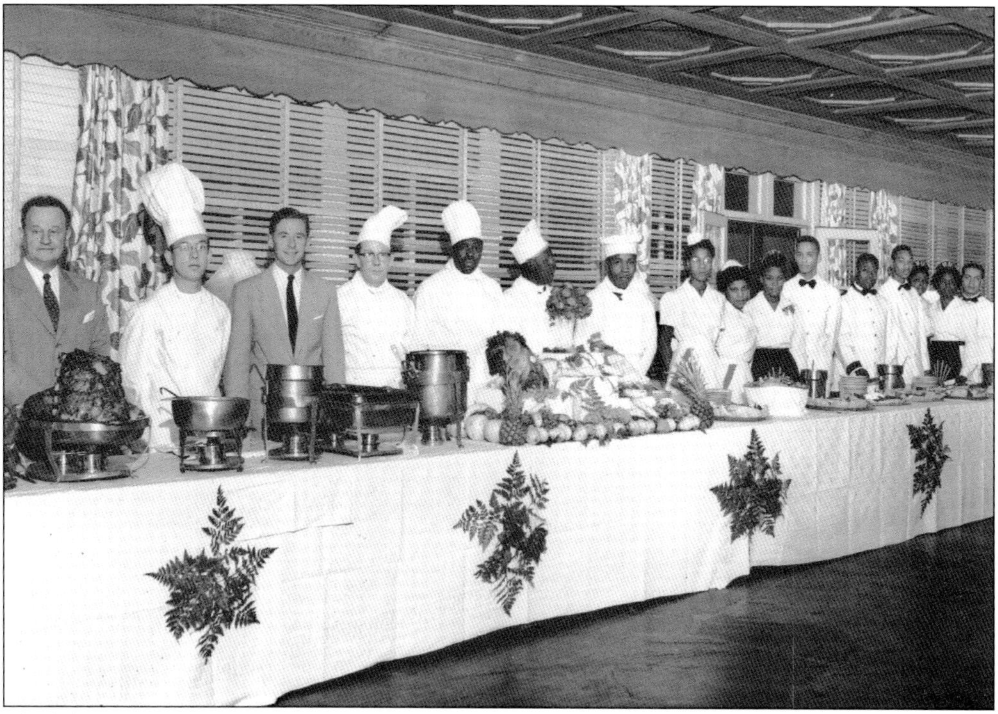

Chefs line up in the Terrace Room at the Ponte Vedra Club in the 1950s. Fine food was also an attraction at the resort for local members and visitors.

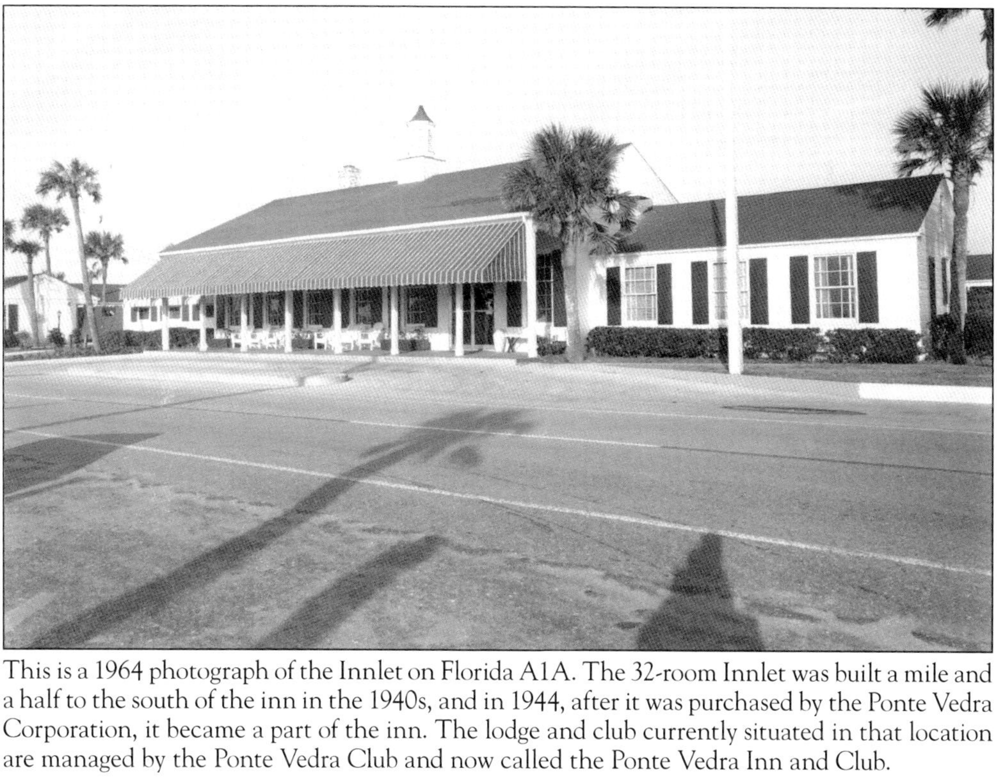

This is a 1964 photograph of the Innlet on Florida A1A. The 32-room Innlet was built a mile and a half to the south of the inn in the 1940s, and in 1944, after it was purchased by the Ponte Vedra Corporation, it became a part of the inn. The lodge and club currently situated in that location are managed by the Ponte Vedra Club and now called the Ponte Vedra Inn and Club.

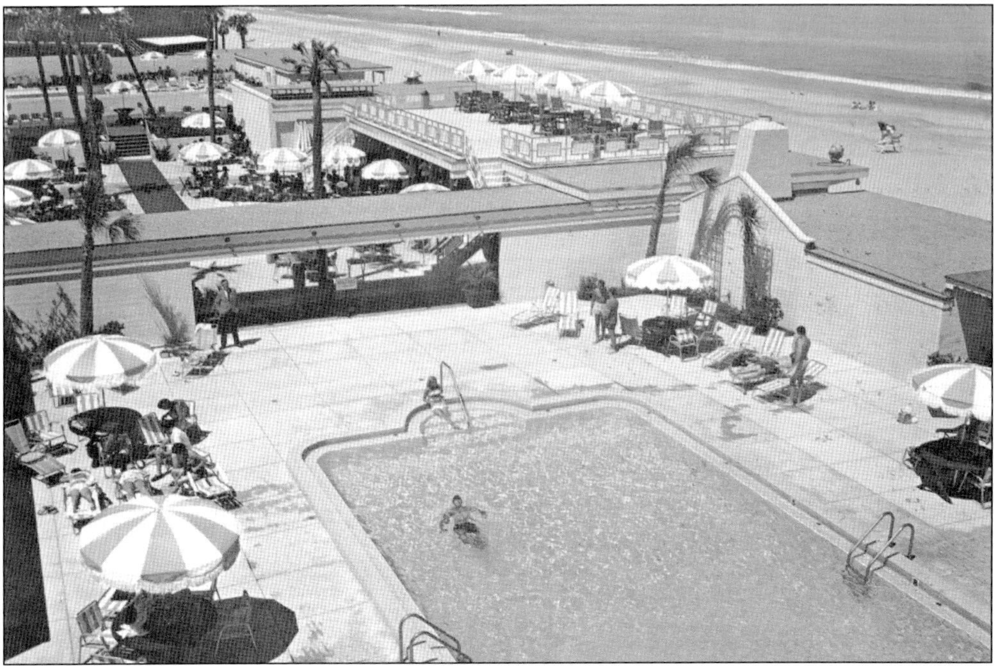

This postcard of a scene at the Ponte Vedra Club pool was issued in the 1950s. Pool scenes were often used in postcards.

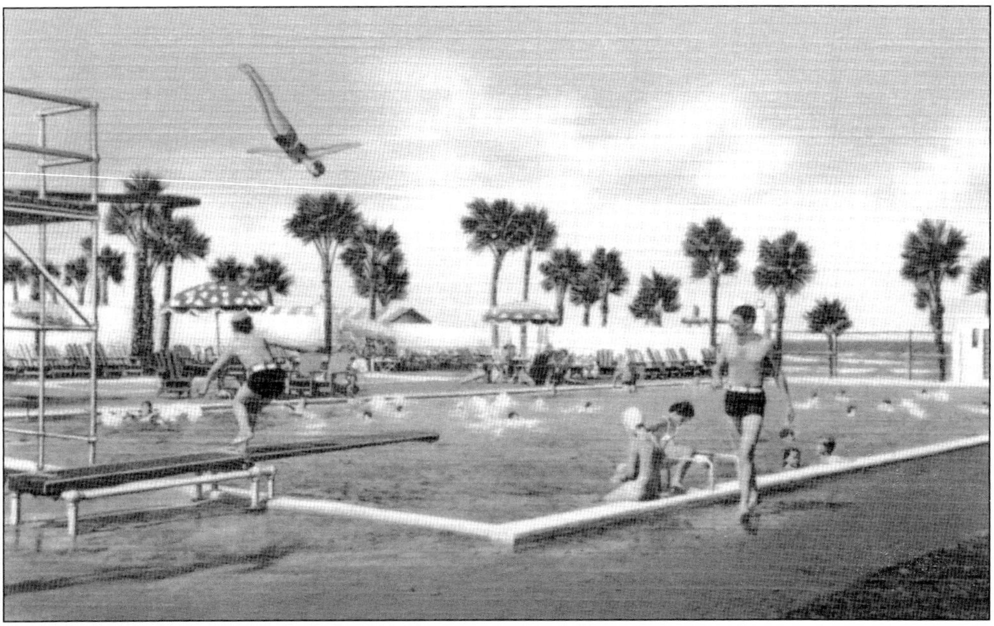

This is another scene at the Ponte Vedra Club pool, which was attractive for its beachside location. The Ponte Vedra Inn and Club today is an American Automobile Association five-diamond resort.

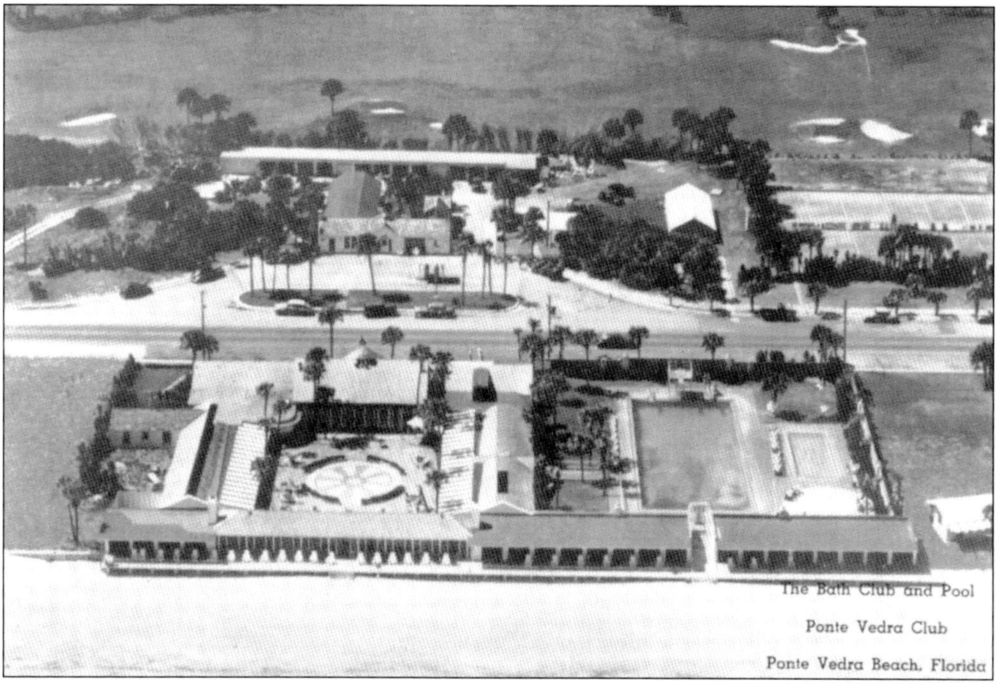


This scene also depicts the Bath Club and pool at the Ponte Vedra Club during its early years. The semitropical weather offered opportunities to swim through most of the year.

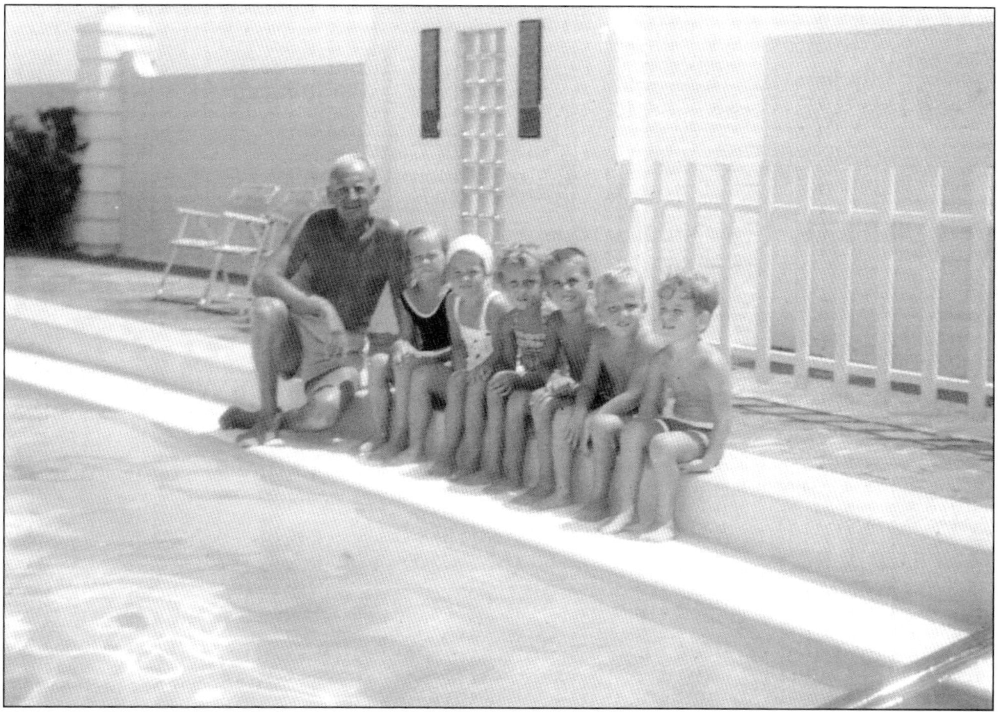

Swim coach Sam Miller poses with six unidentified children during swimming lessons in what appears to be the 1960s. Many local families who were members of the Ponte Vedra Club sent their children for swimming lessons there.

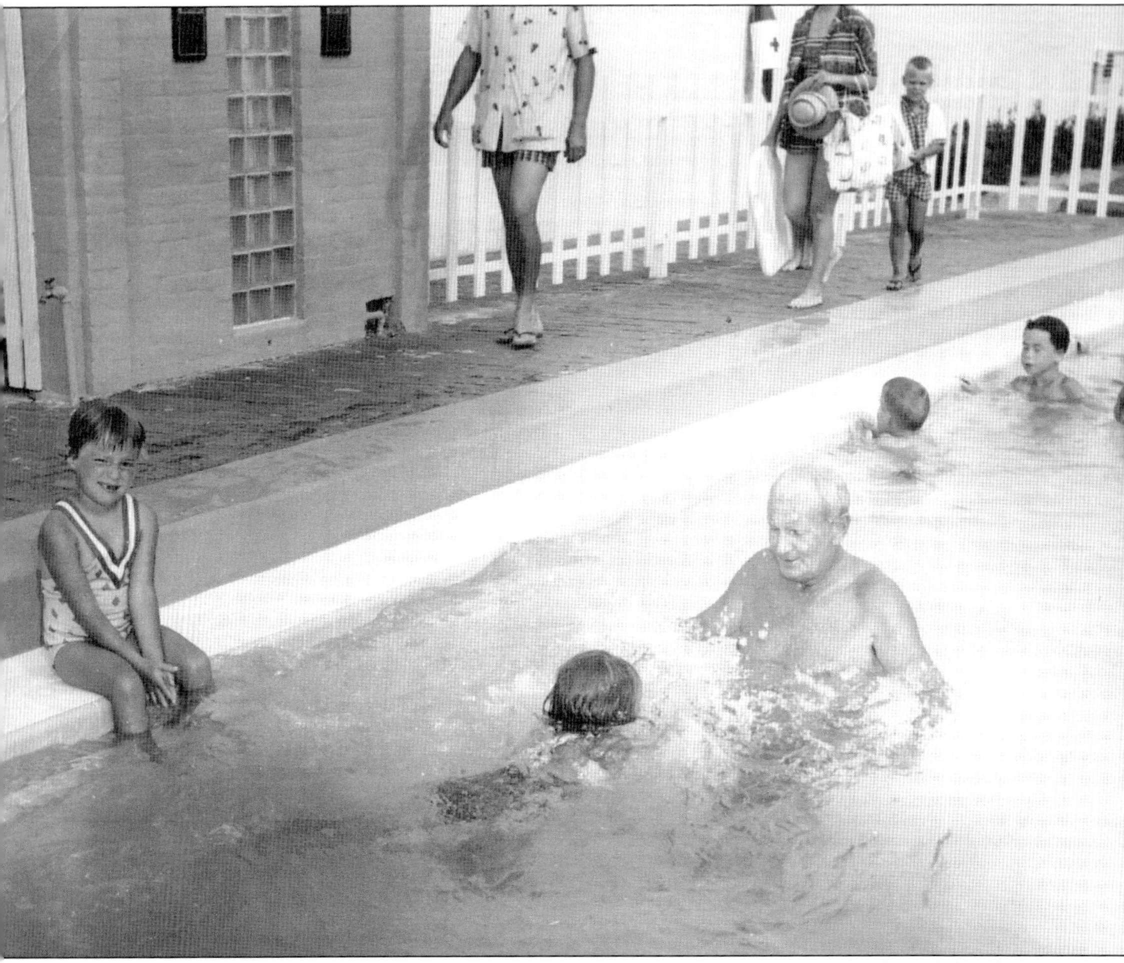

Here, Miller teaches children to swim at the Surf Club pool at the Ponte Vedra Club. The year is not identified, but it appears to be the 1960s. By the middle of the 20th century, the population of Ponte Vedra Beach was growing, and more people were year-round residents. And while the sports of golf and tennis have always been popular in the area and at the club, so was swimming. It is an important skill to have in an area surrounded by the ocean, many lagoons and lakes, and pools. The climate supports swimming most of the year, especially with heated pools, and it grew into a competitive sport among children and teens.

# *Three*

# PALM VALLEY

Palm Valley has always been an important part of the Ponte Vedra Beach area. In fact, since it was given its name and a US post office in 1908, Palm Valley officially existed before Ponte Vedra Beach. The land, west of the beach areas stretching to the present-day Intracoastal Waterway and beyond, was long valued more than the beach coastline because it could be farmed.

During the Spanish period in the 1700s, some families settled in the area north of St. Augustine and established large cattle ranches. The Diego Espinosa family had the largest ranch in the present-day Palm Valley area, so it was known as Diego Plains. Espinosa's house was considered an outpost of the Spanish defenses and known as Fort San Diego.

The land was gradually transformed into small farms in the late 1700s. Many immigrants from the island of Minorca moved there, attracted by bargain land prices.

In 1908, an intracoastal canal was cut through Diego Plains, connecting the San Pablo River to the north to the Tolomato River near St. Augustine. The opened-up water transportation route drew farmers and loggers to the area, which was renamed Palm Valley because of the large numbers of palm trees growing there.

Over the years, a series of bridges were built over the Intracoastal Waterway, and some residents began harvesting palm fronds to sell to churches around the country for Palm Sunday.

In 1916, the Shore Sawmill was built on the northwest side of the waterway at Cracker Landing, also called Craddock Landing. Then, several years later, Prohibition gave residents another source of income, even though it was illegal. They made moonshine in homemade stills hidden deep in the swamps and woods. The moonshine industry continued to thrive even after Prohibition ended, until the high price of sugar put an end to it.

After World War II, as more people were attracted to Florida and the Ponte Vedra Beach area, parts of Palm Valley were gradually transformed into attractive, manicured communities.

There is no longer a Palm Valley post office, as the area is part of Ponte Vedra Beach zip code 32082. There are no more stills, sawmills, or cattle ranches. But Palm Valley continues to exist, even though there are no official lines that indicate where it begins and where it ends.

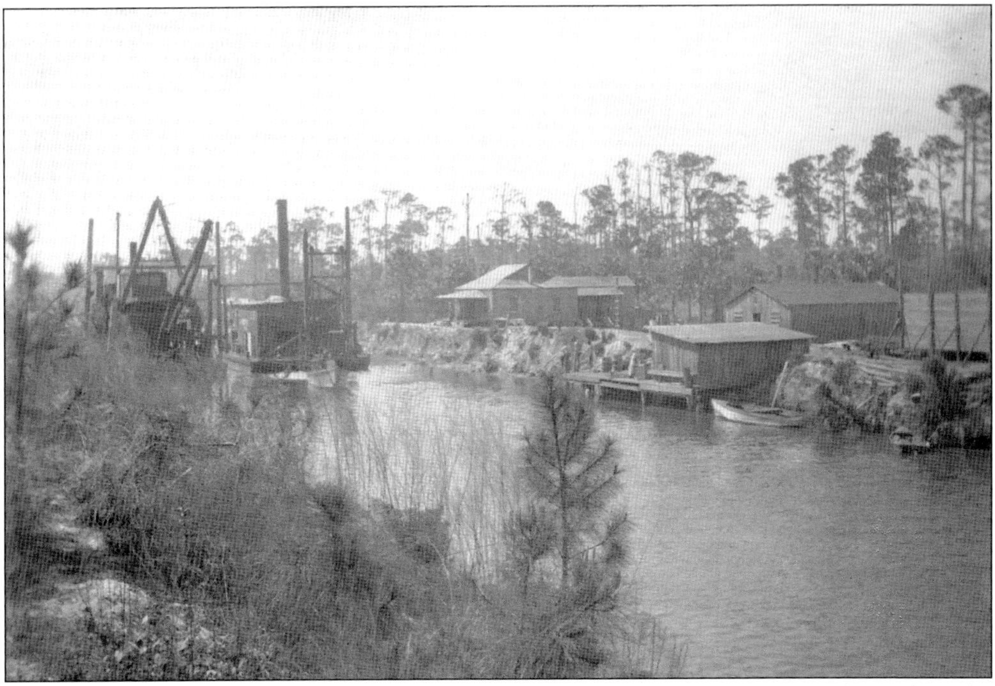

This is an April 1916 image of the Shore Sawmill in Palm Valley. The mill was located on the west side of the Intracoastal Waterway, then known as Pablo Creek, in an area called Cracker Landing, which some locals called "Graddock Landing."

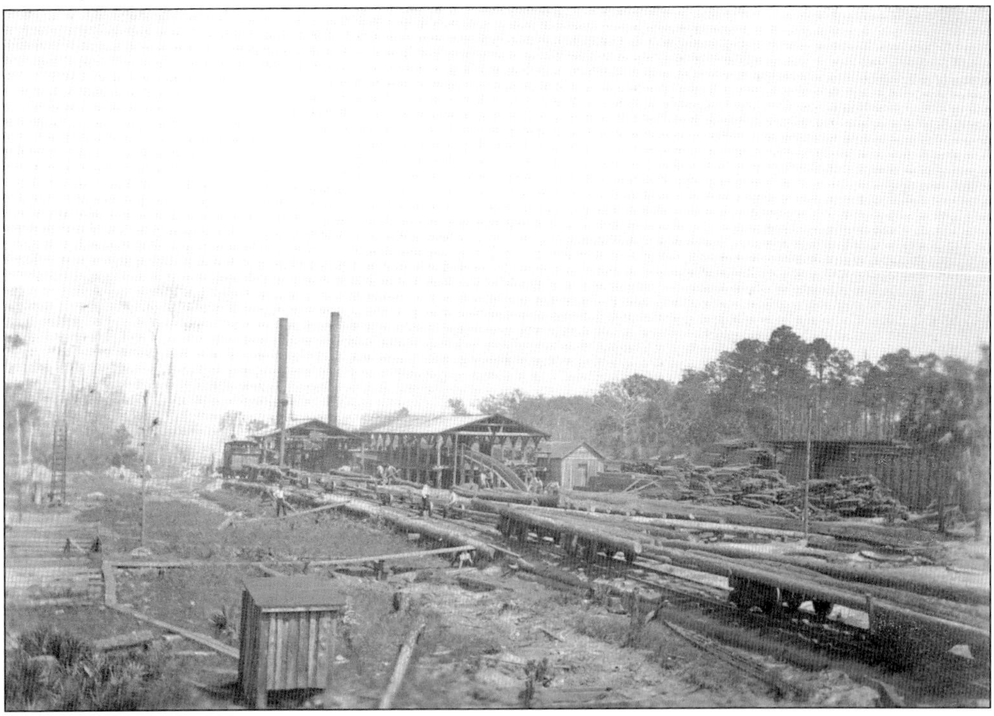

Dredging took place along Pablo Creek in Palm Valley in April 1916. The canal is being widened in front of Shore Sawmill, where some area residents worked.

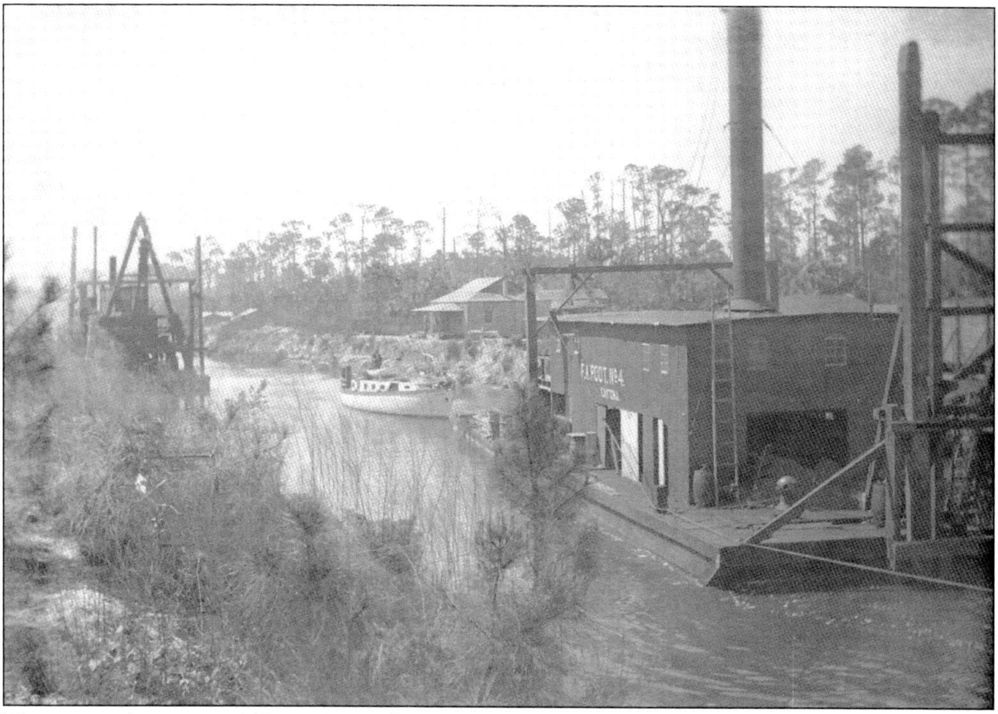

This is another view of Shore Sawmill in 1916 in Palm Valley, a community located to the west of the oceanfront town of Mineral City. The sawmill was located in an area surrounded by pine trees.

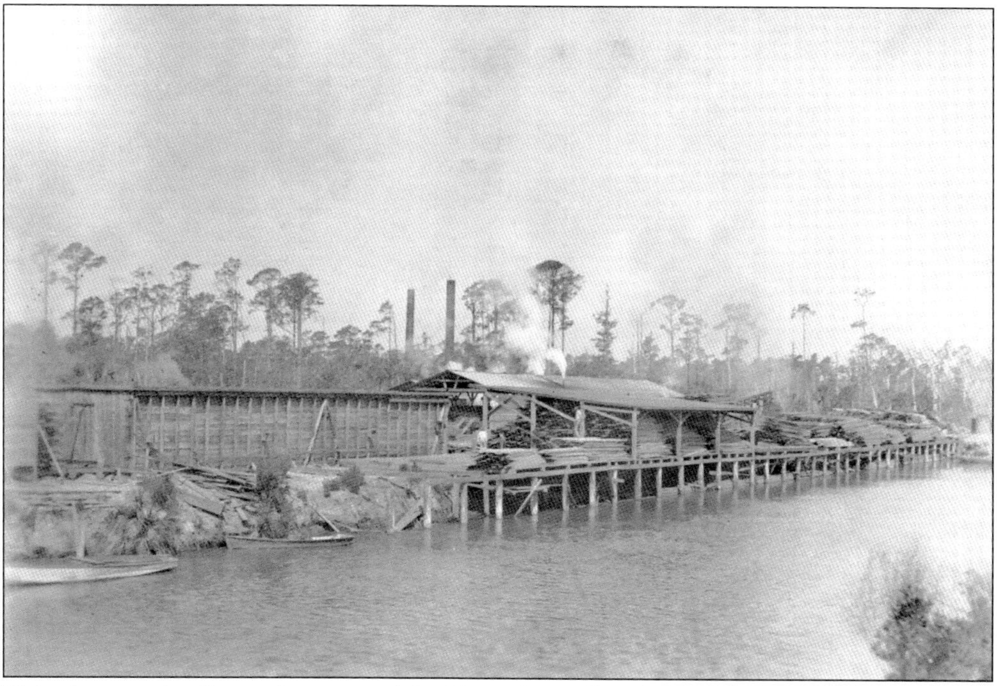

This photograph offers a clear view of the Shore Sawmill in Palm Valley in 1916. Lumber from the area was hauled to Pablo Beach.

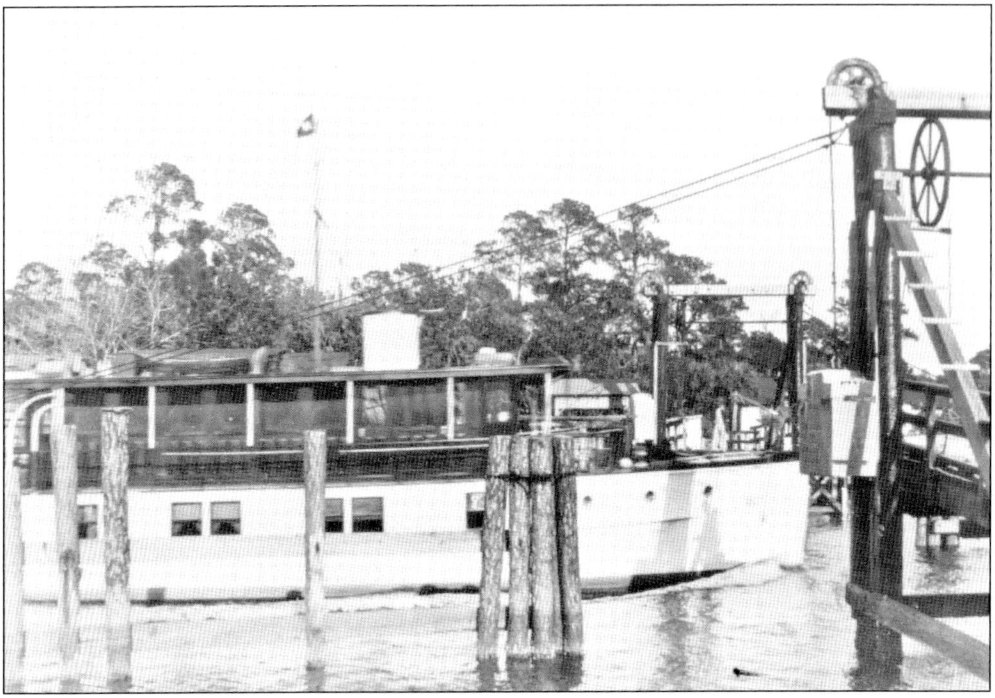

This photograph, taken in either 1934 or 1935, is of the Barge Bridge that crossed the Intracoastal Waterway in Palm Valley. There have been a series of bridges in that area over the years.

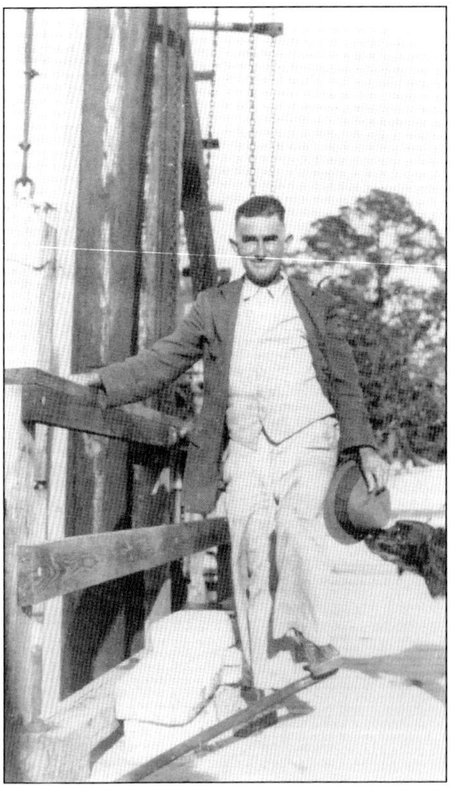

George Oesterreicher stands on a bridge crossing the Intracoastal Waterway in 1935. The Oesterreicher family lived in Palm Valley for many years, along Twenty Mile Road, about two miles north of County Road 210. Oesterreicher and his family ran a fish camp at the Intracoastal Waterway.

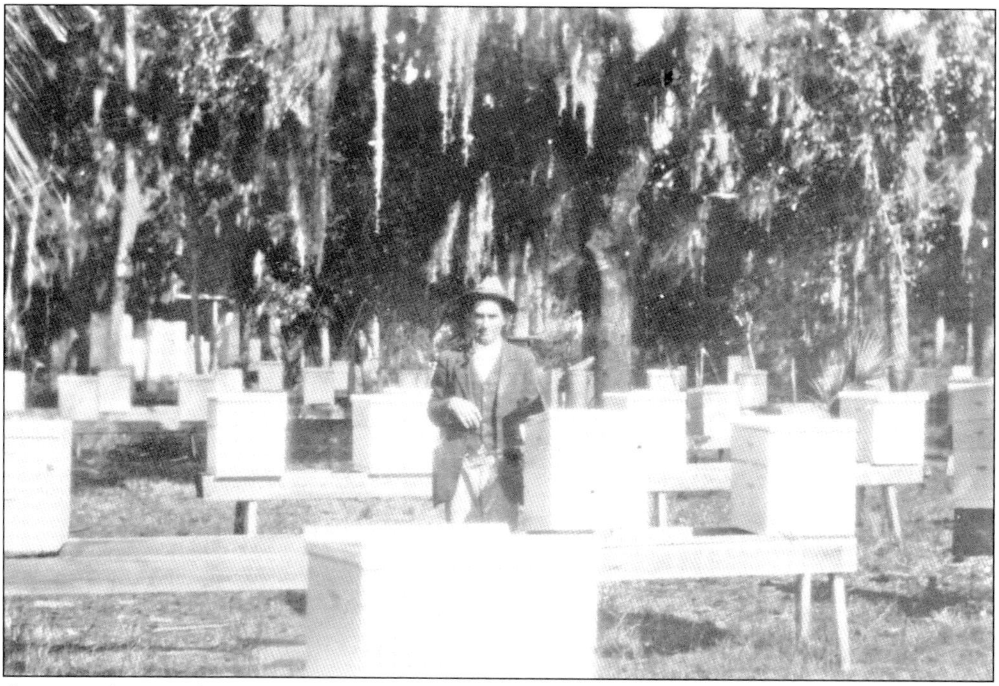

Oesterreicher stands near some beehives in 1935 in Palm Valley. He was part of a family that long lived in the area. The family's homestead was built in 1873, when the area was known as Diego.

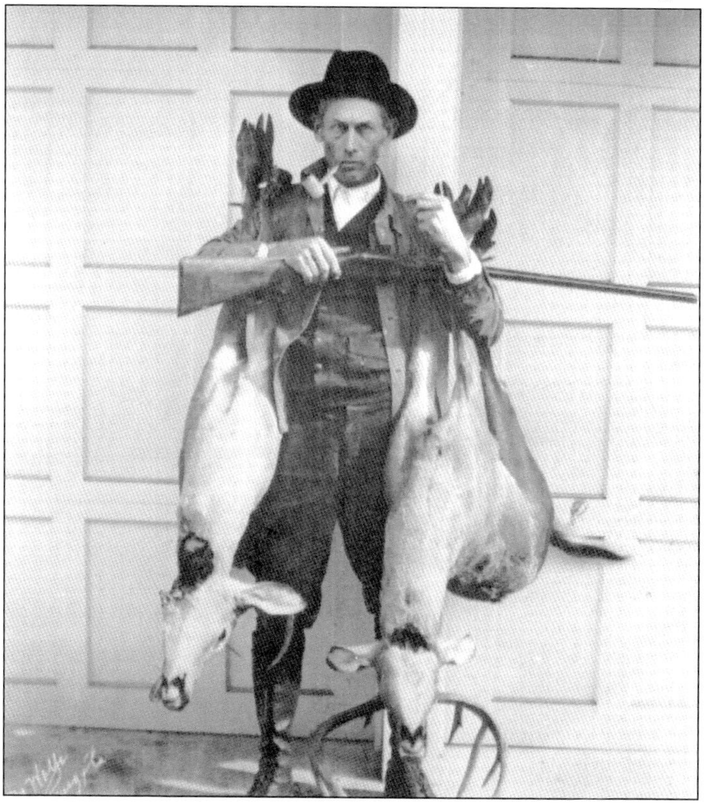

Francis Hayman poses with two deer he shot during a hunting trip in Palm Valley on December 26, 1935. Hunting and fishing were popular in Palm Valley, as it was a remote wooded area close to the Intracoastal Waterway.

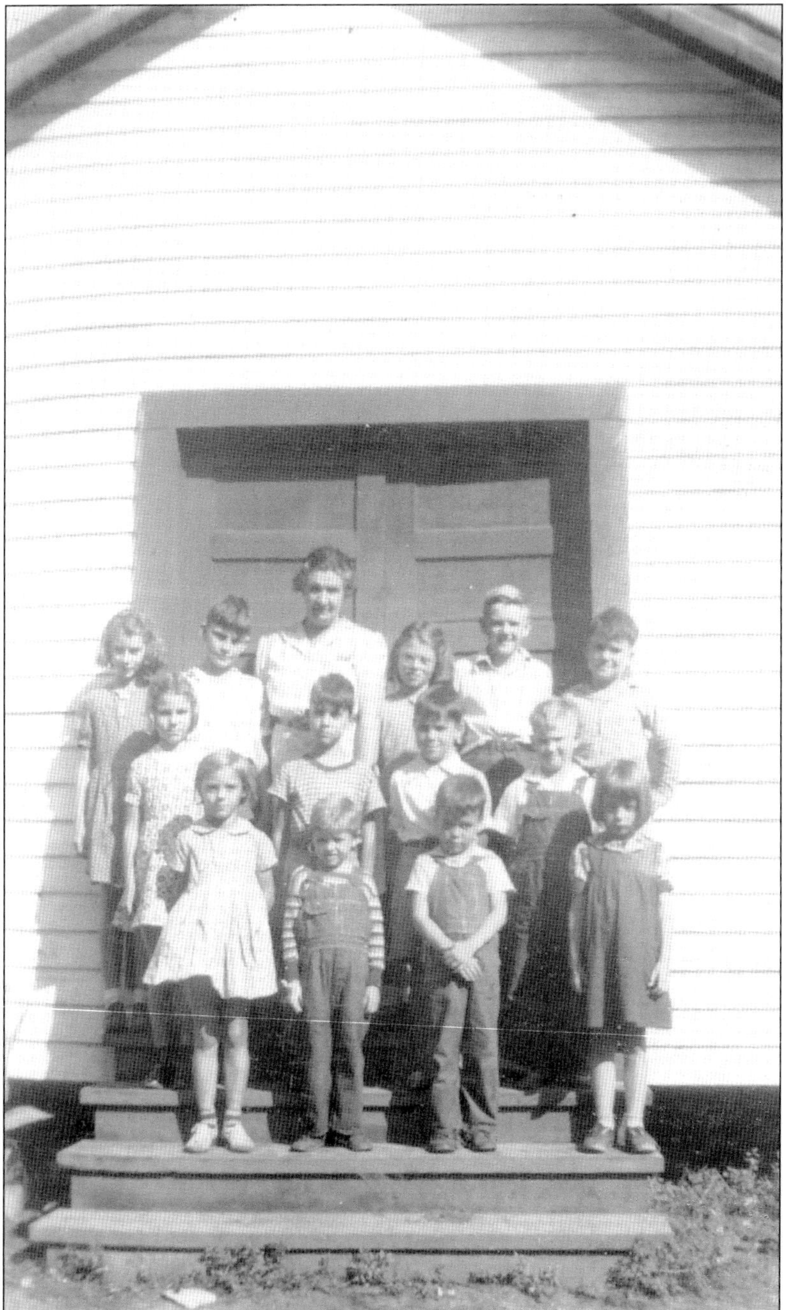

Teacher Florence Hartstuff stands with her class at the Palm Valley School. While the year is not identified, it appears to have been taken in the 1930s or 1940s. The area was sparsely populated, and the teacher probably taught all the grades, as the children appear to be different ages. Palm Valley's first school opened in 1882, just west of what is now the Intracoastal Waterway. That two-room school held four classes of children, and after it burned, a second wooden schoolhouse was built in that location. It was used until 1927, when the area's third schoolhouse was built east of the Intracoastal Waterway in 1928.

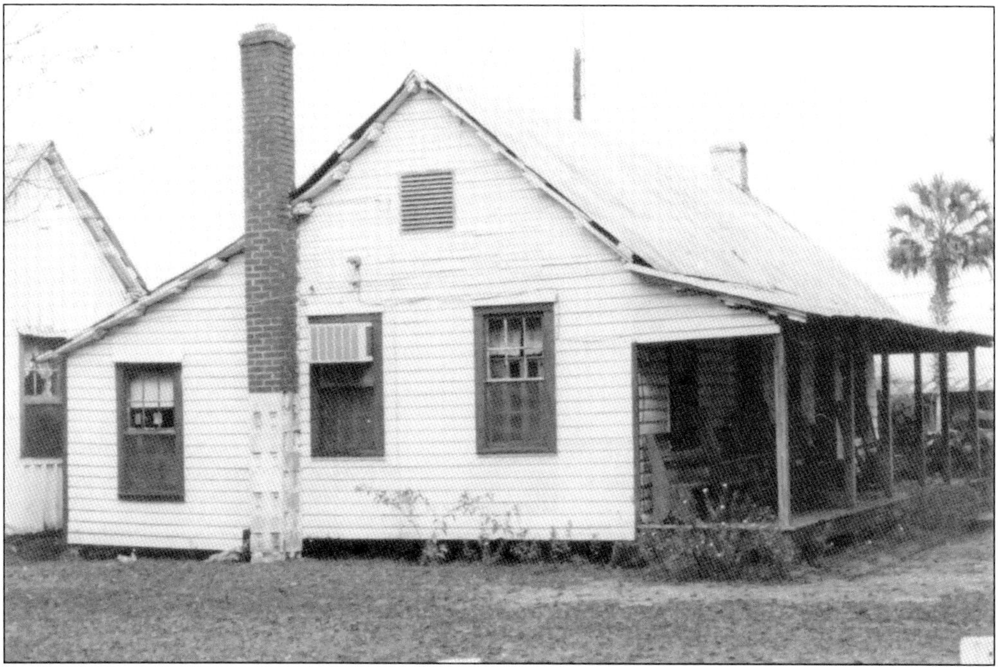

This is a photograph of the Oesterreicher family homestead, built in Palm Valley in 1873, when the area was then known as Diego. The kitchen is located in the building to the left. The home was built with two rooms but two more were added in 1905. The home had no electricity, indoor plumbing, or window screens until 1942.

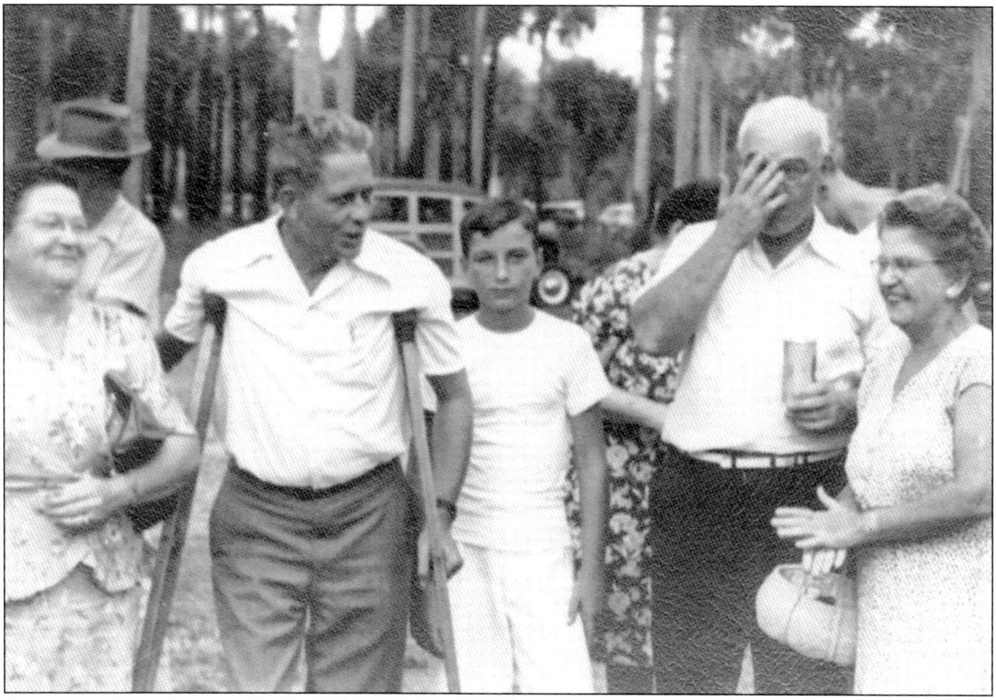

A group of people attends a social gathering in Palm Valley sometime during the mid-1900s. Two of the people are identified as Dr. Earl H. Roberts, second from left, and Anna Purcel, far right.

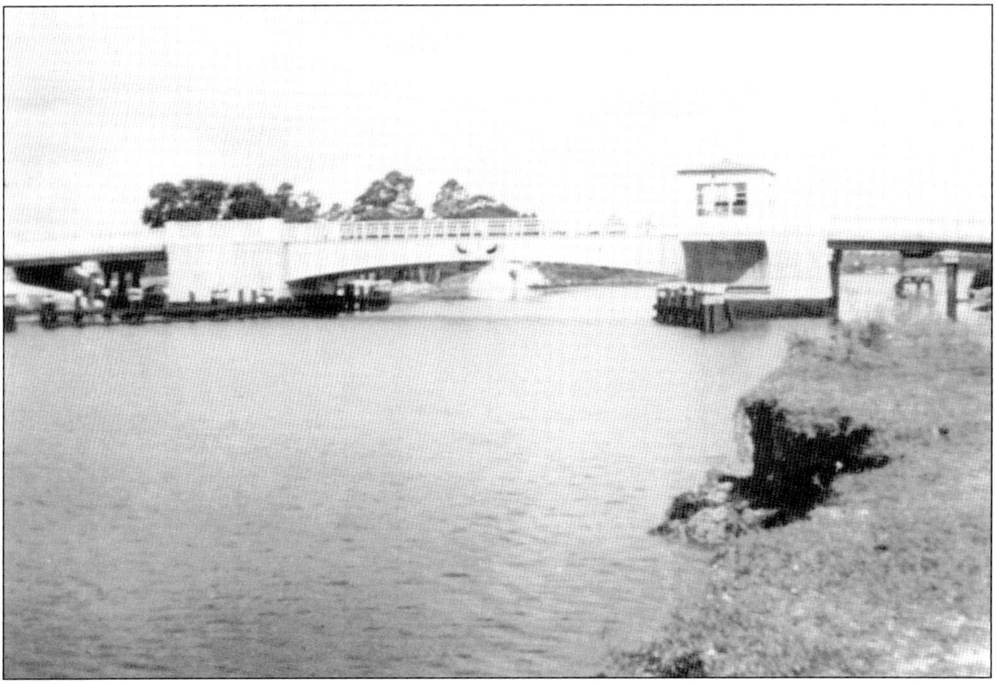

This is a wide-angle shot of the Palm Valley Bridge around 1950. The drawbridge served vehicles traveling across the Intracoastal Waterway for many years, until it was recently replaced by a high four-lane bridge.

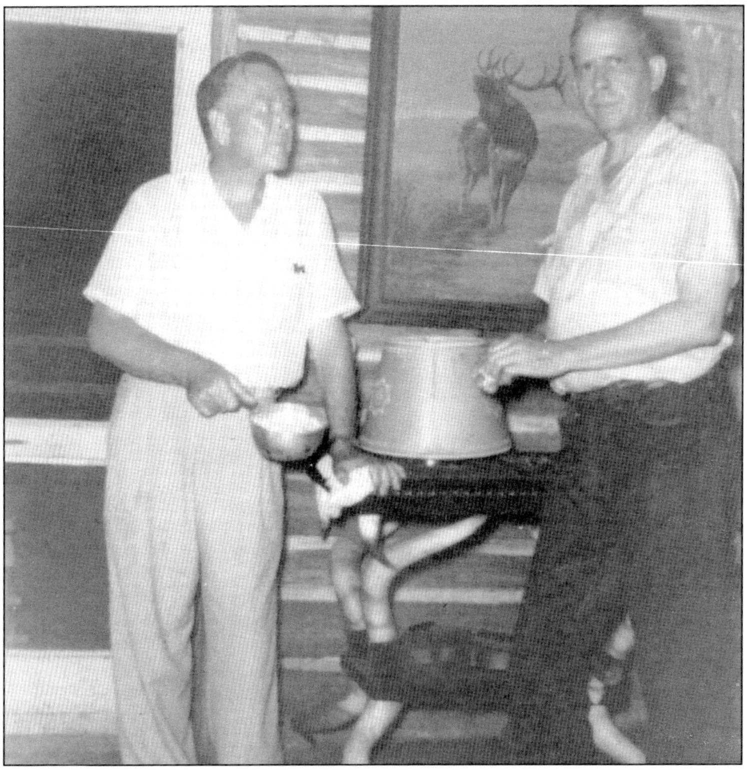

Two men identified as Elvin Watkins and Dr. Earl H. Roberts stand inside a home in Palm Valley on June 15, 1953. The home is identified as the "20 Mile Roberts Ranch." Twenty Mile Road was an important route through Palm Valley.

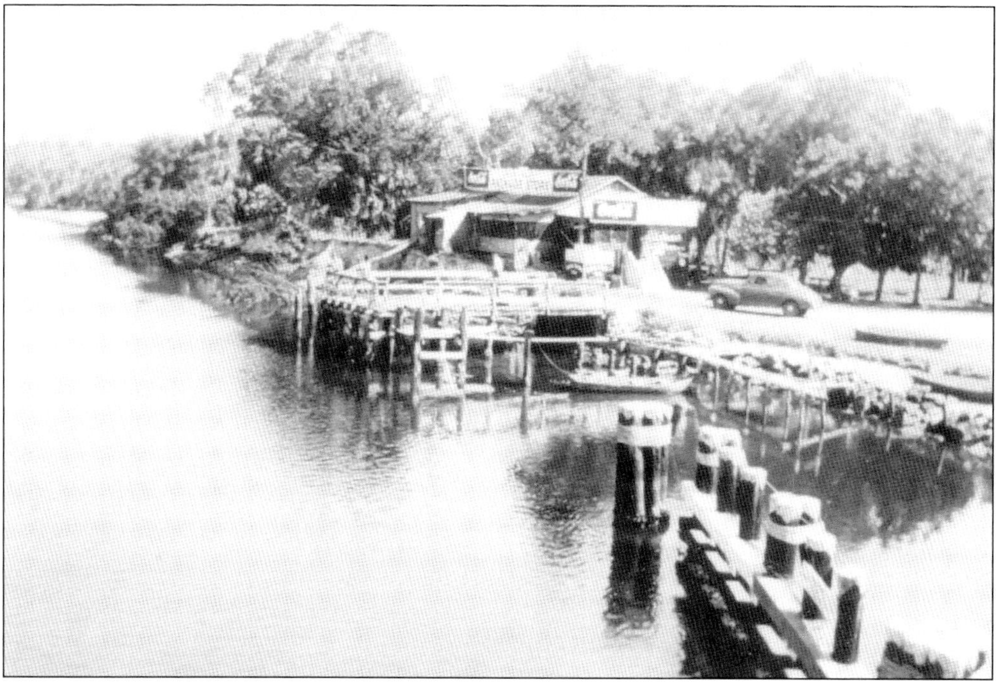

This photograph shows the Palm Valley Fish Camp around 1950. The business, which featured a package store, was located on Palm Valley Road, also called County Road 210, on the eastern shore of the Intracoastal Waterway.

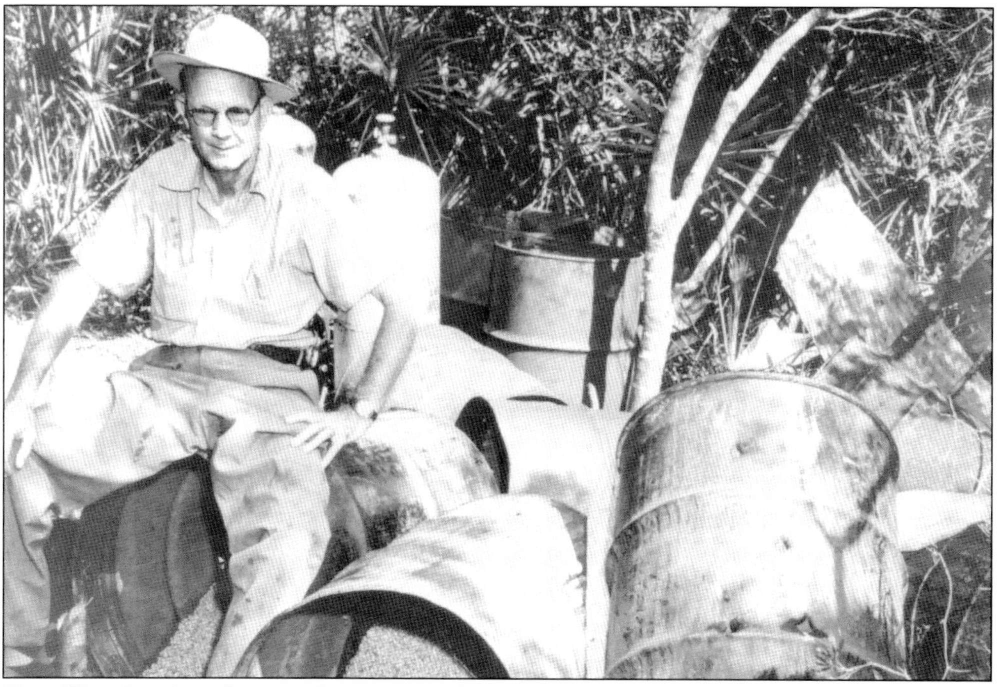

Sheriff Roy Landrum Jr. poses for a picture after raiding and destroying an illegal moonshine still in Palm Valley in 1950. Families in the area began making illegal whiskey in the woods during Prohibition and continued long after it ended.

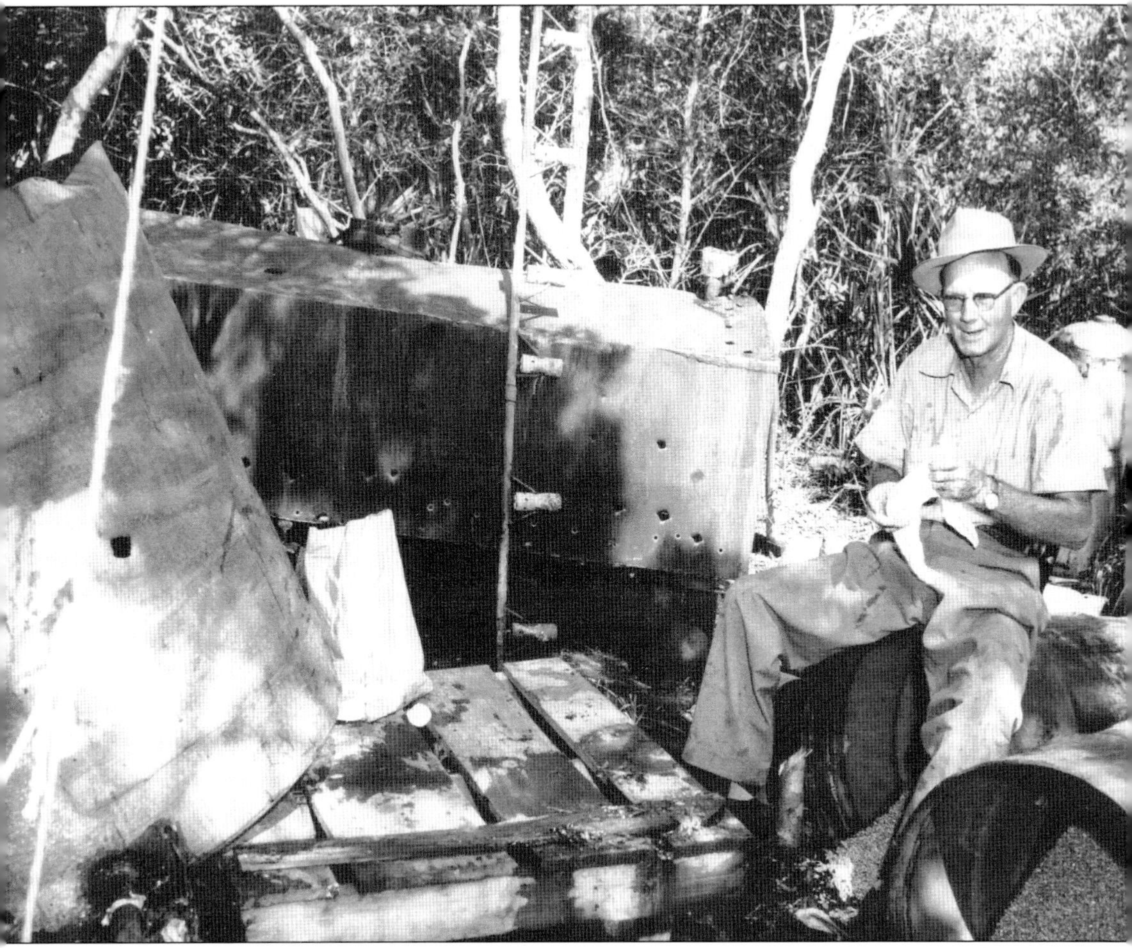

St. Johns County deputy sheriff Roy Landrum Jr. raids and destroys an illegal whiskey still in 1950. The Palm Valley area was an ideal location for making moonshine, offering an abundant supply of water and many places to hide in the woods and marshes. Lawmen found and raided stills on a regular basis for decades, but moonshiners managed to stay in business anyway by moving to another location. Always on the lookout for the revenue men, the lawmen who were on the lookout for illegal stills, moonshiners made their product with corn, rye, and a lot of sugar. High sugar prices eventually put an end to the moonshine business, not the revenue men.

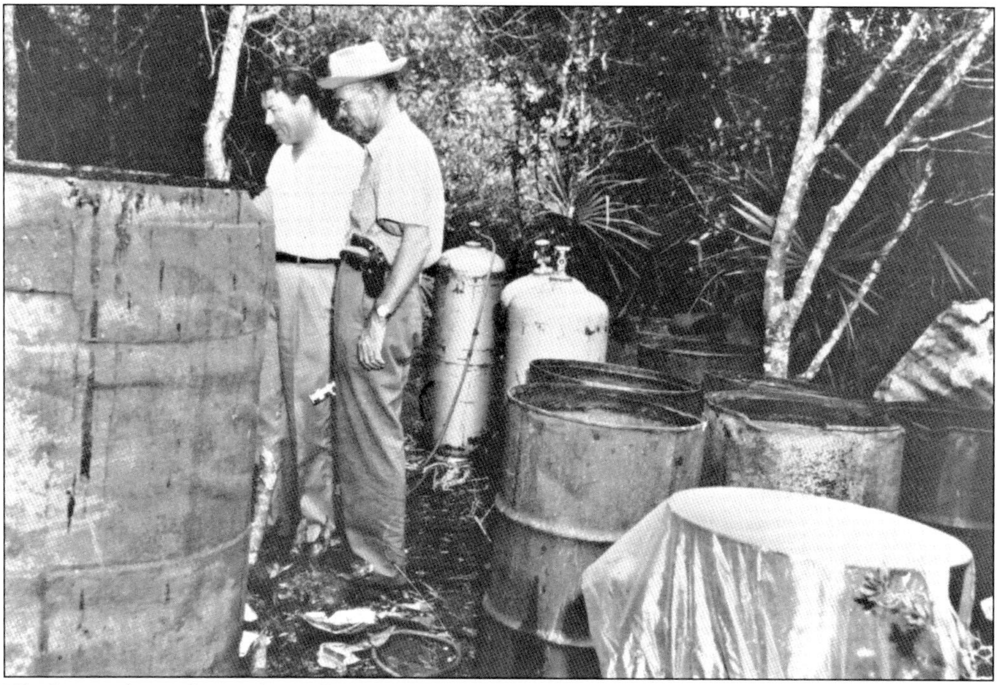

The law raids a still in Palm Valley in 1950. For Deputy Sheriffs Roy Landrum Jr. and Cecil Wilds, it was an important part of their jobs and kept them busy.

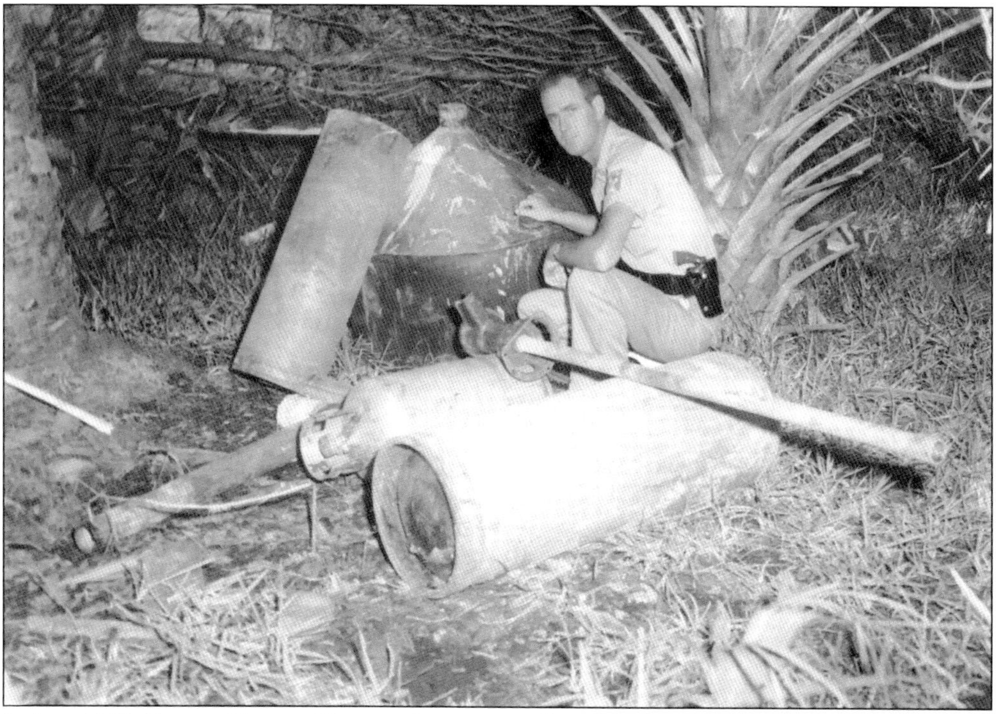

In late 1955, Deputy Everett Heaney destroys an illegal still and equipment in Palm Valley. Prohibition had ended more than 20 years earlier, but Palm Valley residents still found making their own whiskey profitable.

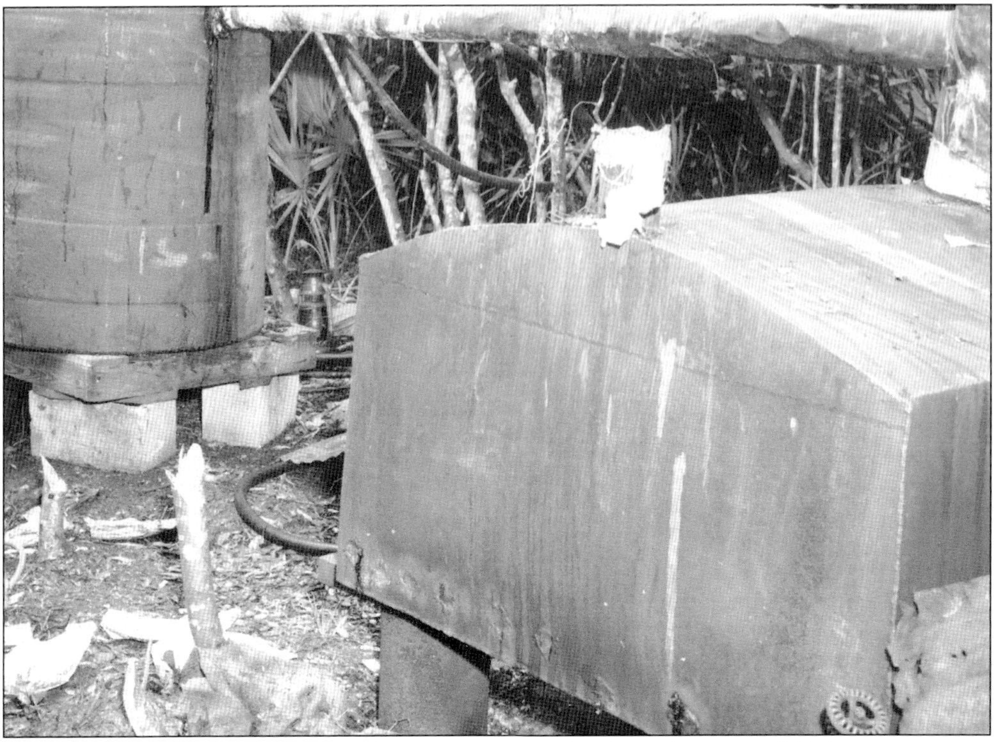

This is a close-up photograph of an illegal moonshine still in Palm Valley in 1955. Lawmen seemed to enjoy having a photographer document their success in finding and destroying stills.

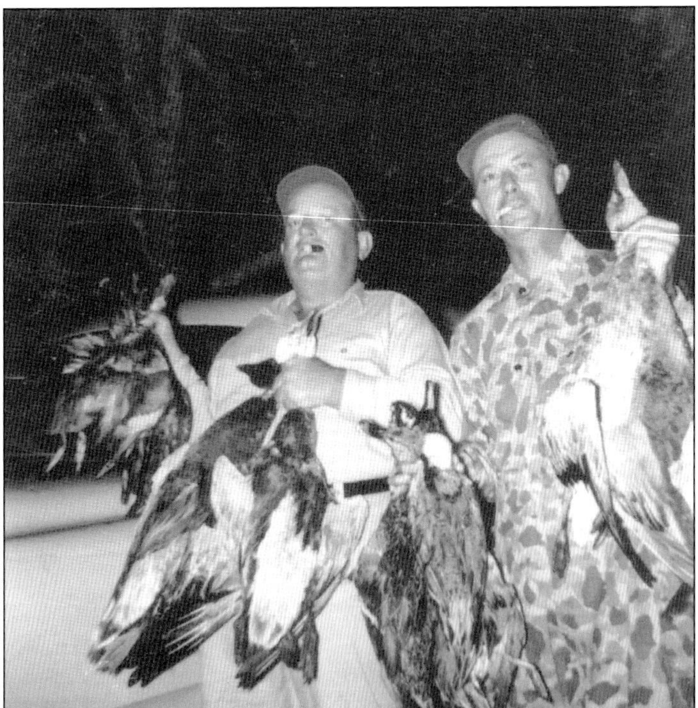

Edward McCormick and Sonny Hulett pose with their catch after returning from a duck-hunting trip in Palm Valley in 1957. Life in Palm Valley was a world away from the life of Ponte Vedra Beach residents at that time.

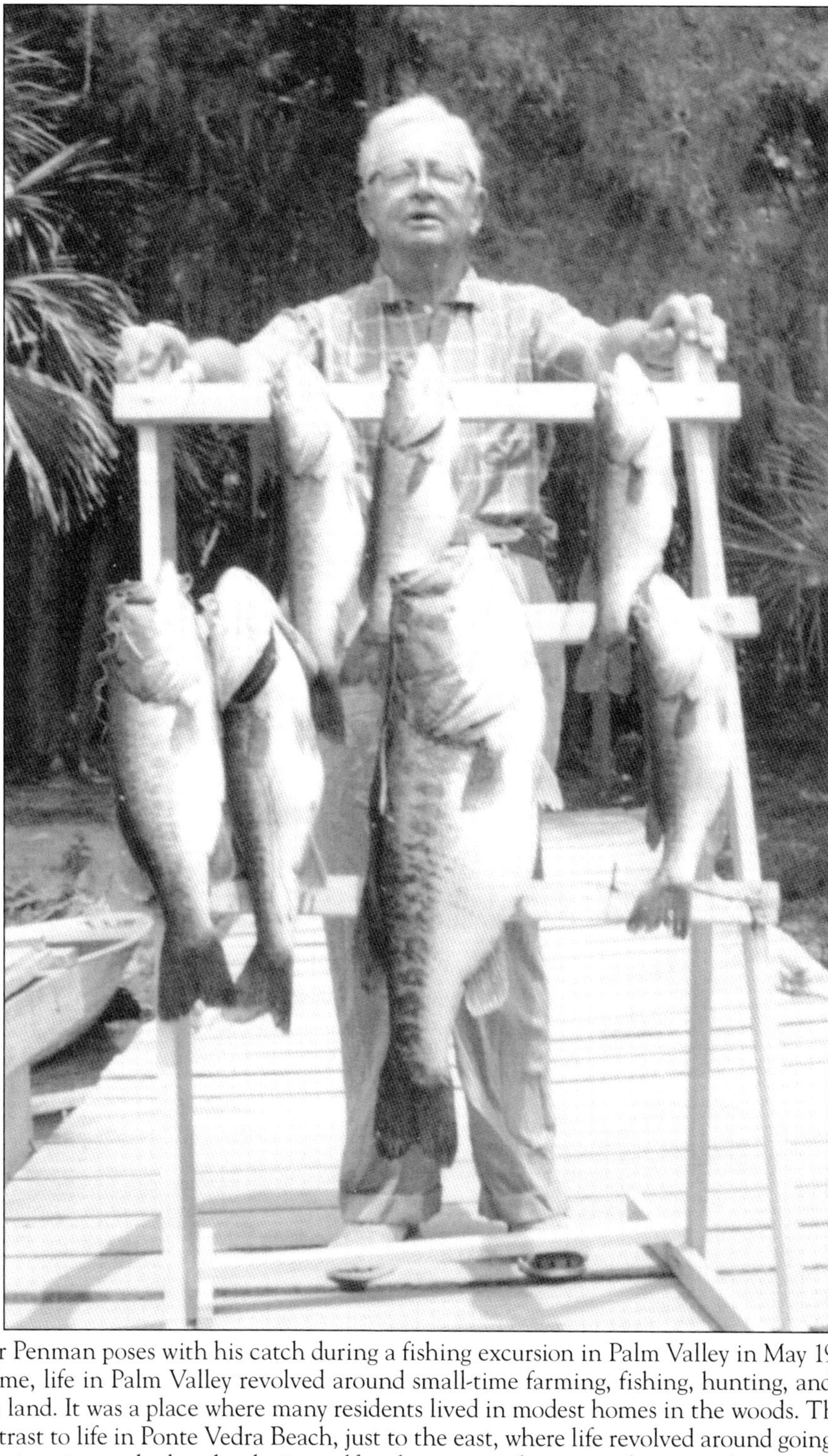

Arthur Penman poses with his catch during a fishing excursion in Palm Valley in May 1963. At that time, life in Palm Valley revolved around small-time farming, fishing, hunting, and living off the land. It was a place where many residents lived in modest homes in the woods. That was in contrast to life in Ponte Vedra Beach, just to the east, where life revolved around going to the pool, swimming at the beach, playing golf and tennis, and going to dances and parties. It was a place where many residents lived in oceanfront homes.

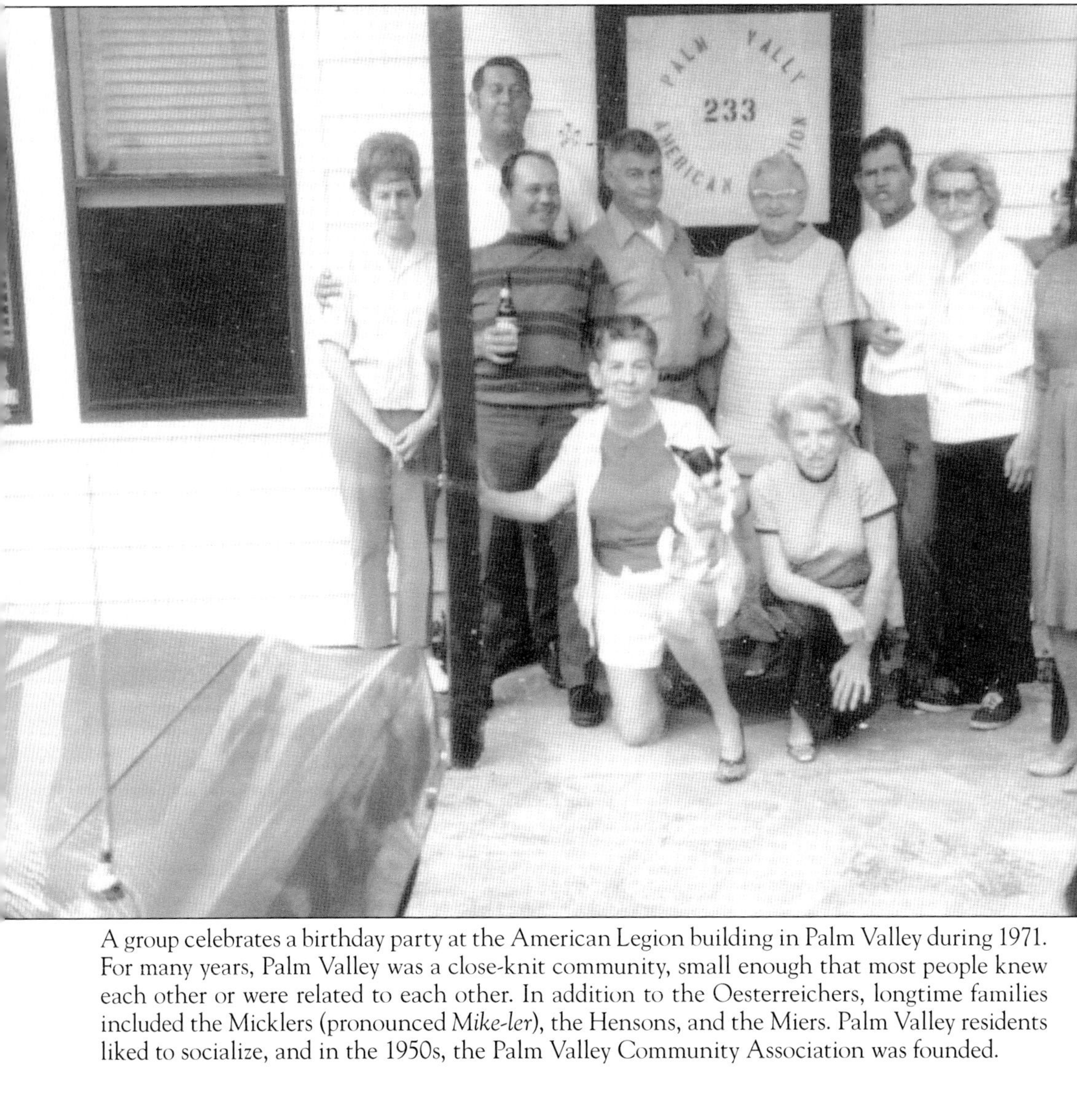


A group celebrates a birthday party at the American Legion building in Palm Valley during 1971. For many years, Palm Valley was a close-knit community, small enough that most people knew each other or were related to each other. In addition to the Oesterreichers, longtime families included the Micklers (pronounced *Mike-ler*), the Hensons, and the Miers. Palm Valley residents liked to socialize, and in the 1950s, the Palm Valley Community Association was founded.

# *Four*

# World War II

On June 17, 1942, a German submarine approached the Ponte Vedra Beach coastline carrying four saboteurs and explosives. The men, who had all lived in the United States at one point and therefore spoke English, loaded the explosives into a rubber dingy and rowed ashore in the dark of night.

They were part of Operation Pastorius, sent to infiltrate the country and destroy factories, bridges, power plants, tunnels, and waterworks in several states during World War II. Four other saboteurs had landed on a beach on Long Island in New York four nights before.

When the Florida saboteurs got to the beach under the light of a thin sliver of moon, they dug holes in the sand to bury four boxes of explosives. They noted the spot because they planned to come back to get them at an opportune time.

They wore bathing suits and German marine caps with Nazi swastikas, which they thought would give them prisoner-of-war status if they were caught. After burying their cargo, they headed north along the beach to Jacksonville Beach, carrying street clothes under their arms. After the sun came up, they acted like tourists to blend in, swimming and relaxing on the beach, even cheerfully waving to a passing police car.

Around 11:00 a.m., they put their clothes on and caught a bus to Jacksonville, where they checked into a hotel and went shopping. All eight saboteurs were caught after one of the Long Island gang turned himself in. They were all tried in court and found guilty. The two who aided authorities were imprisoned, and the other six were executed.

That was the most exciting event that occurred in Ponte Vedra Beach during the war, but residents helped the war effort by keeping their lights off so the coast was dark at night; this action ensured that any enemy ships out at sea would not have targets to aim at. The residents also visited an American Red Cross station at the Ponte Vedra Club to help with projects to aid servicemen.

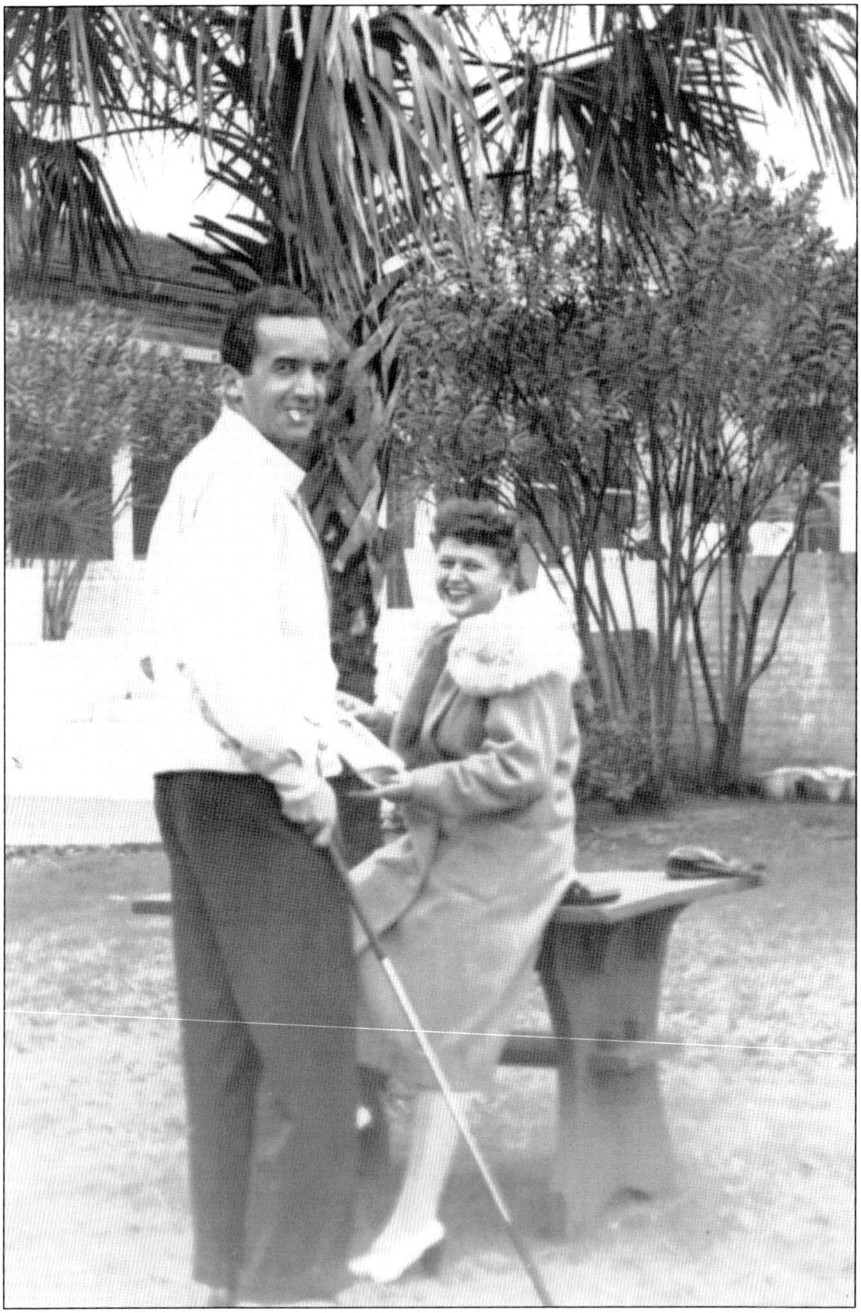

Famous journalist Edward R. Murrow and Jonnie Norris relax at the Ponte Vedra Club on December 27, 1941. Murrow stayed at the club that Christmas, shortly after making his well-known World War II–era "This is London" broadcast. The Ponte Vedra Beach resident helped war efforts in various ways. All buildings along the coast were required to have windows facing the ocean blacked out, to prevent light from shining on American ships at sea along the shore. In the era before air conditioning, that meant blocking out cooling ocean breezes if the lights were on or living in the dark. In addition, the Coast Guard set up a barracks on Ponte Vedra Boulevard, and the mounted patrol kept its horses in stables across the street.

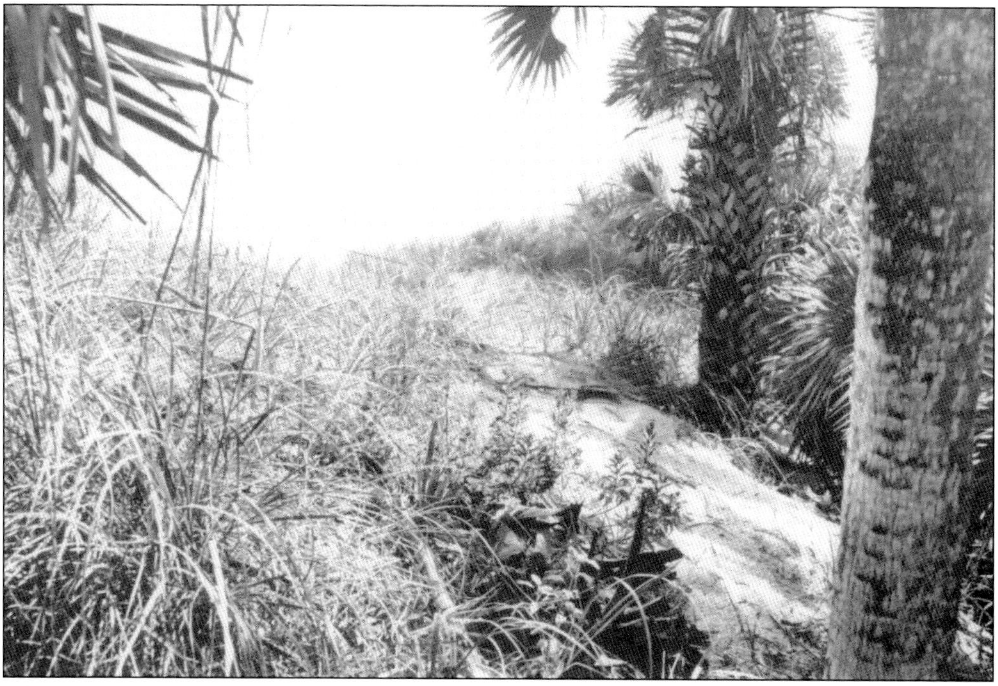

This is a photograph of the beach where German saboteurs buried explosives in Ponte Vedra Beach during June 1942. After rowing ashore from a submarine, they buried their cargo at night in an area in the 900 block of Ponte Vedra Boulevard and planned to retrieve it later. During their mission, called Operation Pastorius, they planned to destroy important sites around the United States.

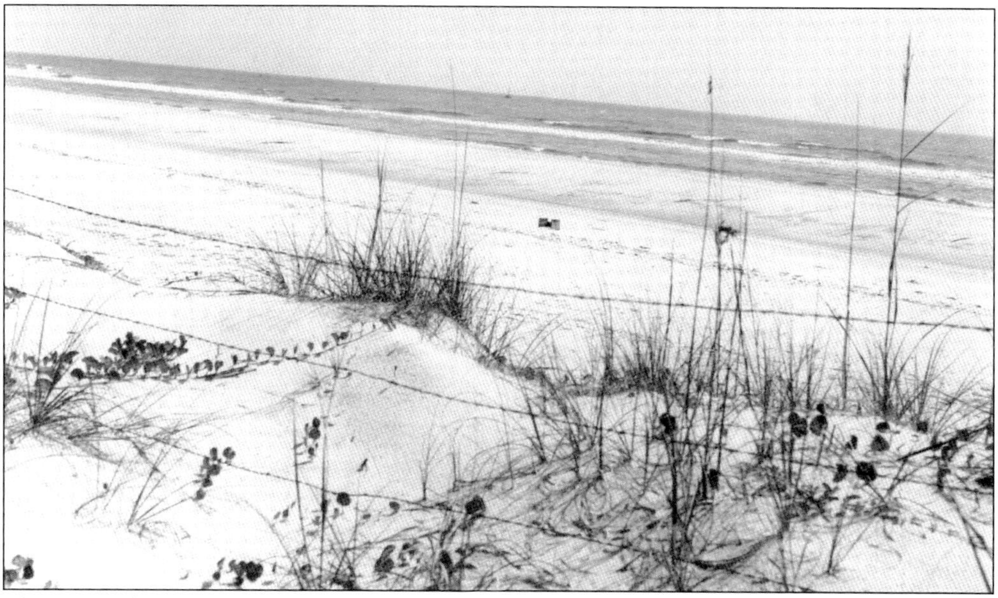

This image shows the dunes where four German saboteurs buried explosives in Ponte Vedra Beach in June 1942. They were on a mission to destroy important sites in the United States but were captured before they could do so. Four other saboteurs also snuck ashore in Long Island, New York, that month, and one of them turned himself in, leading to the arrest of all the others.

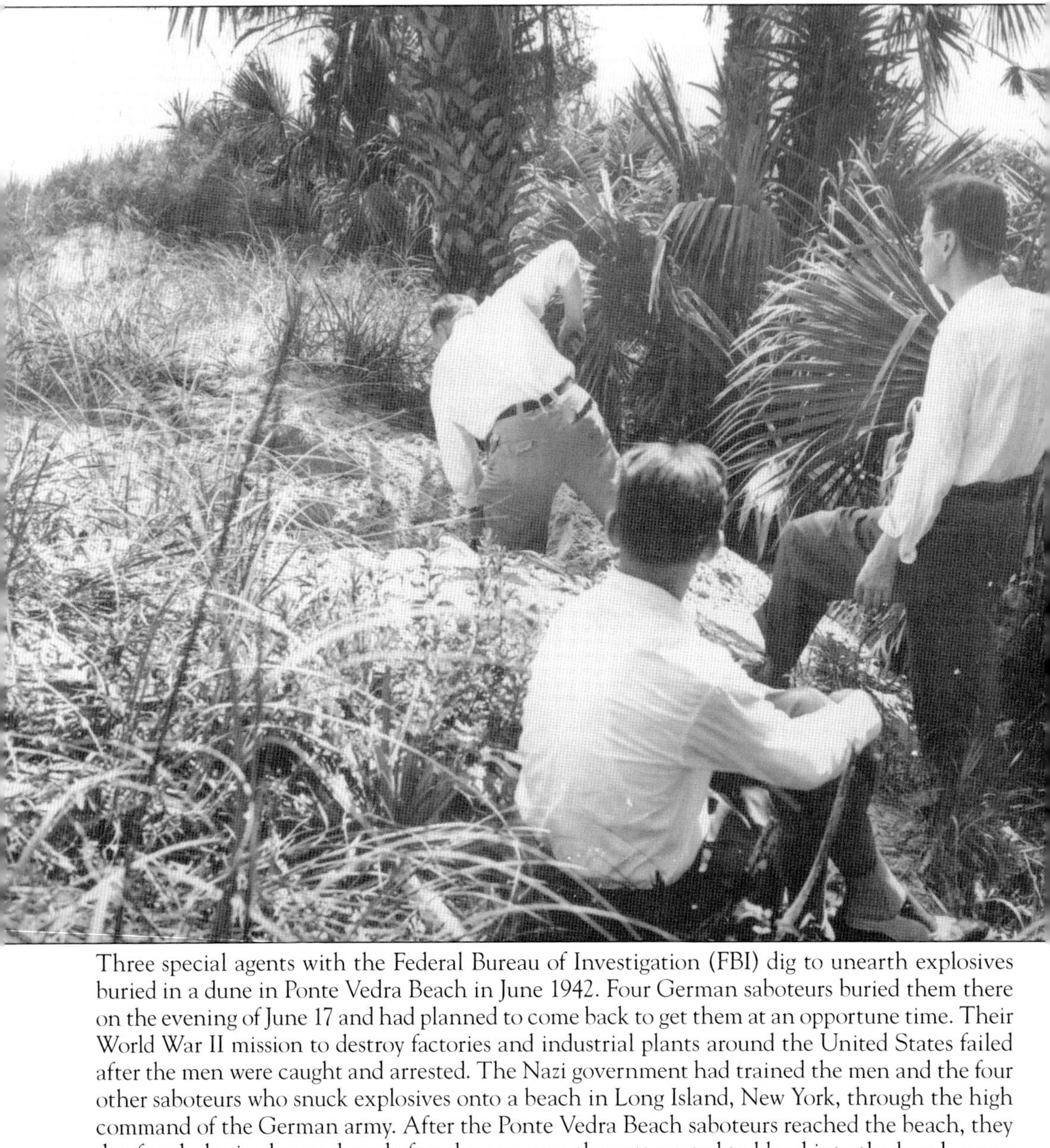

Three special agents with the Federal Bureau of Investigation (FBI) dig to unearth explosives buried in a dune in Ponte Vedra Beach in June 1942. Four German saboteurs buried them there on the evening of June 17 and had planned to come back to get them at an opportune time. Their World War II mission to destroy factories and industrial plants around the United States failed after the men were caught and arrested. The Nazi government had trained the men and the four other saboteurs who snuck explosives onto a beach in Long Island, New York, through the high command of the German army. After the Ponte Vedra Beach saboteurs reached the beach, they dug four holes in the sand, and after the sun rose, they attempted to blend into the beach scene while walking north to Jacksonville Beach, where they boarded a bus to Jacksonville.

A special agent with the FBI works to unearth explosives buried on the beach in Ponte Vedra Beach by German saboteurs during World War II. The Germans selected a spot near a grove of palm trees that they thought would be easy to find again.

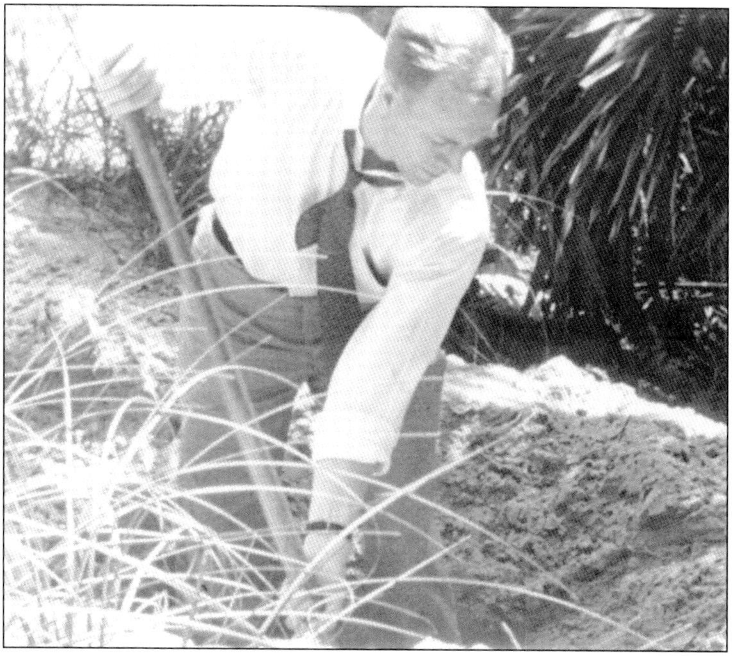

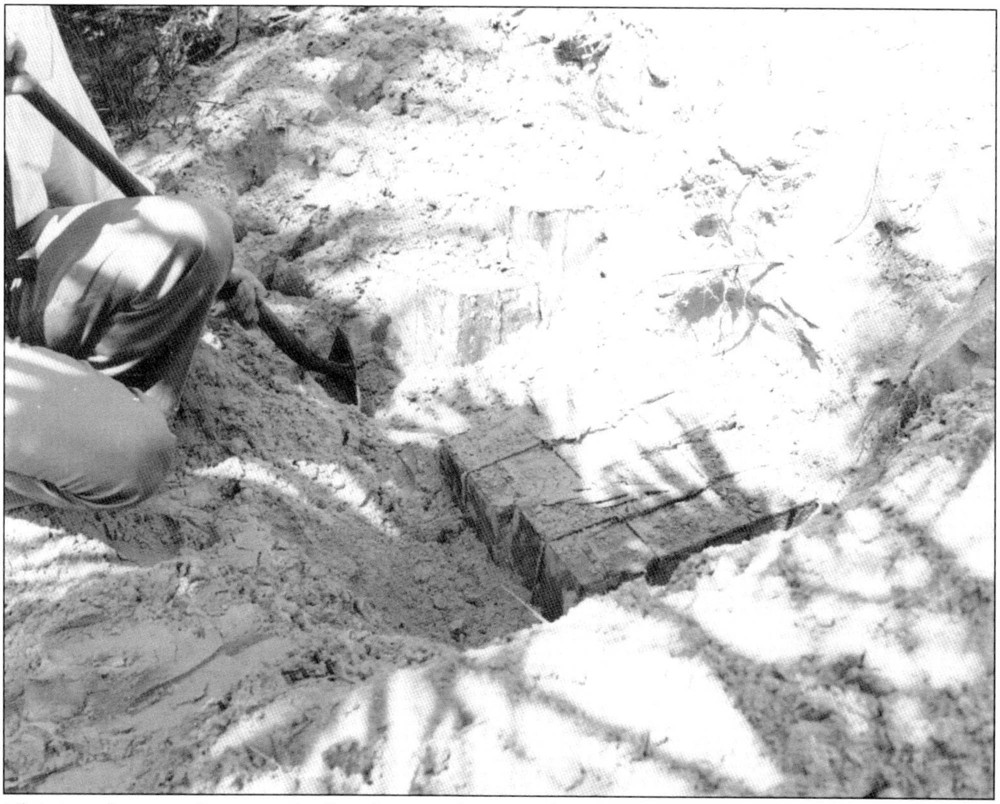

This is a close-up photograph of explosives that were buried in the sand on a Ponte Vedra Beach by German saboteurs in 1942. An FBI agent holds a shovel used to unearth the package of explosives, which had not been there long.

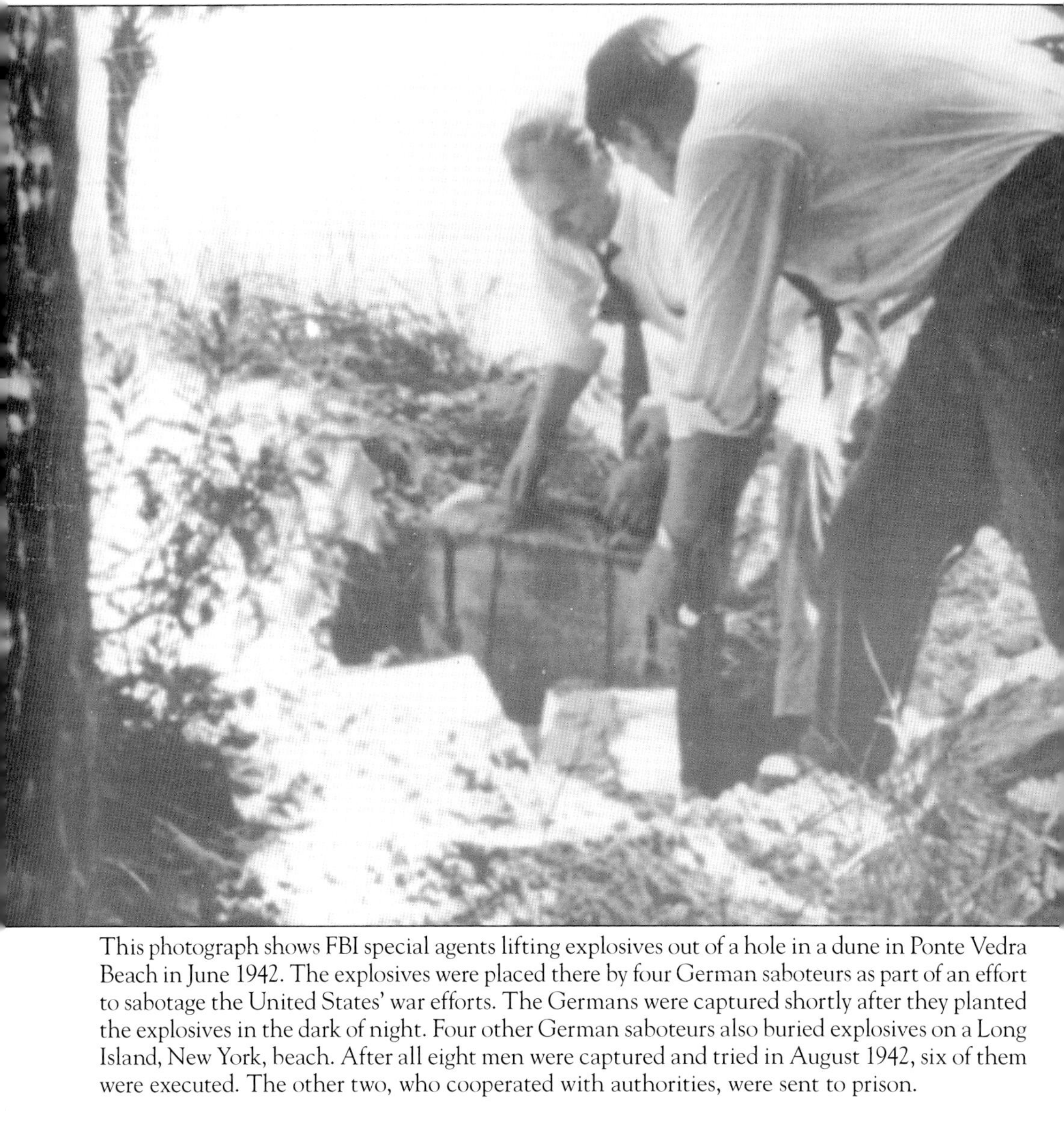

This photograph shows FBI special agents lifting explosives out of a hole in a dune in Ponte Vedra Beach in June 1942. The explosives were placed there by four German saboteurs as part of an effort to sabotage the United States' war efforts. The Germans were captured shortly after they planted the explosives in the dark of night. Four other German saboteurs also buried explosives on a Long Island, New York, beach. After all eight men were captured and tried in August 1942, six of them were executed. The other two, who cooperated with authorities, were sent to prison.

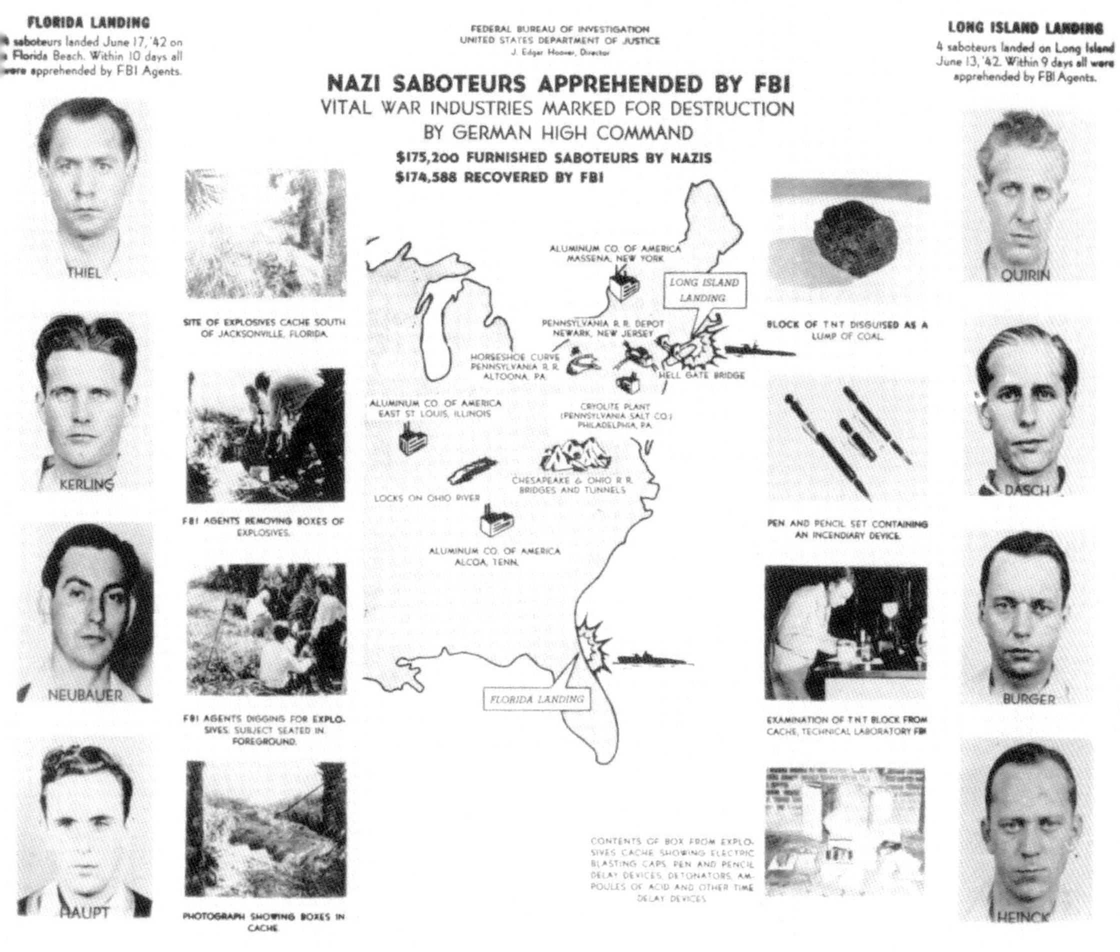


A composite photograph features mug shots of all eight of the German saboteurs who brought explosives into the United States during Operation Pastorius. The image also includes a map of all the targets around the country that the saboteurs planned to destroy, as well as other photographs taken during the investigation. A World War II Operation Pastorius marker currently sits on the grounds of the Ponte Vedra Inn and Club, telling the story of the historical event. The marker is north of the actual location where the event took place.

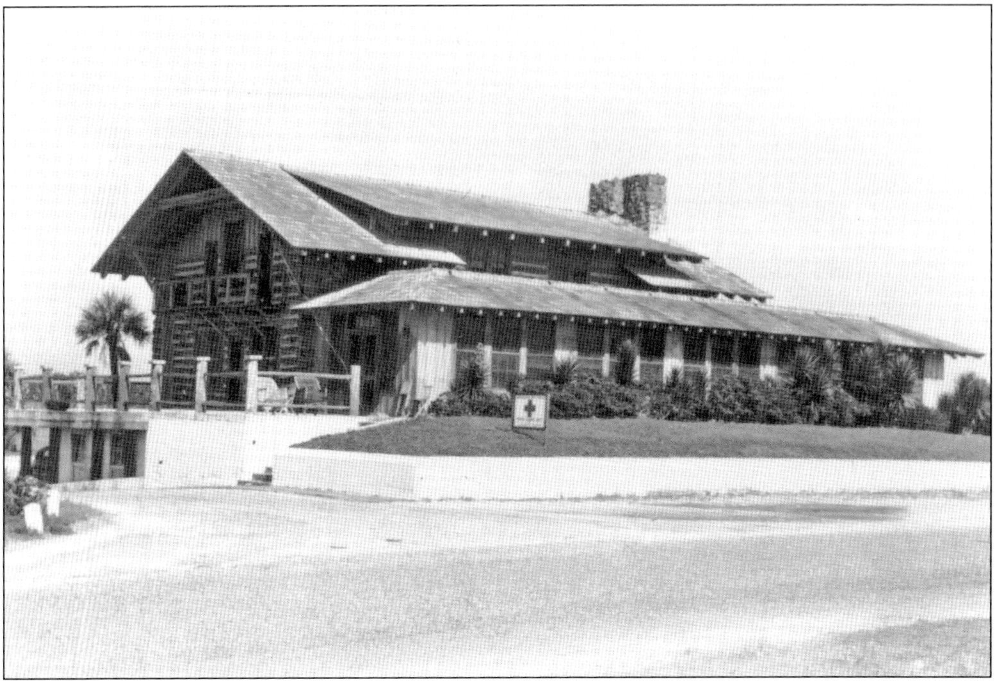

This is a photograph of the American Red Cross station located at the Ponte Vedra Club during World War II. The golf clubhouse was converted into the Red Cross station to assist the war effort.

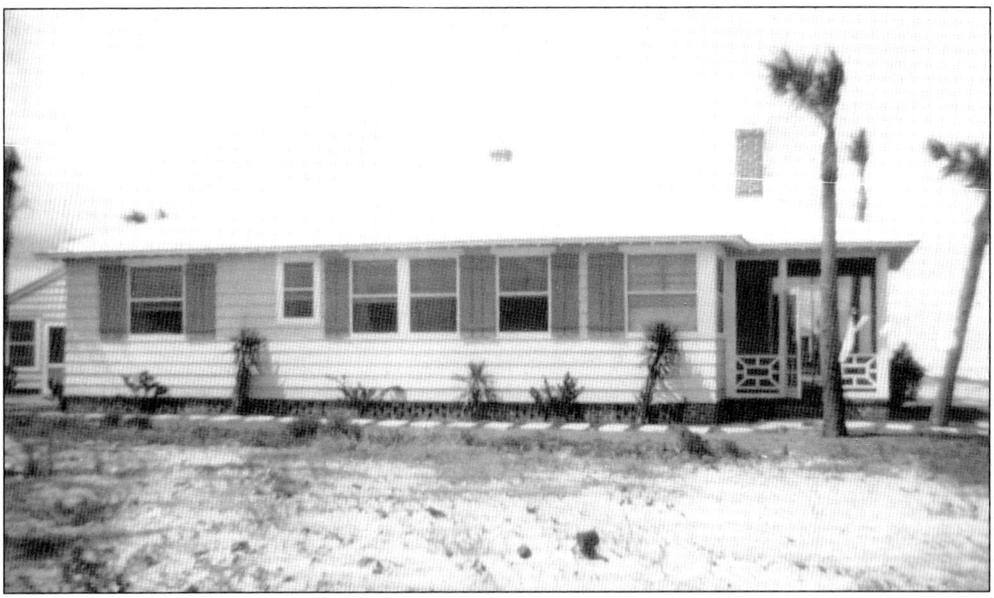

US Coast Guard barracks were situated at 557 Ponte Vedra Boulevard during World War II. This picture was taken on September 1, 1942. Horses for the mounted patrol were kept in stables across the street.

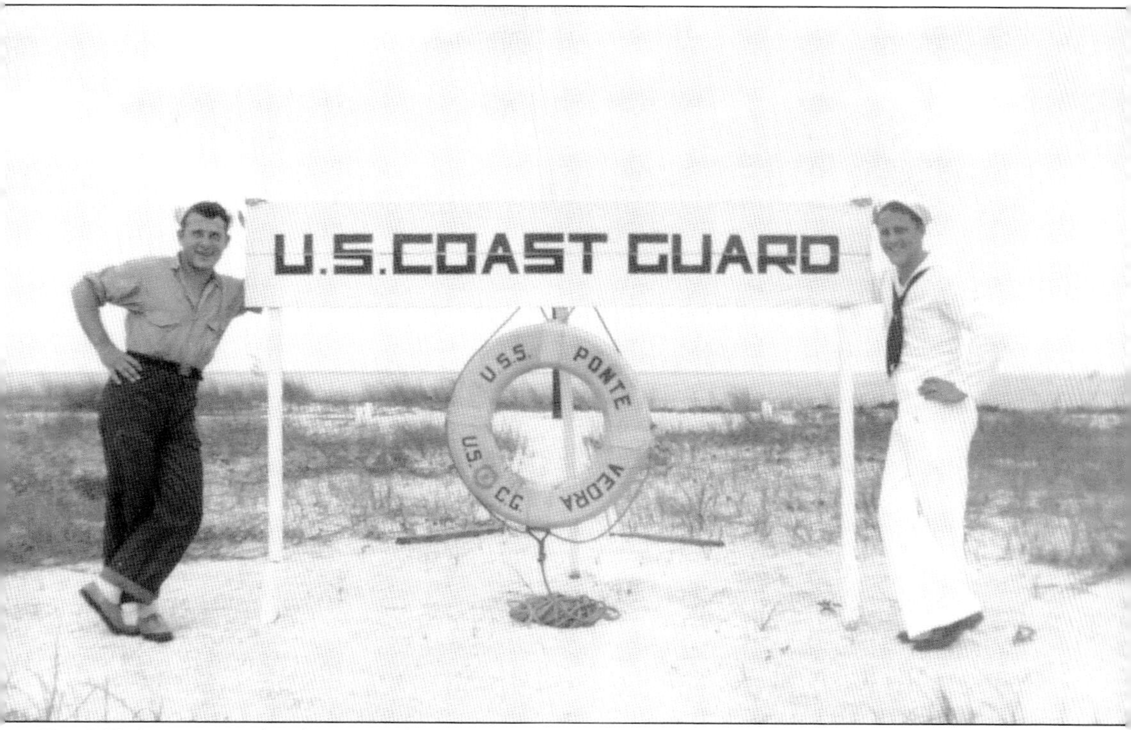


Two US Coast Guard sailors pose for a photograph in Ponte Vedra Beach on August 15, 1943. They are identified as Benny P. Buza Jr. and his friend "Ted." The town of Ponte Vedra Beach also saw sailors from Mayport Naval Station during the war. The naval station, located to the north in the town of Mayport, was an important base. After being stationed in the Jacksonville area during the war, some servicemen grew to admire the communities there. A few returned to live in those communities, including Ponte Vedra Beach, after the war.

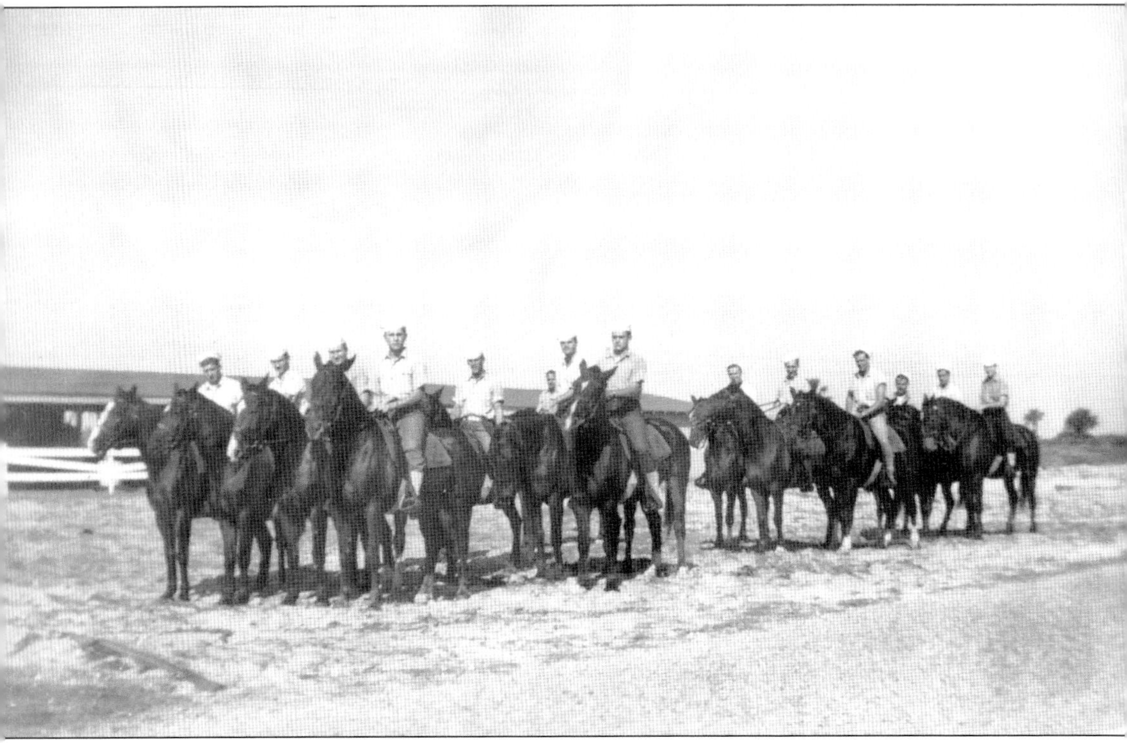

Sailors, identified as most likely being members of the US Coast Guard, pose on horseback in Ponte Vedra Beach during World War II. The Coast Guard kept horses in stables at their barracks in town during the war.

# *Five*

# Beach Scenes

In Mineral City's early days, few people went to the beach to stroll, swim in the surf, or sunbathe. Workers mined minerals there, but some people used the beach for recreation. Some photographs of that time feature beachgoers clowning around on the sand and posing by the ocean in their bathing suits.

Transportation to and from the area was limited, as there were no roads yet, so anyone who had time for recreation did not have to worry about fighting crowds.

Mining engineer George Pritchard built a seaside home for his family near the Sand Plant in 1917 and called it Bonnie Dune. He later sold it to mining executive George Jeffers, who turned it into the Bonnie Dune Lodge in the 1920s.

The Ponte Vedra Club promoted the beach as one of its main attractions. In the 1930s and 1940s, visitors from colder climates went there to swim and get a tan. Some famous people visited, including some movie stars.

The beach at the end of Mickler's Road was also a popular spot. The Mickler family, who were early settlers in Palm Valley, built and ran a fishing pier there in 1935. The 600-foot structure, made with palm tree pilings, jutted 300 feet into the ocean; admission was 25¢. Bait and tackle were sold there, and an ocean breeze–powered windmill on the pier pulled saltwater up to the top to keep live bait fresh. After a storm damaged the pier in 1945, it was torn down.

Now owned by the county, the Mickler's Beach landing is the only public beach access point in Ponte Vedra Beach. It has long been a popular place in the town, because as Ponte Vedra Beach grew and roads were built from Jacksonville to the beaches, more people came for a day to enjoy the beach.

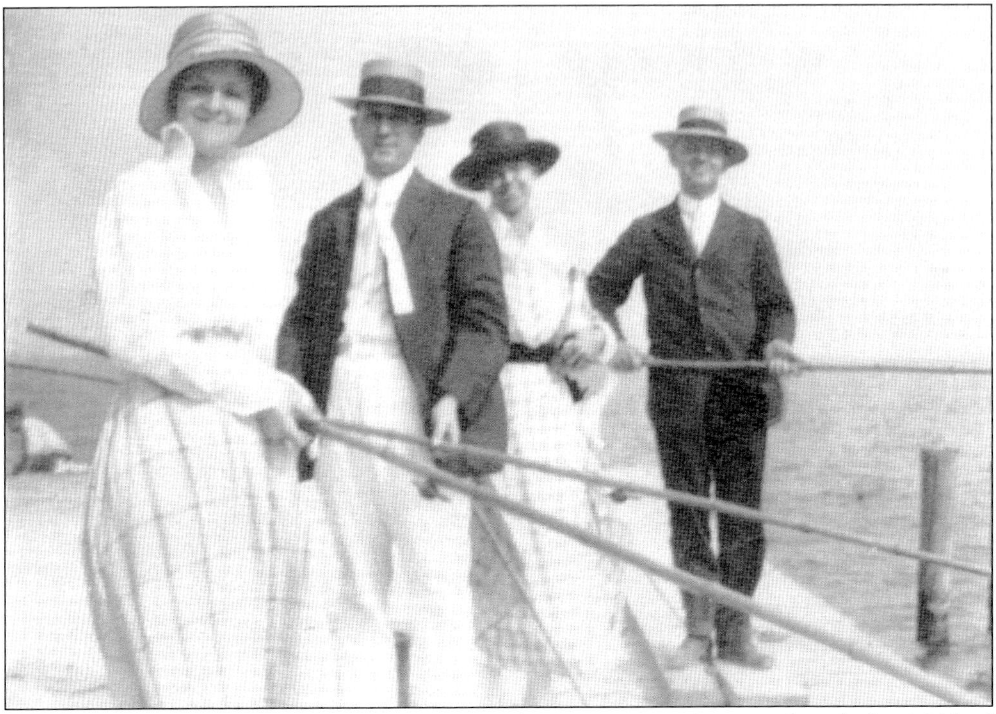

Four people go on a fishing expedition in Mineral City in 1918. They are identified as Mildred Reynolds, Charles McIllvain, Edward Brach, and Nell Branch.

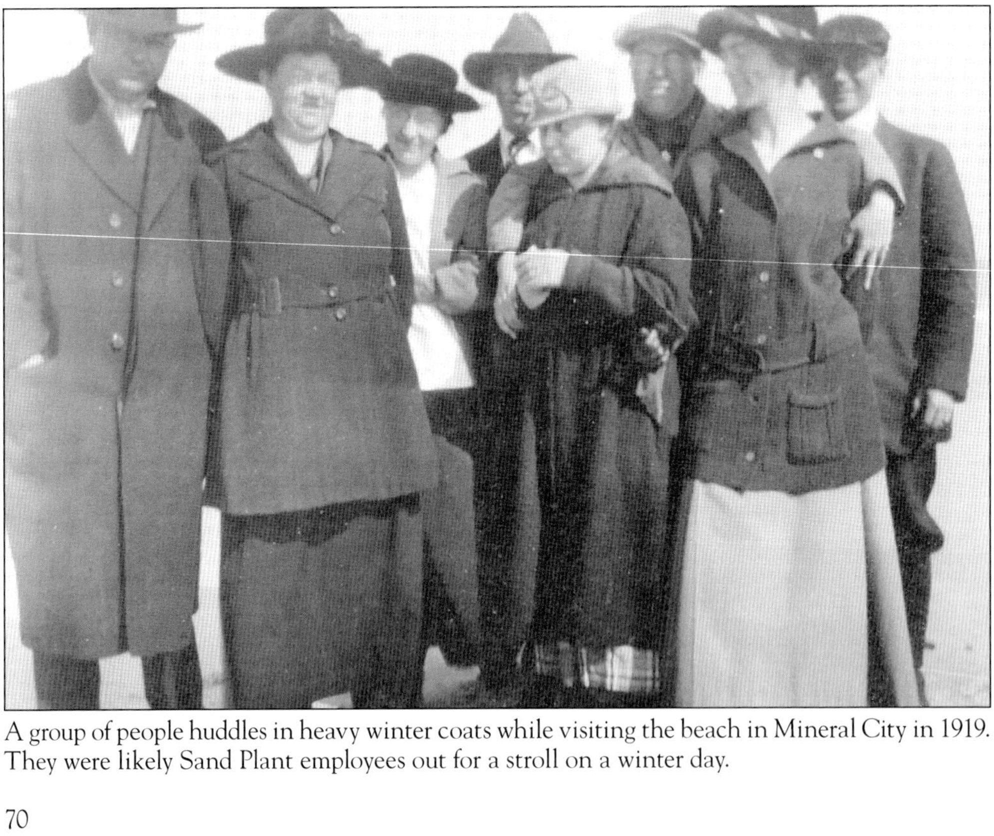

A group of people huddles in heavy winter coats while visiting the beach in Mineral City in 1919. They were likely Sand Plant employees out for a stroll on a winter day.

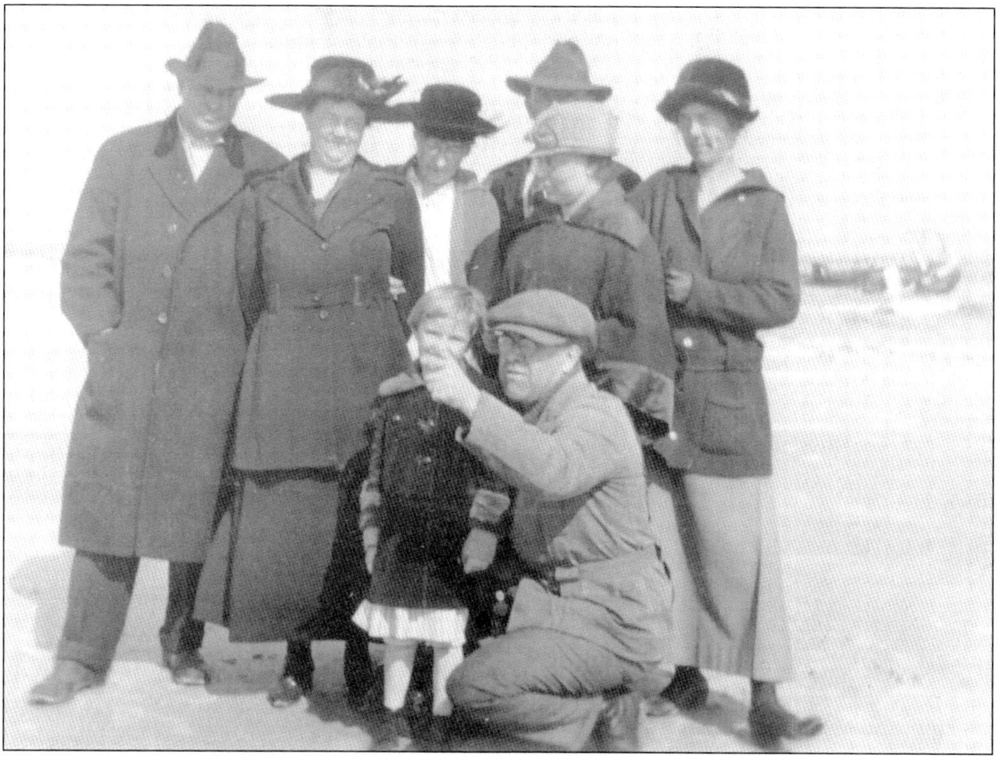

Even during winter, the beach attracts visitors, like here in Mineral City in 1919. They are not identified, but it is obviously a cold day.

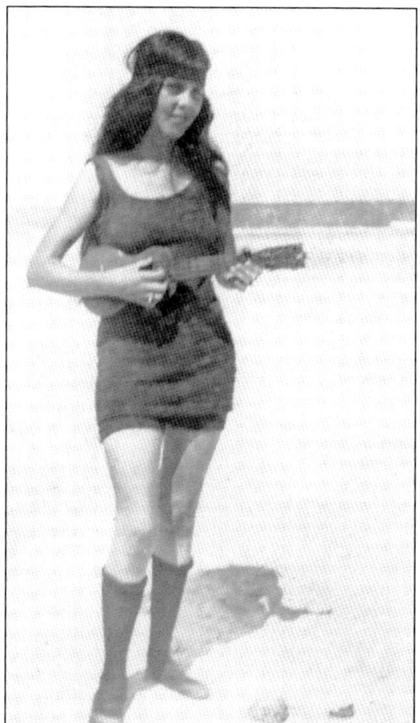

An unidentified girl in a bathing suit poses with a ukulele on a Mineral City beach in 1919. Beachgoers during that time in Mineral City seemed to enjoy posing for pictures while engaged in a variety of activities.

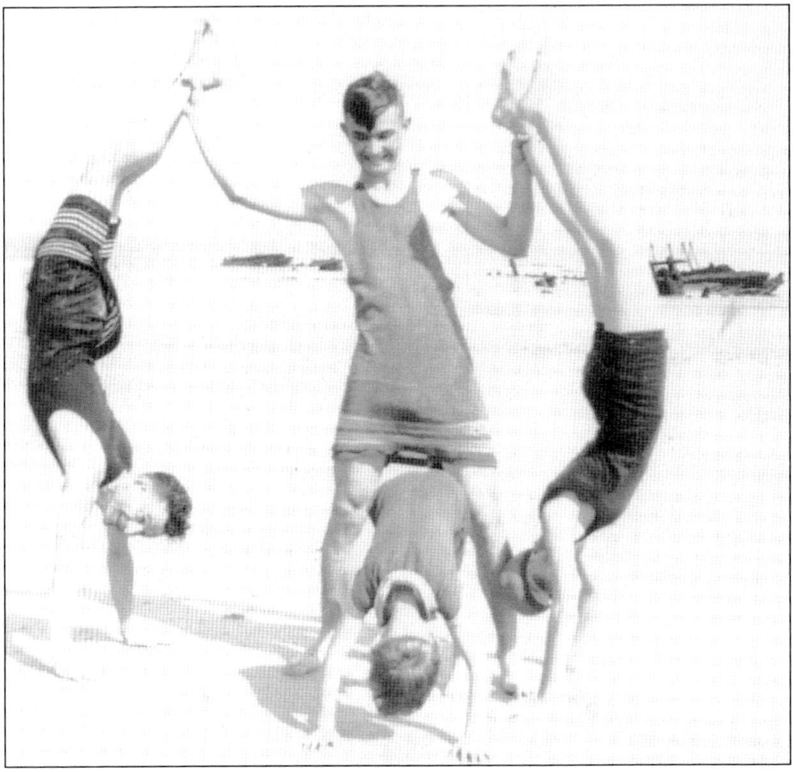

Adults and children clown around on the beach in Mineral City in 1919. They are identified as Marion Jeffers, Mr. Dow, George Jeffers Jr., and Dorothy Jeffers.

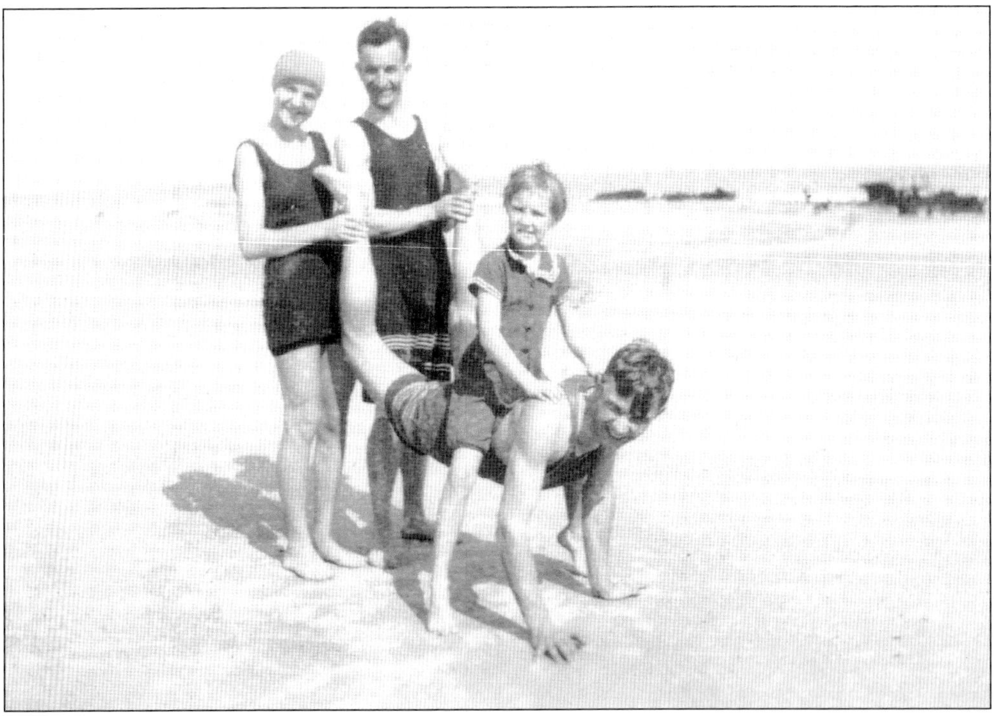

Marion Jeffers, Mr. Dow, George Jeffers Jr., and Dorothy Jeffers strike a pose for the camera in 1919 in Mineral City. The shipwreck of the *Hugh de Payne* can be seen in the background.

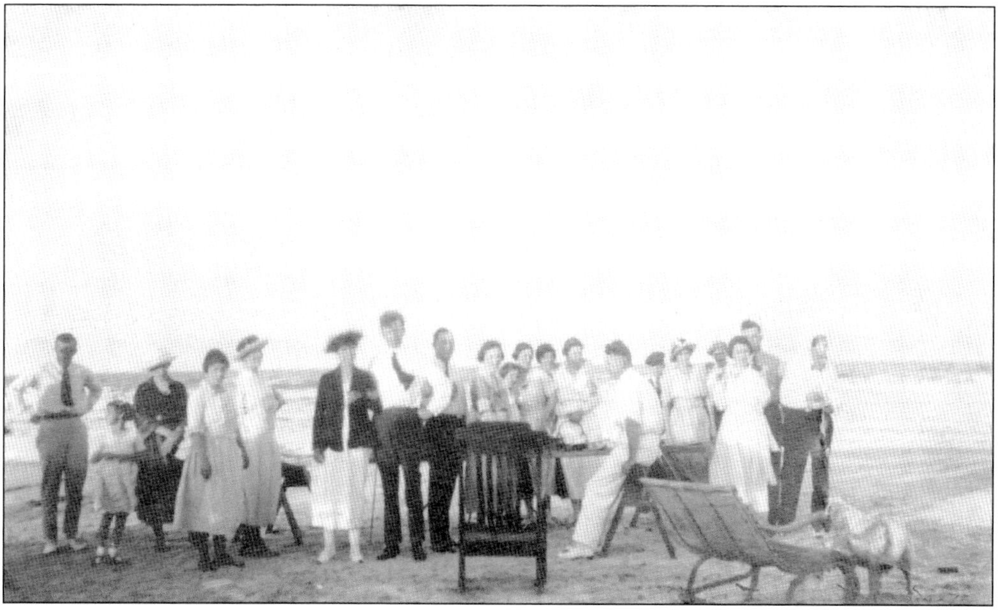

A group of people enjoys a wiener roast and party on a Mineral City beach in 1921. They are not identified but were likely employees of the Sand Plant.

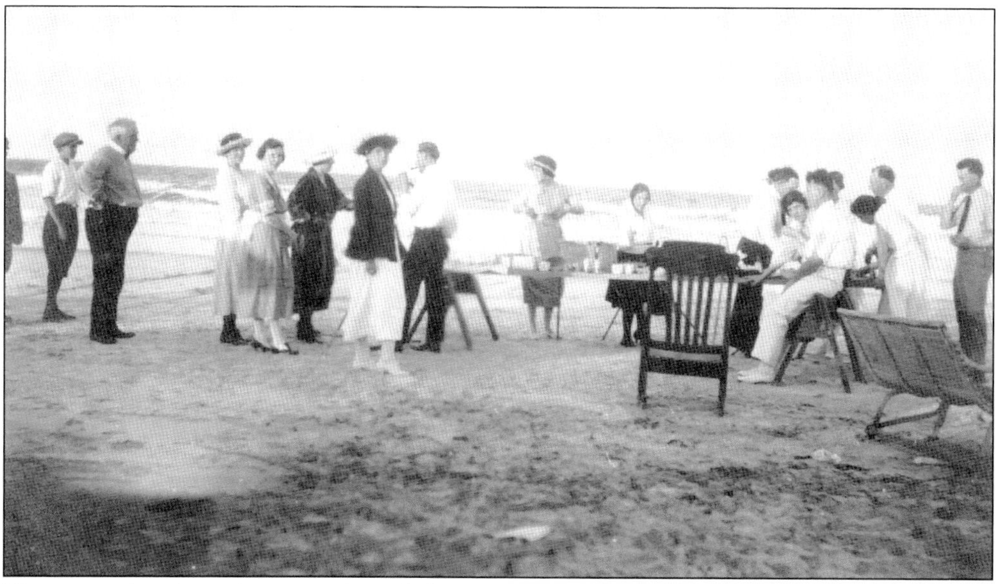

This is another shot of a group of people having a wiener roast and party on a beach in Mineral City in 1921. This image shows that people enjoyed being out on the beach for recreational purposes, just as people have during the decades since.

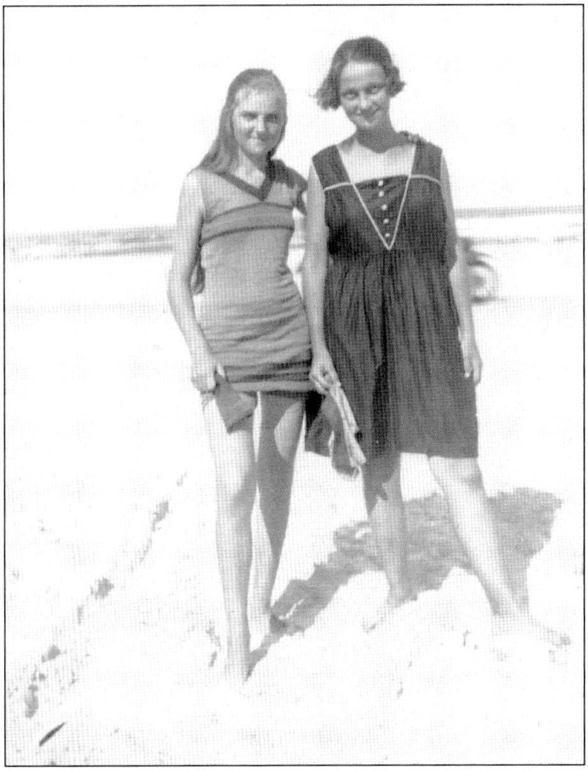

Two young women play around on a beach in Mineral City in 1922. They are identified as Thelma Shad and Mrs. Howard L. Monroe.

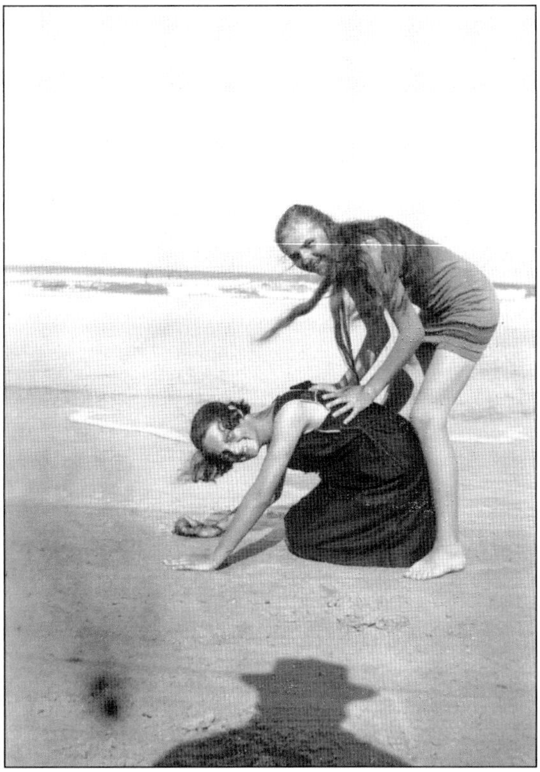

Thelma Shad and Mrs. Howard L. Monroe play leapfrog on a beach in Mineral City in 1922. They seem to enjoy striking poses for the camera.

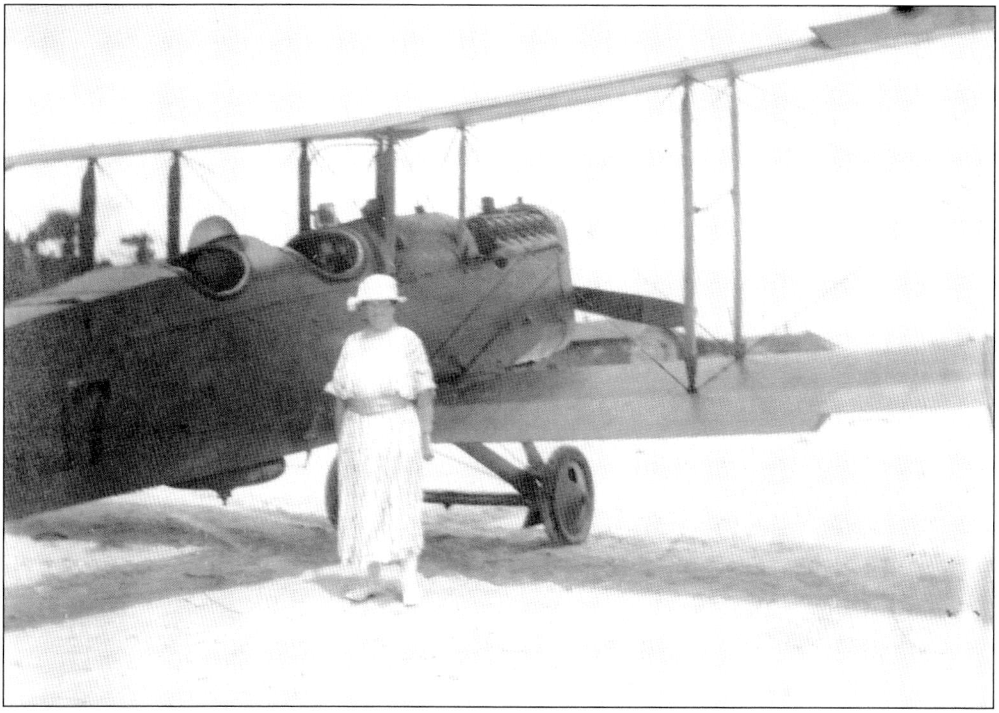

A woman identified as Mrs. George Jeffers poses by an airplane that landed on a beach in Mineral City in 1922. The plane sits in front of the Jefferses' home, Bonnie Dune Lodge

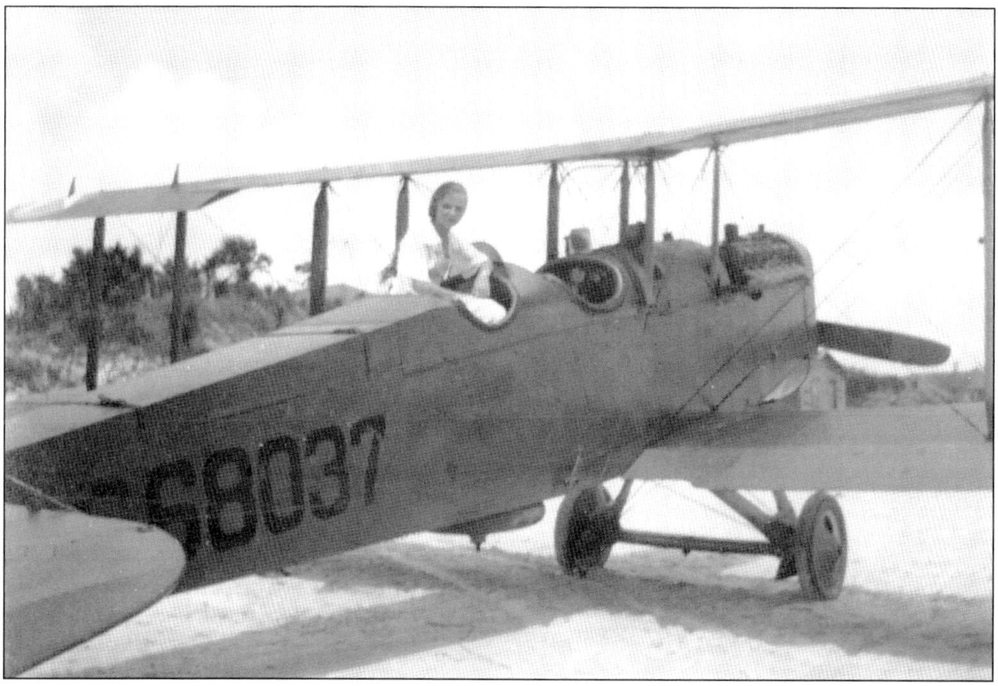


A woman identified as Thelma Shad sits in an open-cockpit airplane on a beach in Mineral City in 1922. The plane sat in front of the Bonnie Dune Lodge, but there is no information about whether Thelma flew the plane or just posed for a picture in it.

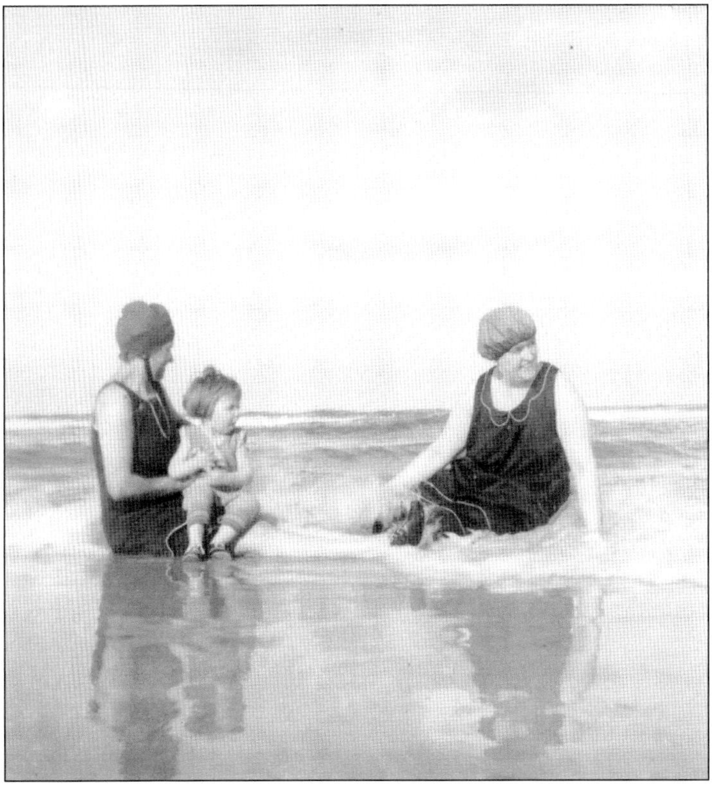

Nelle Pritchard (left) sits at the edge of the ocean in Mineral City one summer day in 1922. She is with her infant son, Allen, and a woman identified as Mrs. Belt. The women are wearing the modest type of bathing suits popular at that time, which look like they might have felt heavy when wet.

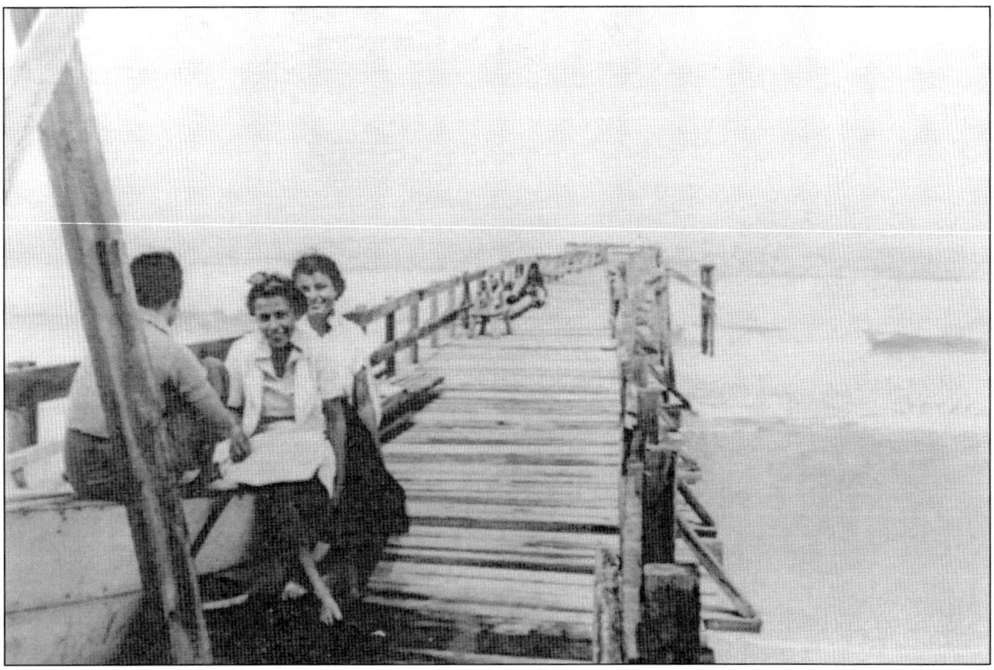

Sid, Edna, and Susan Mickler pose for a picture on the Mickler Pier in 1940 in Ponte Vedra Beach. The Mickler family ran the fishing pier from the mid-1930s to the mid-1940s. It was located at the present site of Mickler's Landing Beach.

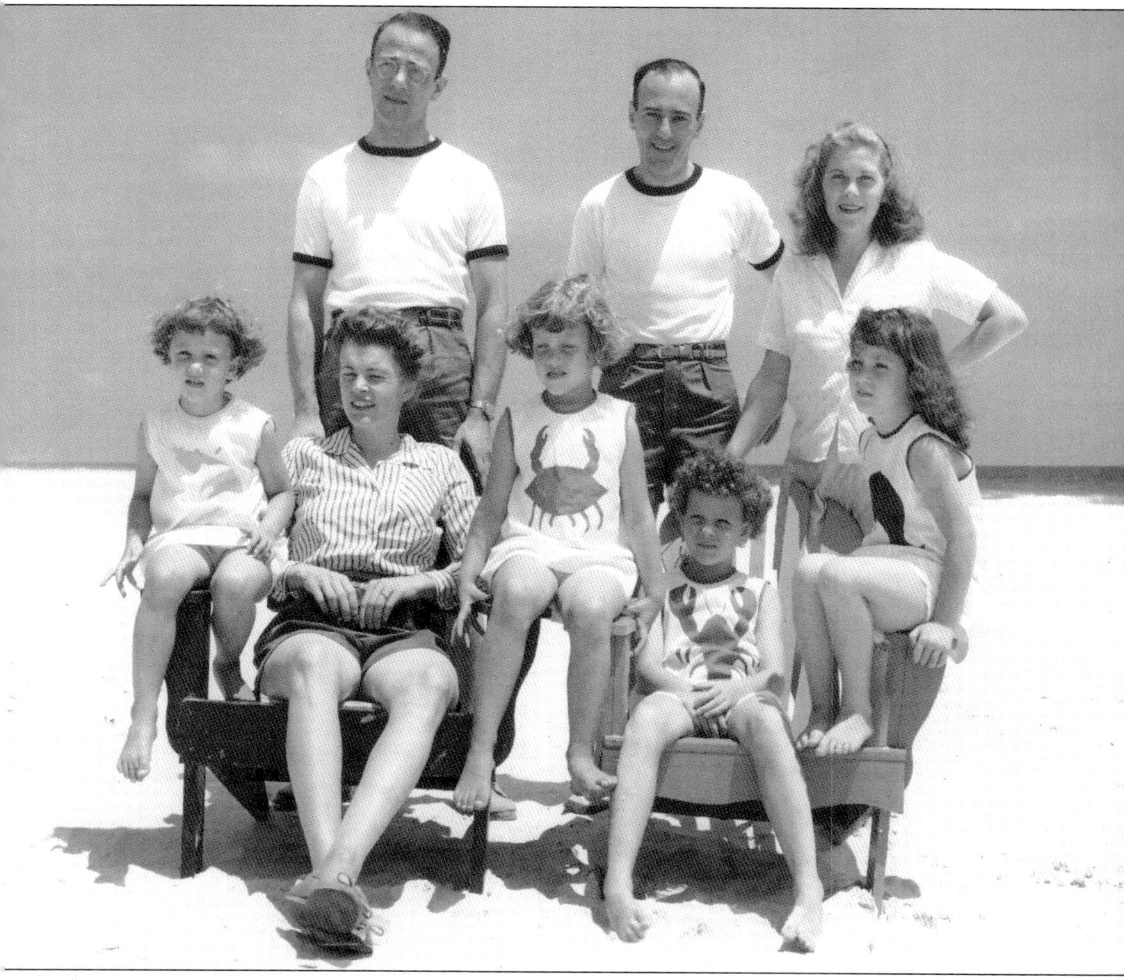

A large group of people poses for a picture on a beach in Ponte Vedra Beach in 1946. By then, bathing suits were baring more skin, making it easier to swim and get a tan. The photograph does not identify where the beachgoers were, although they were likely at the Ponte Vedra Club, which had the most popular beach in town at the time.

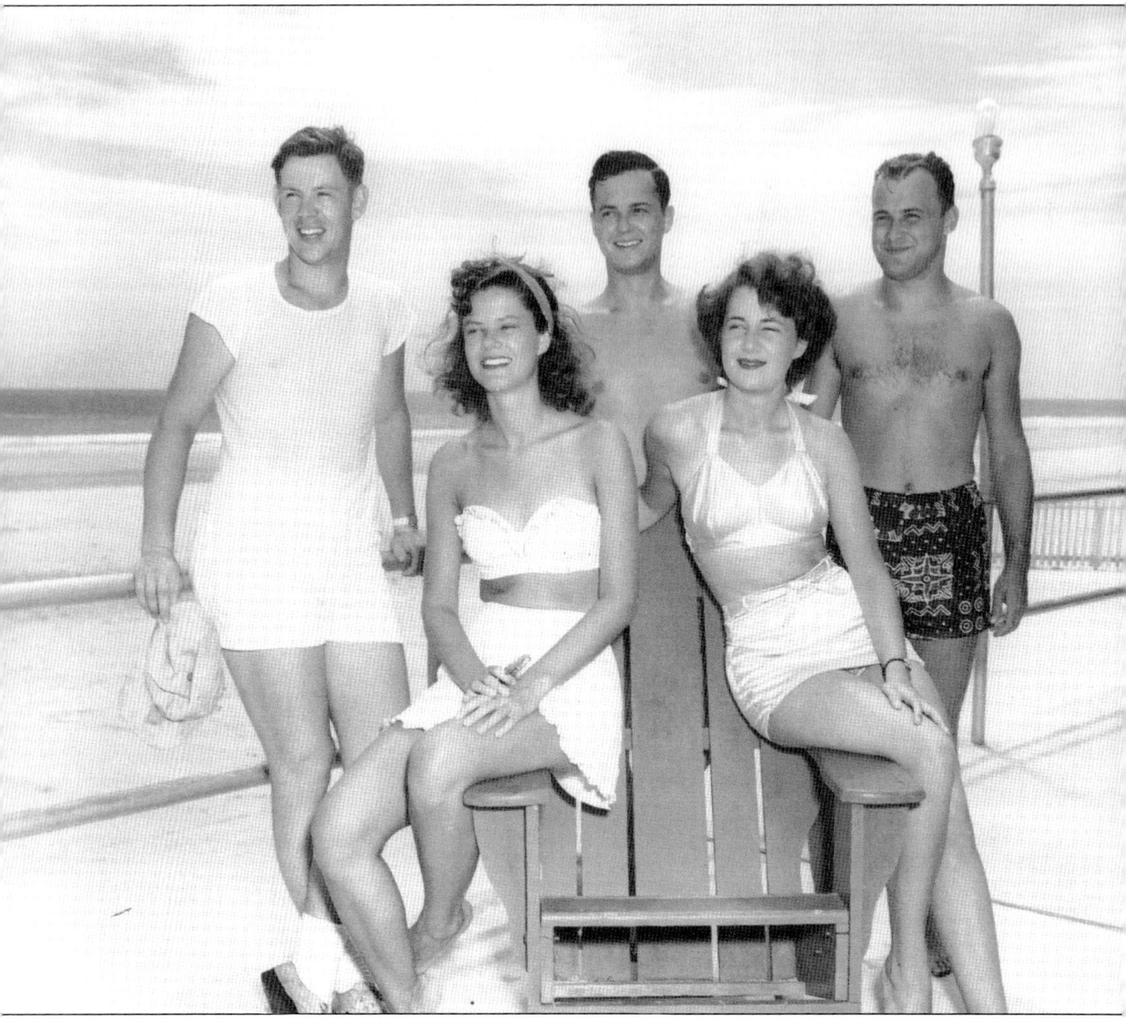

Attractive young men and women pose for a photograph on a beach in Ponte Vedra Beach during July 1947. The image is typical of those captured by popular, successful local photographer Virgil Deane at the Ponte Vedra Club. It illustrates the growing popularity of the club and the beach in the years after World War II.

Three family members relax on a beach at the Ponte Vedra Club in July 1947. Local photographer Virgil Deane took note of when he captured his resort images but did not leave records of the subjects' names.

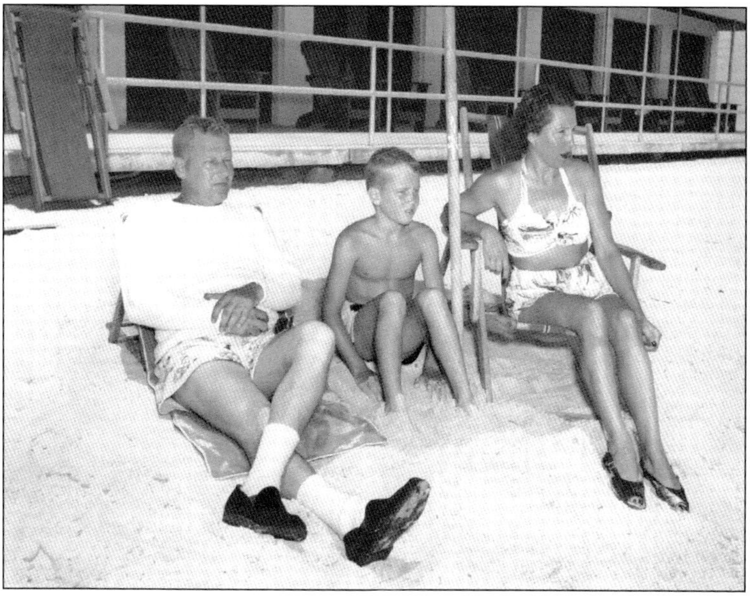

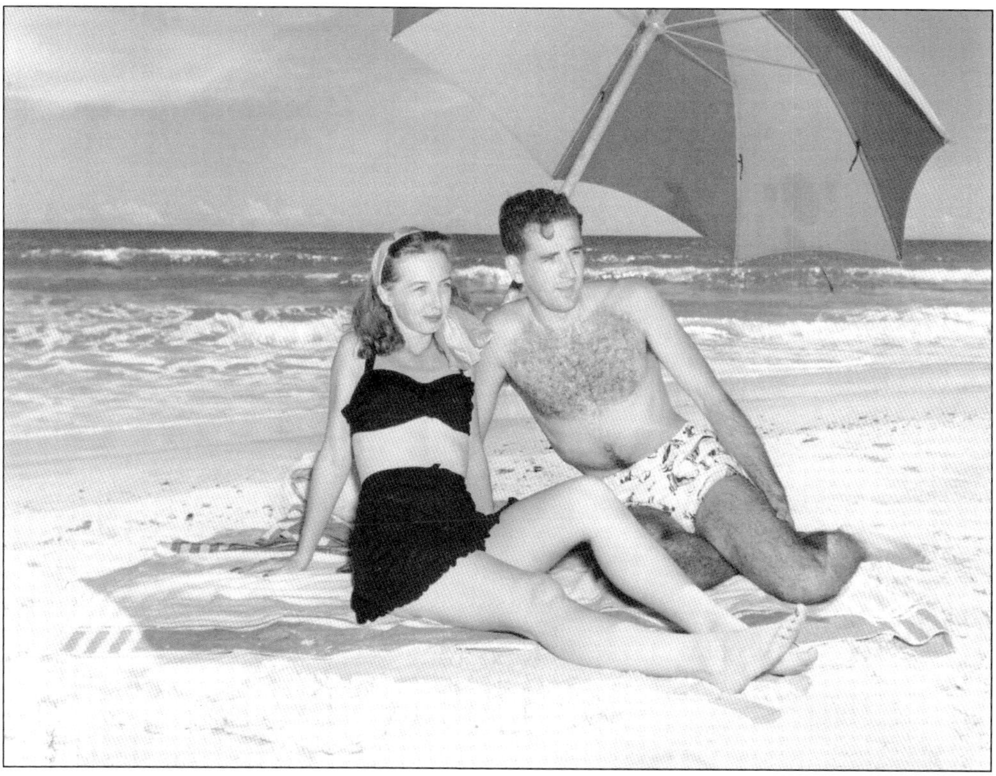

A young couple relaxes under a beach umbrella at the Ponte Vedra Club in the 1940s. Attractive and serene, they look like they are posing for a vacation photograph or an advertisement for the resort.

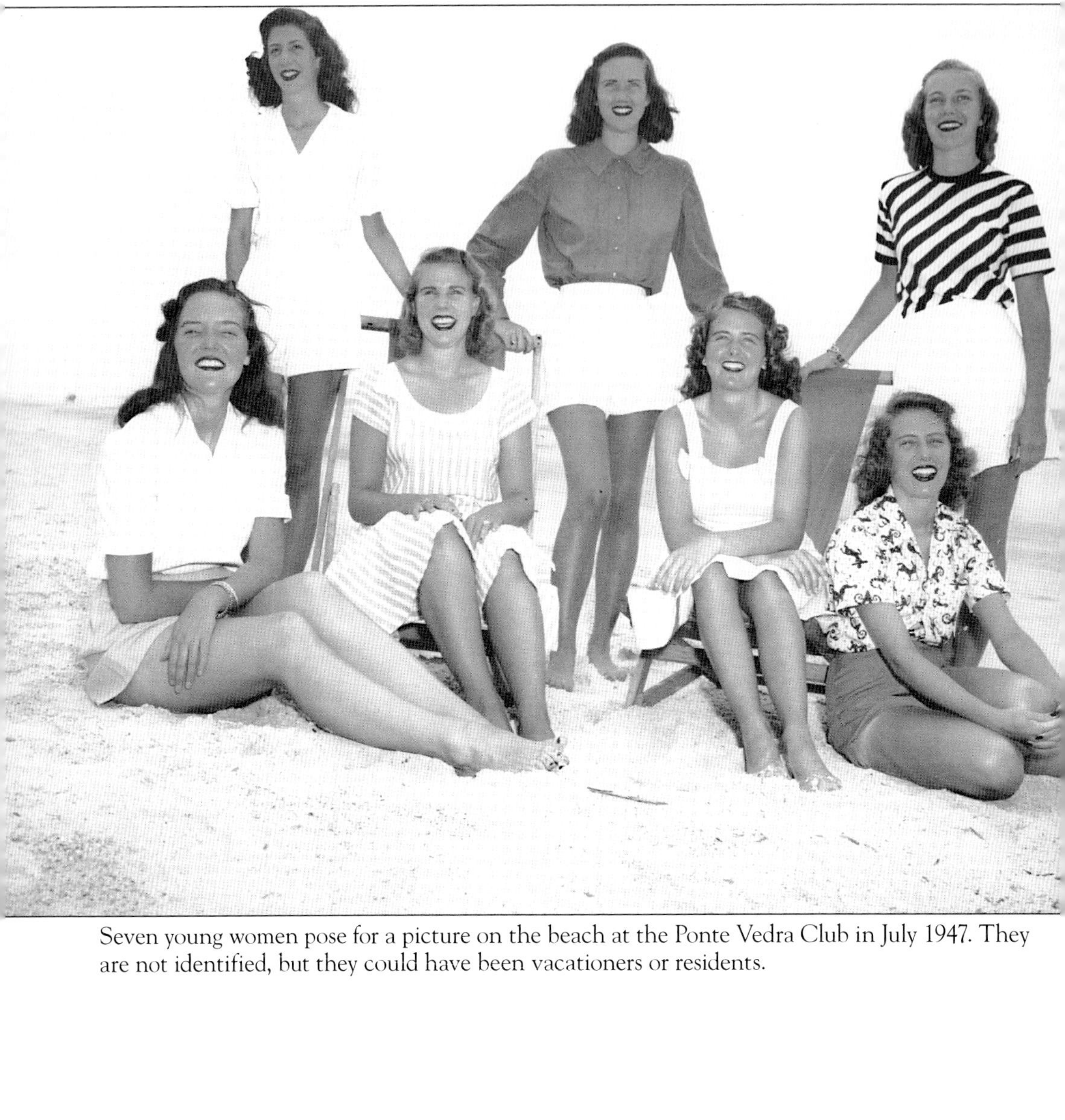

Seven young women pose for a picture on the beach at the Ponte Vedra Club in July 1947. They are not identified, but they could have been vacationers or residents.

Three young women pose for a beach shot in Ponte Vedra Beach sometime in the mid-1900s. Many people liked having their picture taken on the beach to remember the fun.

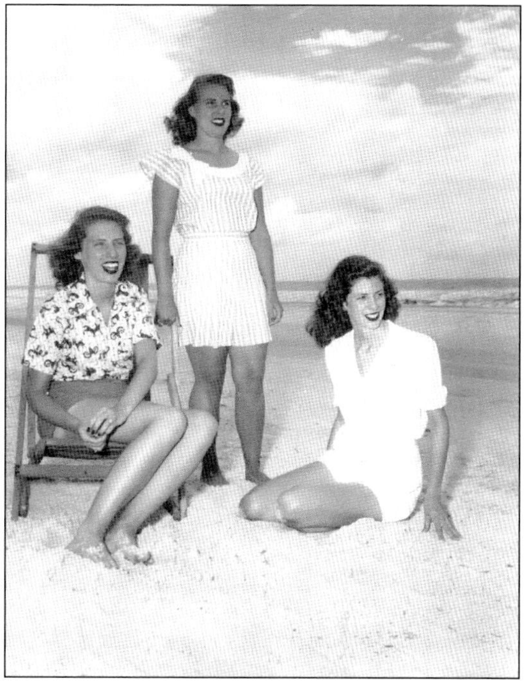

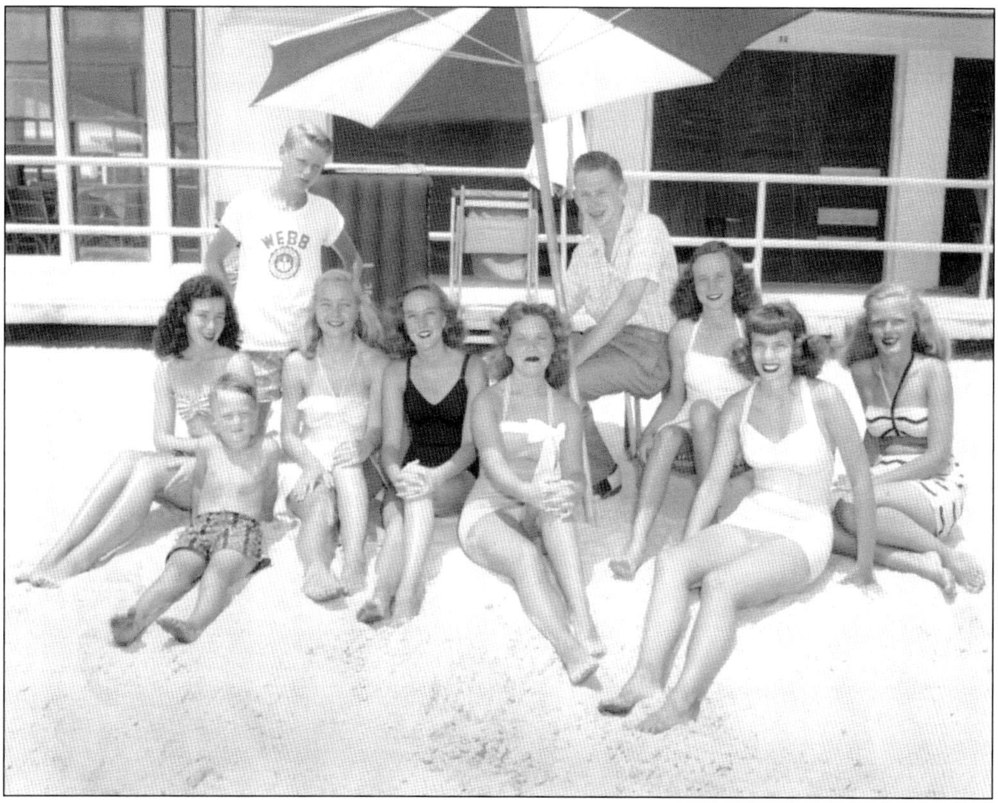

A large group of people poses under a beach umbrella in July 1947 in Ponte Vedra Beach. Photographs such as this made great souvenirs.

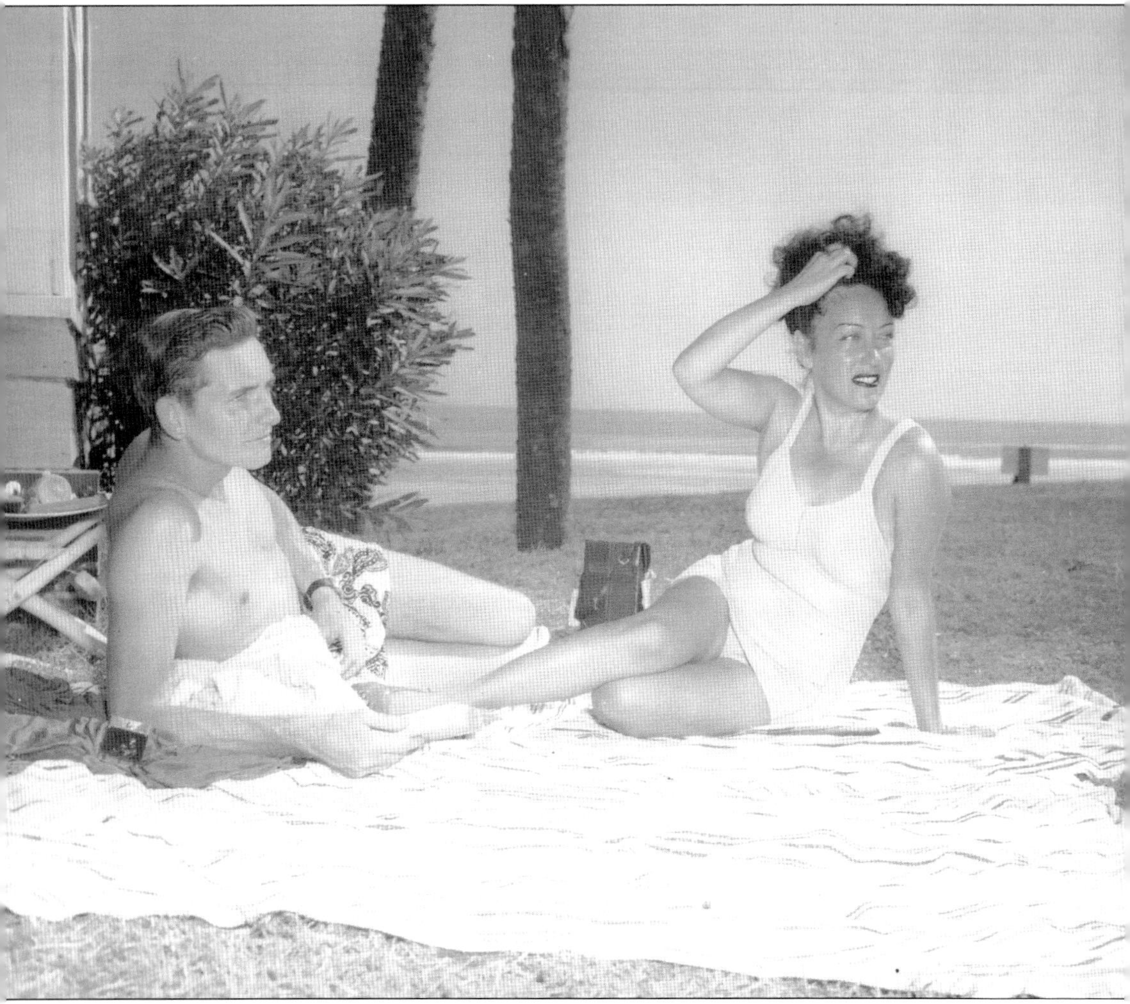

Movie stars Hedy Lamarr (right) and Dana Andrews relax by a beach at the Ponte Vedra Club in the 1940s. Famous and attractive, they seemed to fit into the resort's scene. Lamarr, who was born in 1913 or 1914 in Vienna, Austria, is quoted as saying, "Any girl can be glamorous. All you have to do is stand still and look stupid." She died in 2000 at her home in Orlando, Florida. Andrews, who was born in 1909 and died in 1992, was one of the major Hollywood stars during the 1940s.

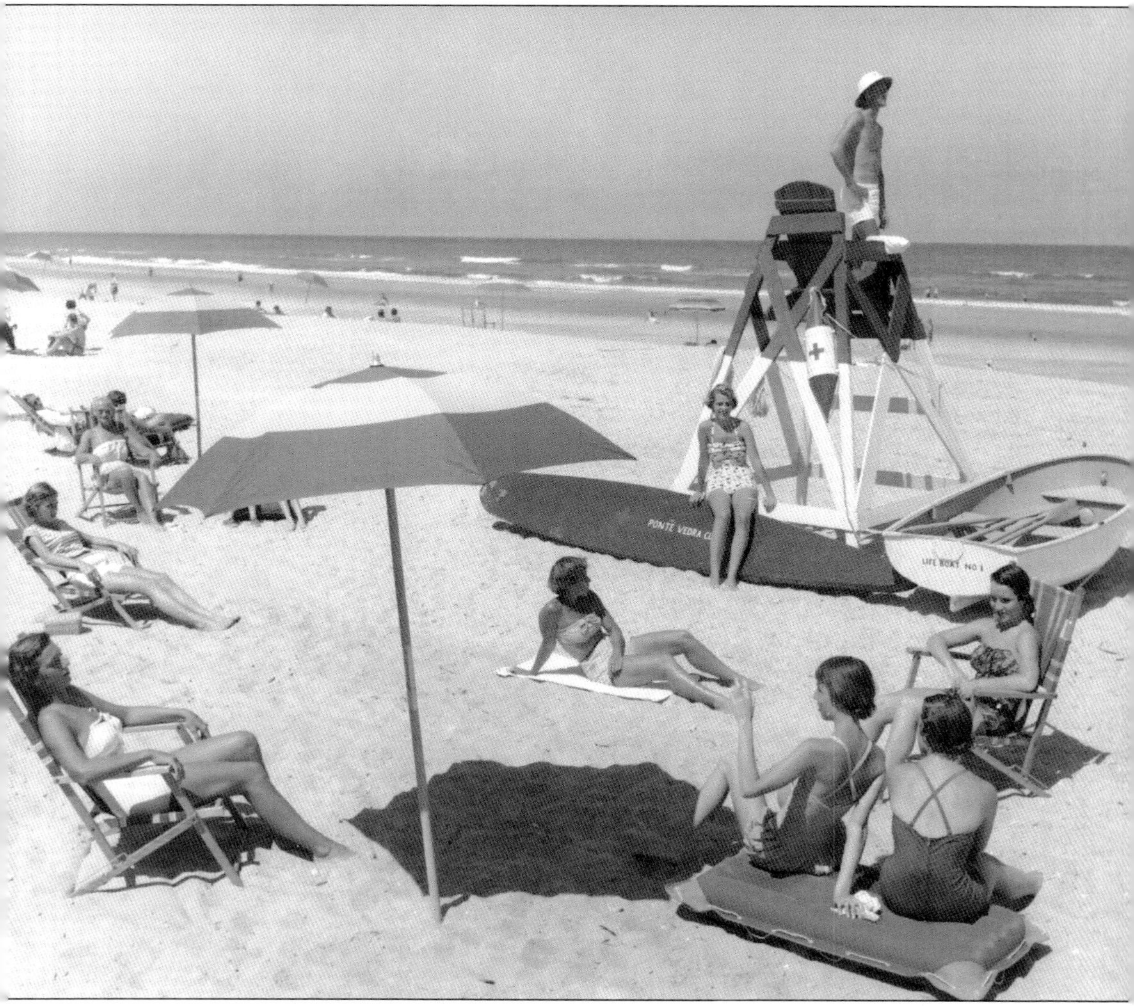


This beach scene records a typical summer day at the Ponte Vedra Club in the 1950s. Jim Stockton retired from complete management of the club in 1948 and turned it over to J.P. LeMaster. Later, in the 1960s, J.P.'s son Edward "Ebbie" LeMaster was elected president of the Ponte Vedra Club, which continued to increase in membership.

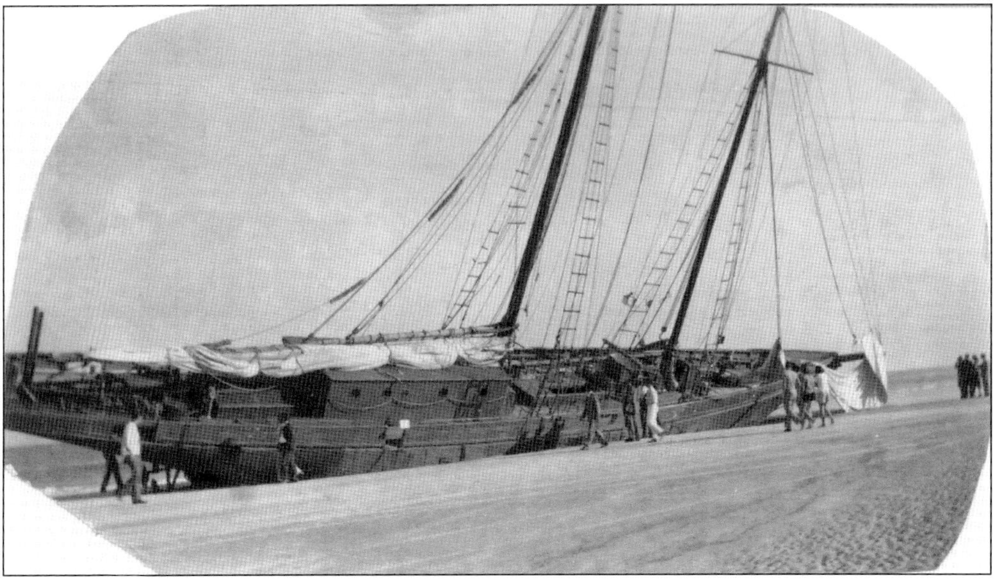

People gather around a two-masted schooner that ran ashore during a storm in December 1947 at Mickler's Landing in Ponte Vedra Beach. Storms along the coast could be dangerous for boats.

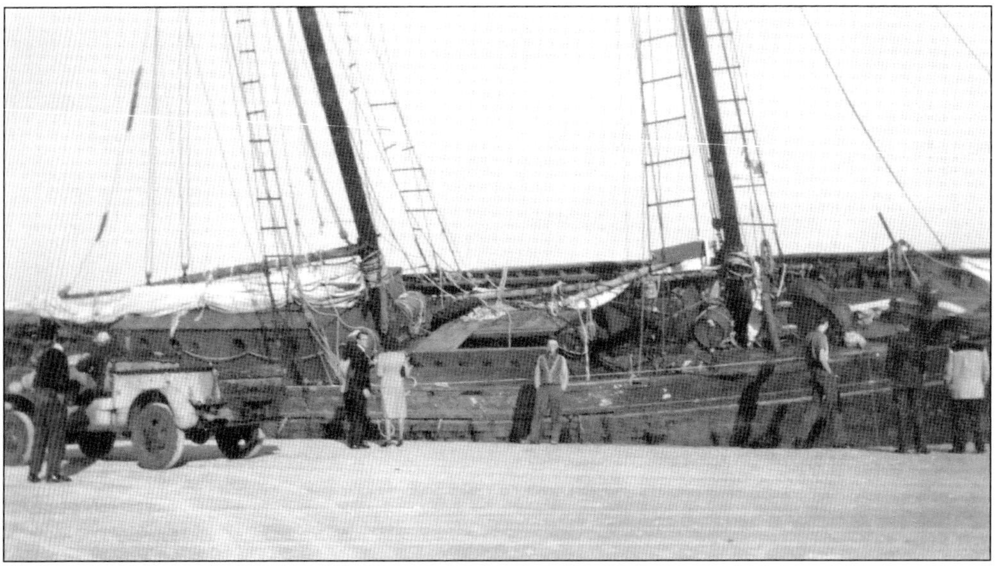

This is a closer shot of the schooner that was beached at Mickler's Landing in December 1947. Storms periodically strike the coast in Ponte Vedra Beach, but the sight of a ship grounded by one was unusual.

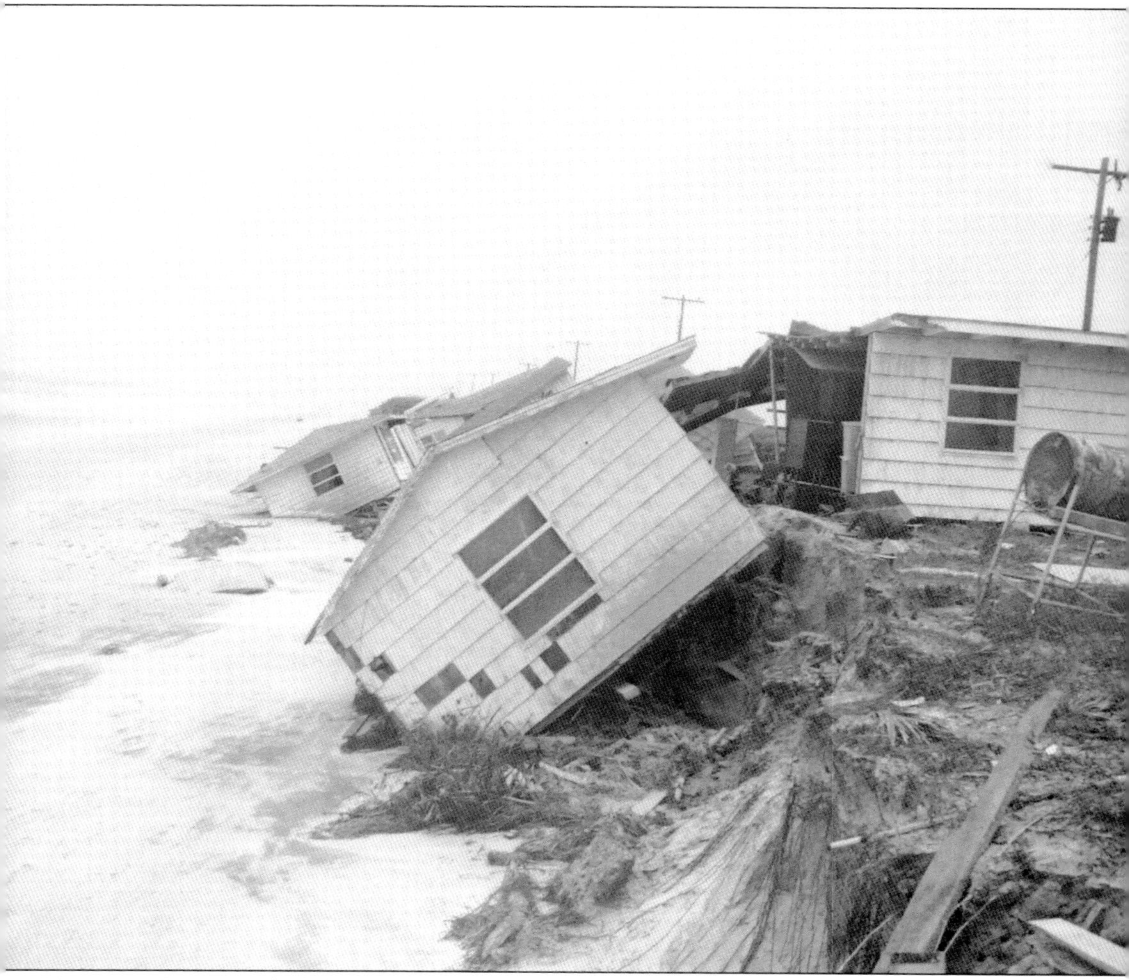

Hurricane Dora wrecked these homes in South Ponte Vedra Beach in 1964. It was the worst hurricane to strike the coast in decades, and none has matched the damage it caused since. Oceanfront homes in Ponte Vedra Beach suffered damage because the storm came ashore to the south near Vilano Beach, but the town quickly recovered and continued to grow.

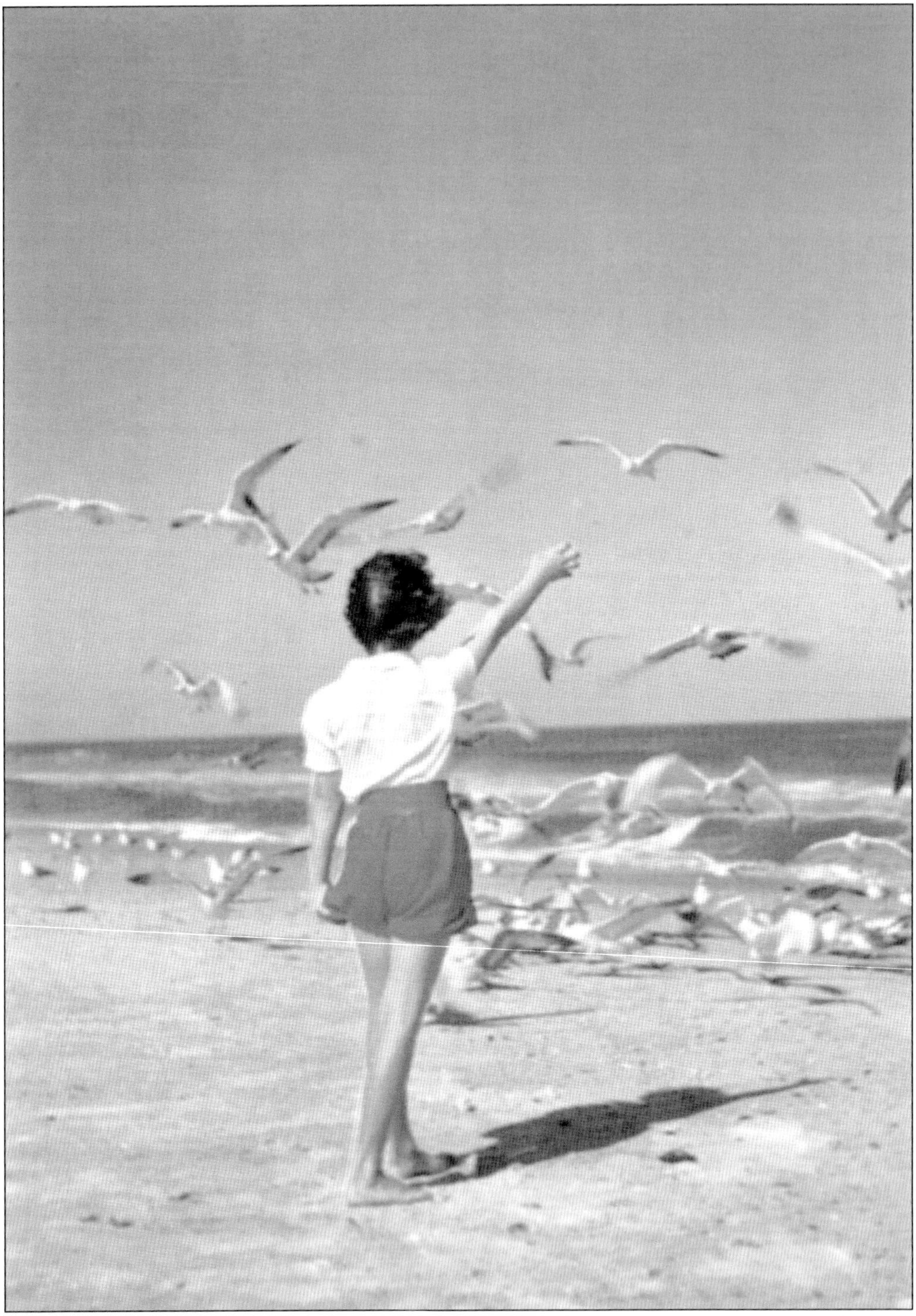

This image of a woman feeding gulls in Ponte Vedra Beach was used in a postcard in the mid-1900s. The woman is not identified, but the photograph, originally in color, captures the feelings of freedom and joy that beachgoers often have while relaxing by the ocean. By the middle of the 20th century, the Ponte Vedra Beach shore was lined with oceanfront homes.

# *Six*

# Golf and Tennis

Golf was an early recreational pursuit in Ponte Vedra Beach and has continued to be an important one.

Since the Mineral City mining plant was so remote and removed from the rest of civilization, the National Lead Company built a nine-hole golf course near the ocean to give the workers something to do during their off-hours.

That original course was redesigned and expanded over the years after the Ponte Vedra Club was built. As more communities sprang up around Ponte Vedra Beach, more golf courses followed.

Golf has also long been an important spectator sport in the town. In the late 1970s, the PGA Tour was looking to relocate its national headquarters from Washington, DC. Brothers Paul and Jerome Fletcher, important local developers, liked the idea of moving the tour to Ponte Vedra Beach, so they sold 415 acres to Commissioner Deane Beman for $1.

The tour headquarters opened in the fall of 1980, and soon after the Tournament Players Club at Sawgrass Stadium Course was completed, along with a large clubhouse. The first PGA tournament, now known as The Players Championship, was held there in 1982. The world's best golfers play there every May, attracting thousands of people to the area.

Tennis has also long been a popular sport in town. The Ponte Vedra Club built tennis courts for its guests, expanding the number of courts, along with players, through the years. Those courts have hosted many tournaments.

As Ponte Vedra Beach grew, many new communities also built their own tennis courts. Tennis arrived in a big way after Paul and Jerome Fletcher donated 11 acres near the PGA Tour headquarters to the Association of Tennis Professionals (ATP) in the 1990s. The ATP built a national headquarters building there, as well as tennis facilities. Although the ATP later sold its facilities and is no longer headquartered in Ponte Vedra Beach, tennis continues to be popular with people of all ages.

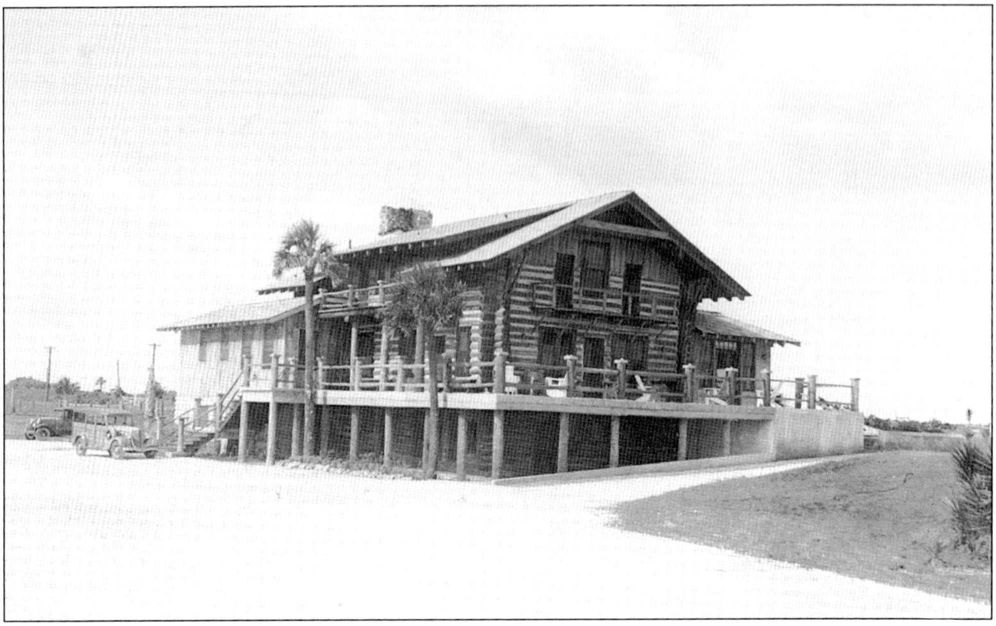

Golfers who visited Ponte Vedra Beach in the 1920s and 1930s stayed in the log cabin clubhouse built by the National Lead Company. As the golf course grew, the 12-room clubhouse/inn was not large enough for all the visitors, so it was replaced by the Ponte Vedra Club Inn in 1937.

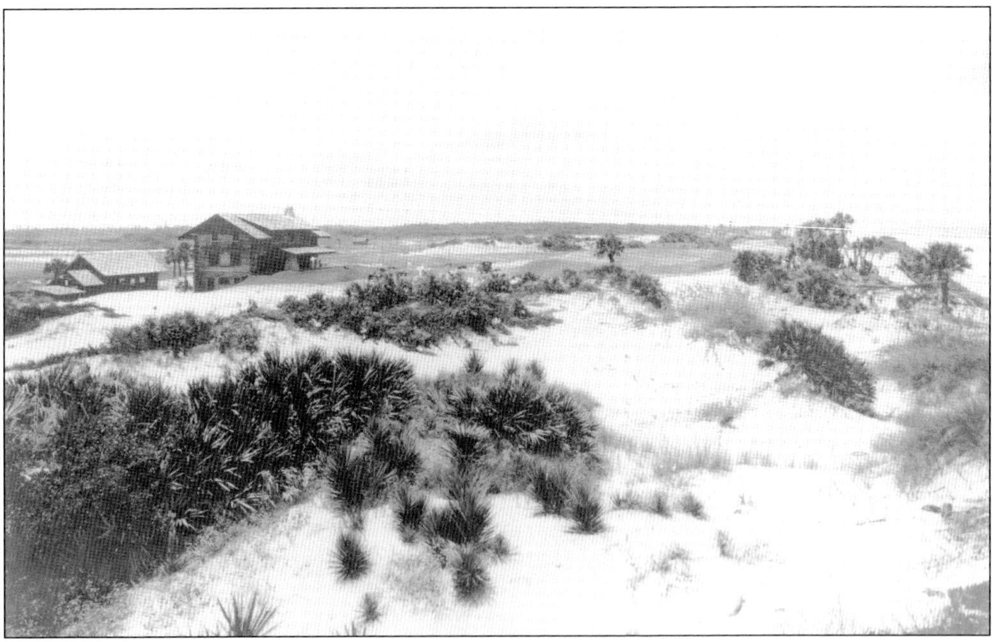

This 1928 photograph shows the National Lead Company mining operation in Mineral City and the Jacksonville Beach Golf Links Clubhouse built for the company's employees when they played golf on the company-constructed seaside golf course.

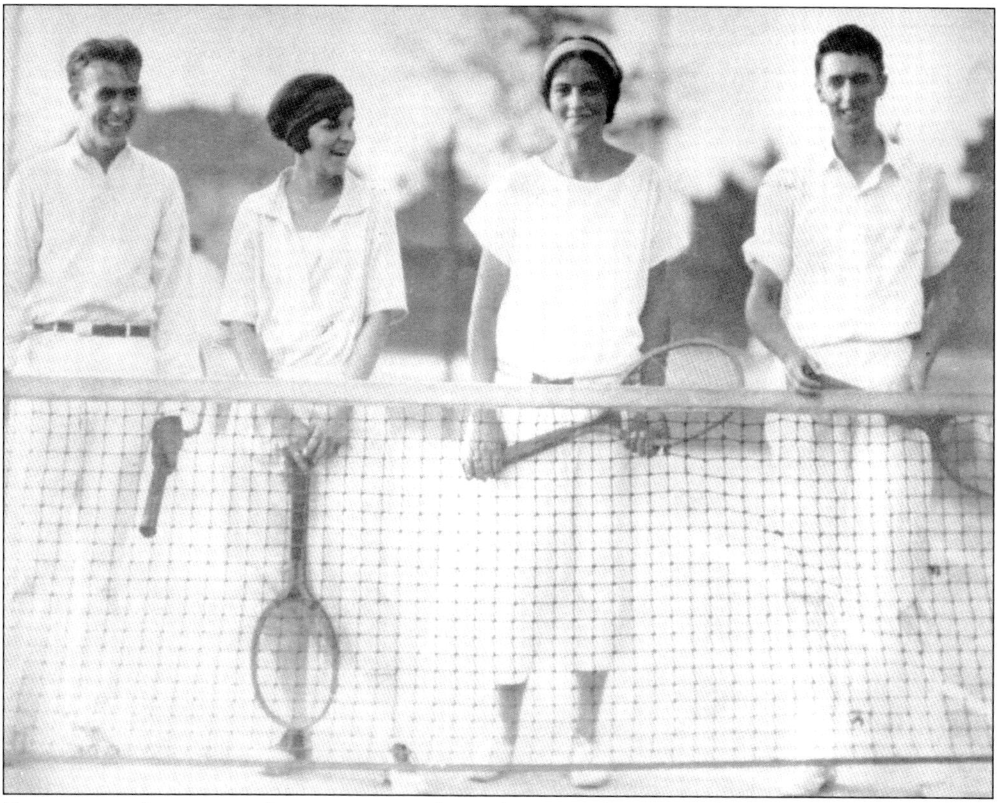

Four tennis players pose for a picture in the early years of Ponte Vedra Beach. Tennis has long been a popular sport in the town. When visitors were not golfing or swimming, they were often playing tennis.

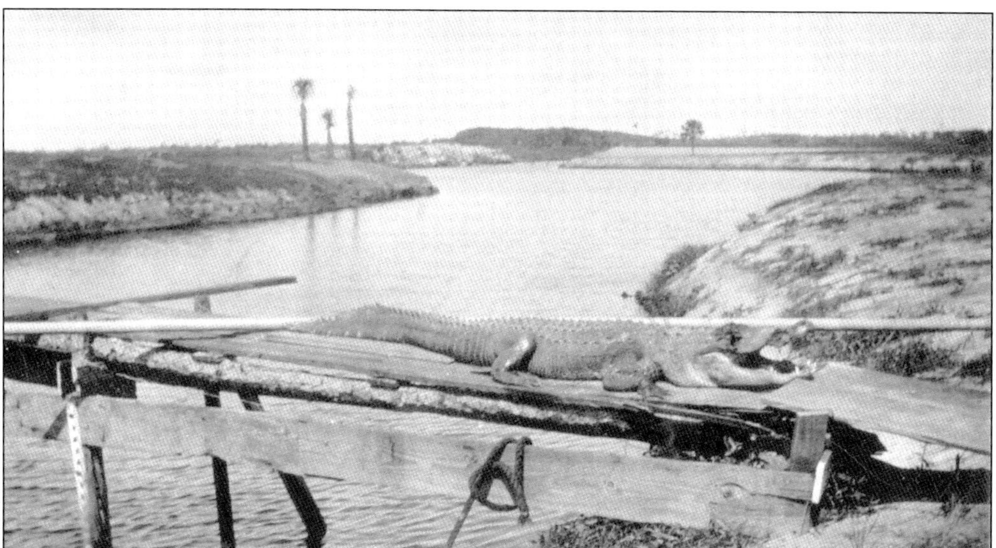

An alligator poses on a plank of wood during construction of an early Ponte Vedra Beach Golf Course.

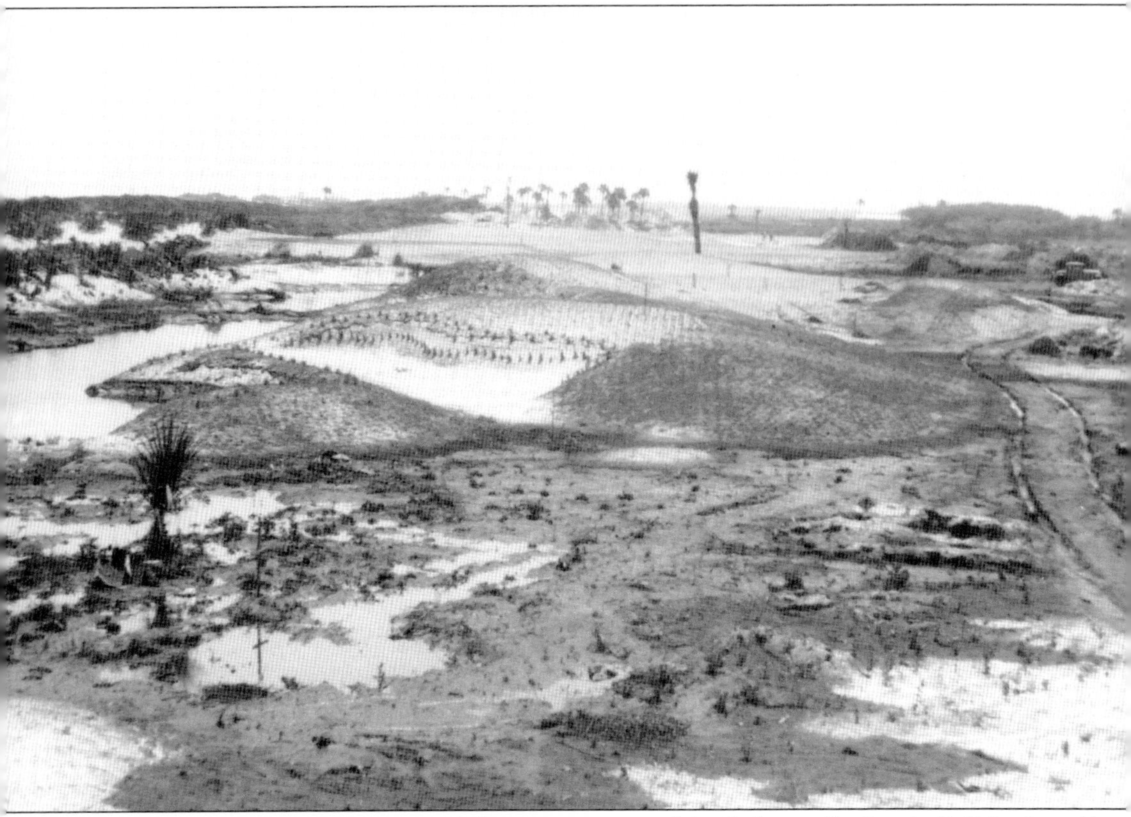

A photographer in 1928 captured the construction of the Jacksonville Beach Golf Links golf course, built by the National Lead Company. The course was an expansion of an earlier nine-hole course constructed for the recreational use of the company's employees.

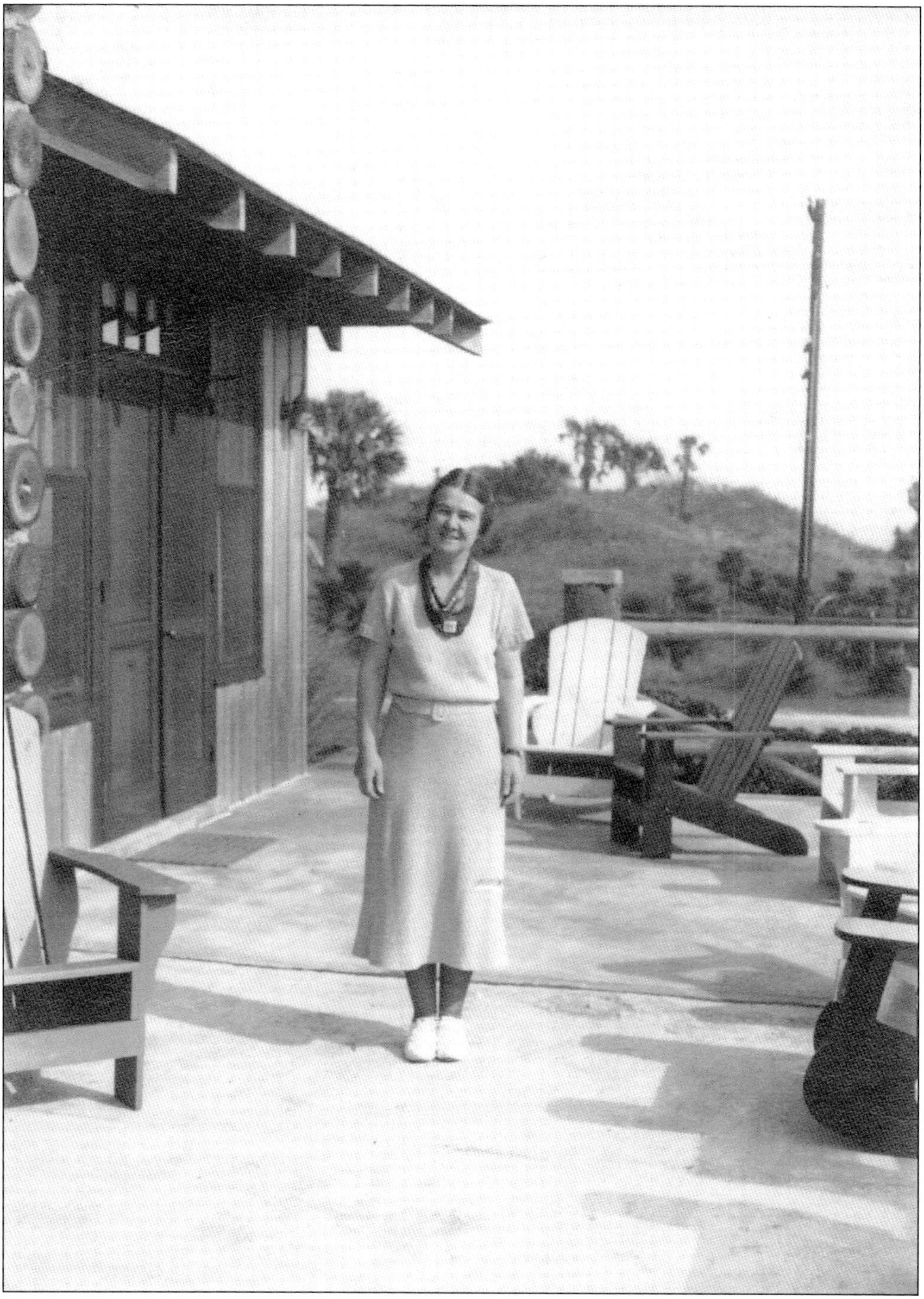

Inez Carson poses for a picture in Ponte Vedra Beach in 1930. As manager of the Jacksonville Beach Golf Links golf course, she served an important role in the small town.

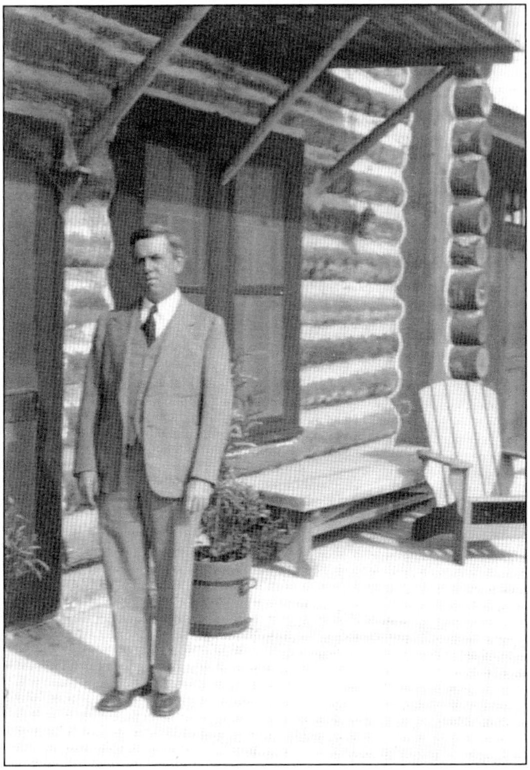

Robert Angus, a National Lead Company employee, stands on a log cabin porch at the Jacksonville Beach Golf Links golf course in Ponte Vedra Beach in 1930.

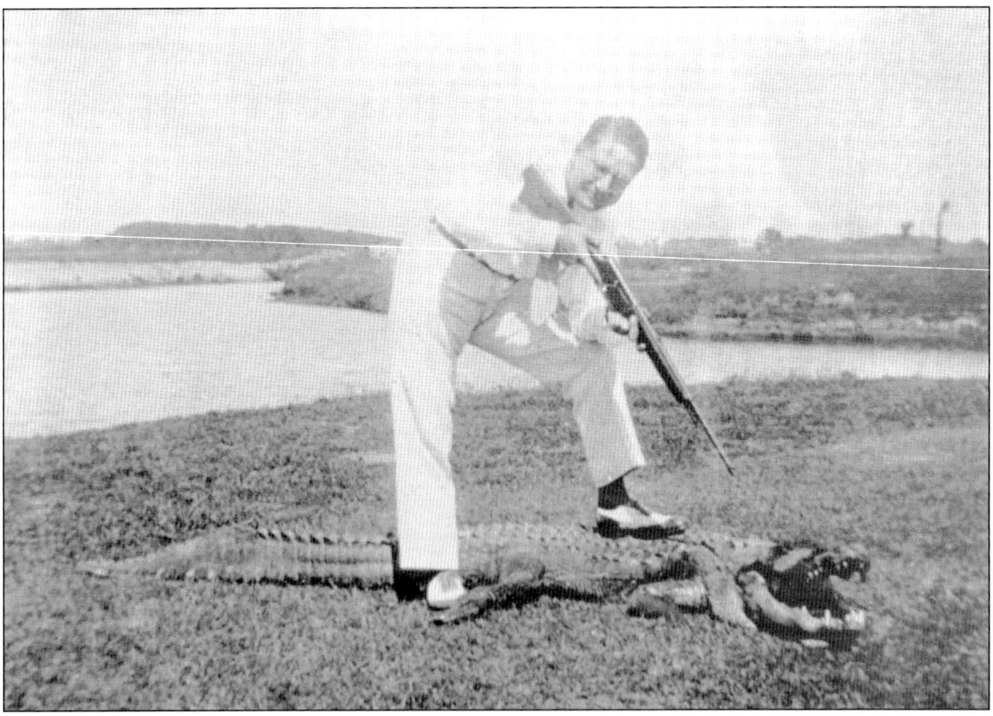

Col. Joseph Stehlin aims a gun at an alligator in front of a golf course in Ponte Vedra Beach in 1932. Since they are native to the area, alligators were a popular sight around the golf course.

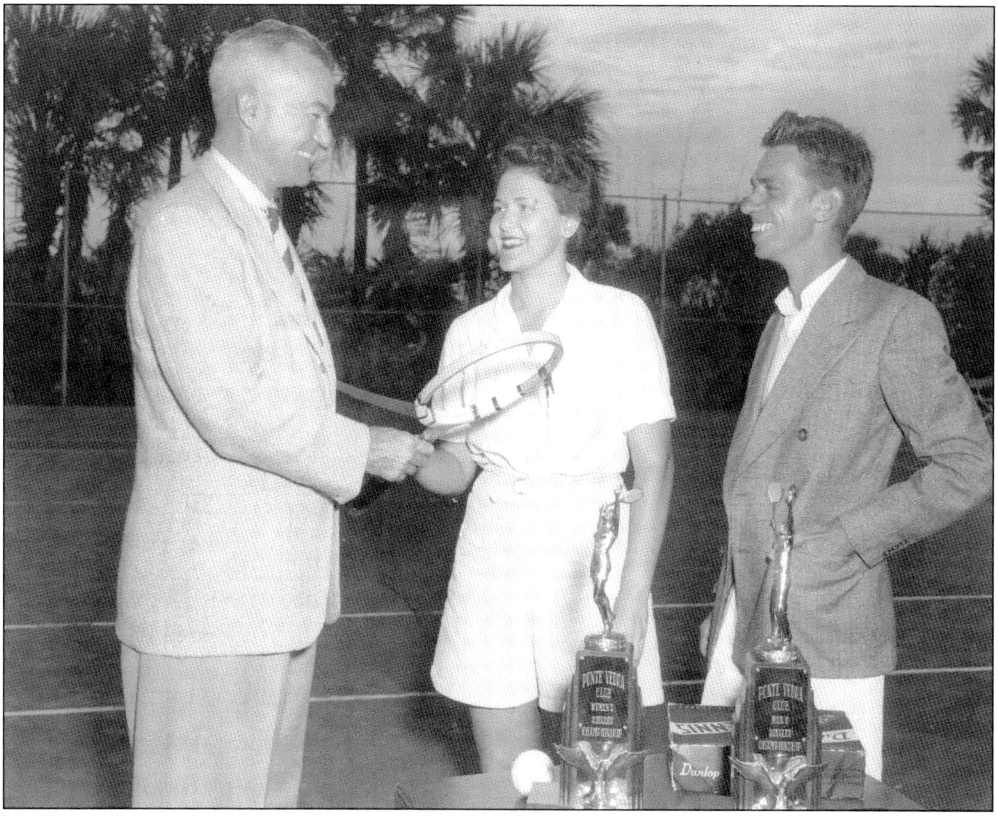


Tennis players are photographed at a net in Ponte Vedra Beach in 1946. They are not identified, but the image is typical of the type taken by area photographer Virgil Deane.

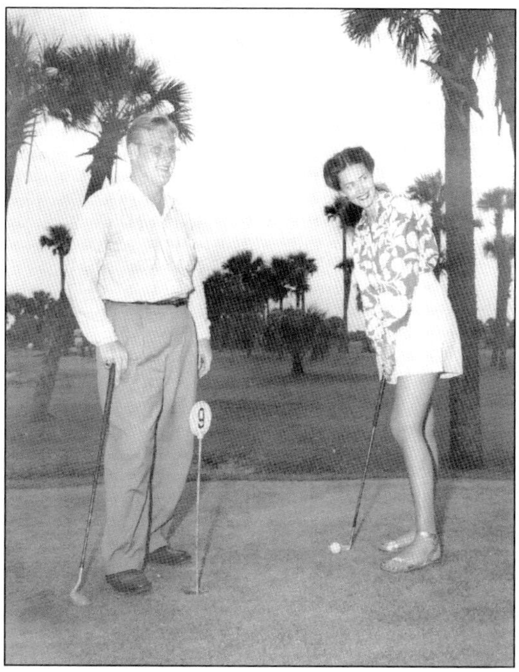

An unidentified man and woman play golf in Ponte Vedra Beach in 1948. As golf grew in popularity throughout the country, it did as well in Florida.

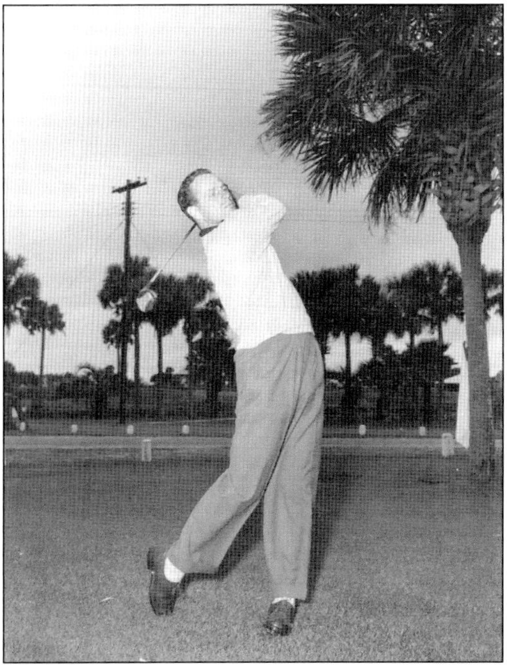

A man has his picture taken while playing golf in Ponte Vedra Beach in 1949. The Ponte Vedra Club golf course was redesigned by Trent Jones in the late 1940s and was listed as one of the nation's best courses.

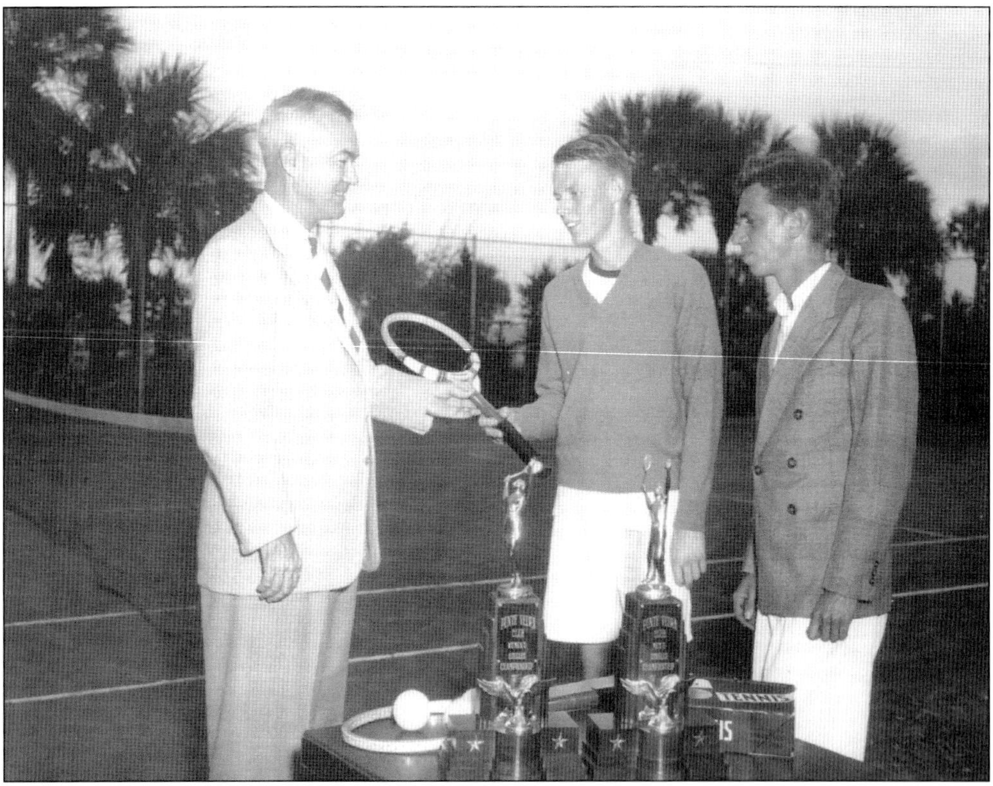

Three tennis players participate in a championship in Ponte Vedra Beach in the 1940s. Tennis tournaments were an important part of the social sports scene, and photographers were usually on the scene, as well.

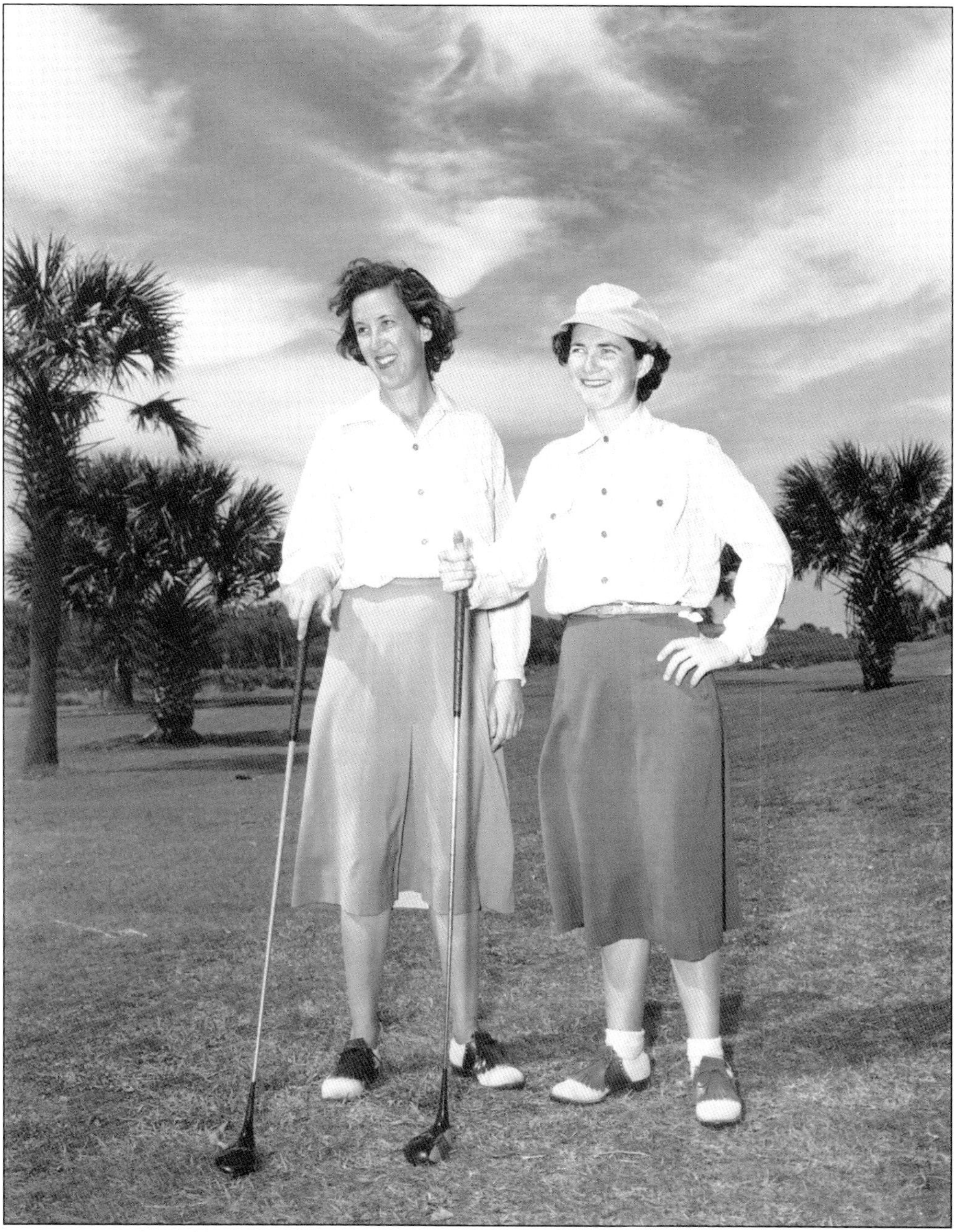

Two women play golf in Ponte Vedra Beach in 1949. In the years after World War II, golf increased in popularity among women.

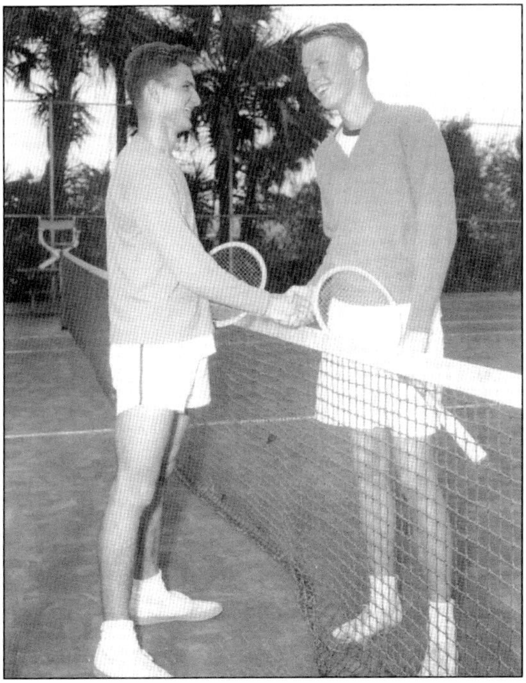

Two young men shake hands at a tennis net in Ponte Vedra Beach in the mid-1900s. The number of tennis tournaments increased with the growth of the sport in town.

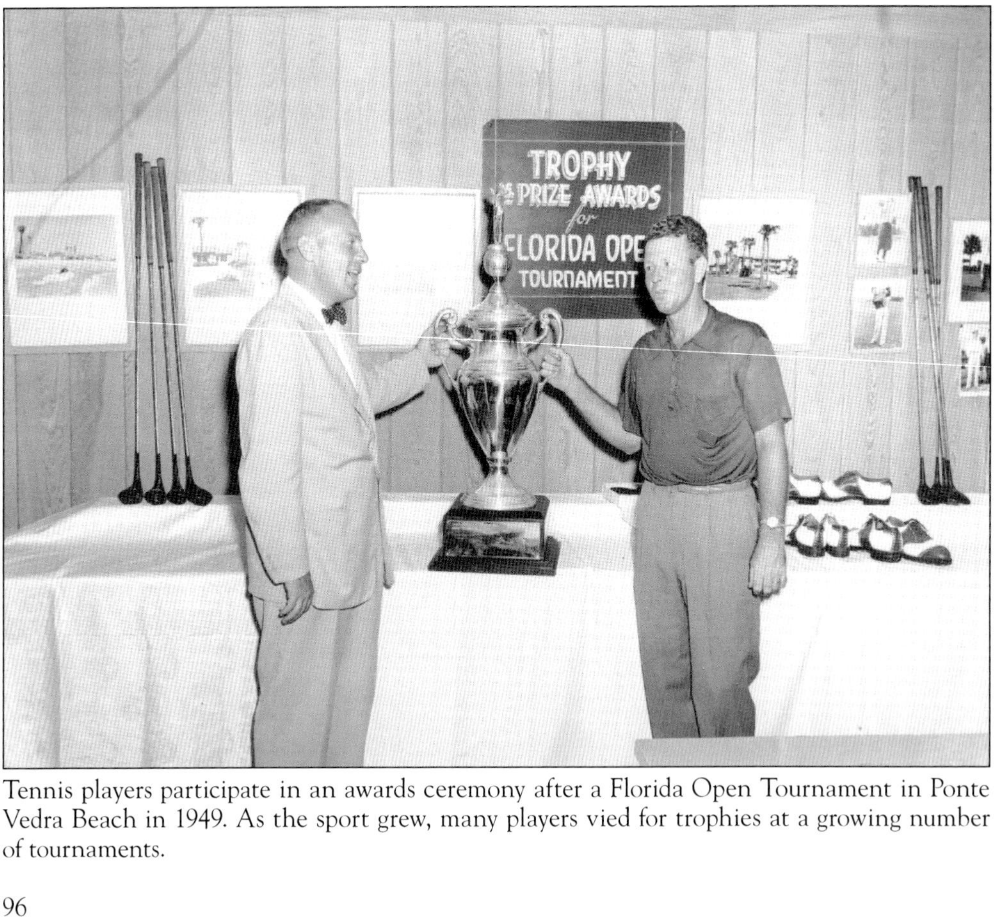


Tennis players participate in an awards ceremony after a Florida Open Tournament in Ponte Vedra Beach in 1949. As the sport grew, many players vied for trophies at a growing number of tournaments.

Tennis players pose for a group shot in Ponte Vedra Beach in the mid-1900s. The northeastern Florida climate proved ideal for the sport.

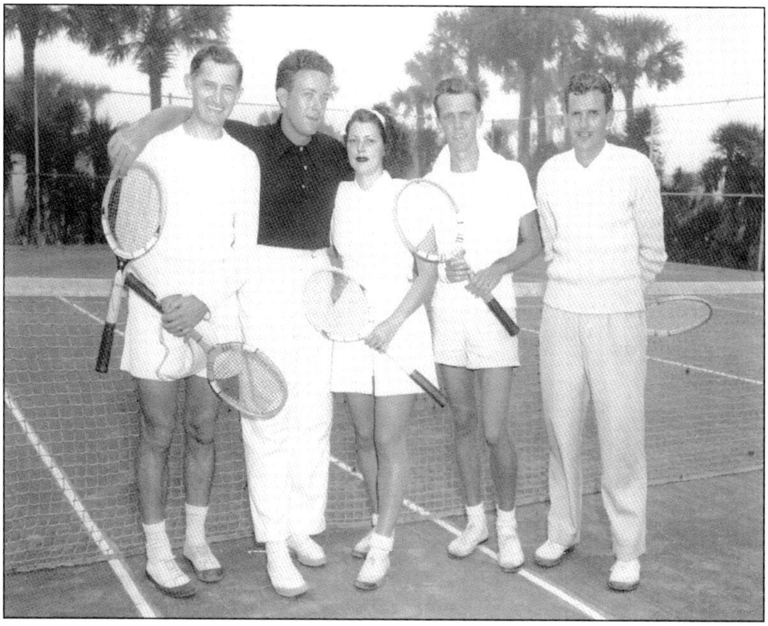

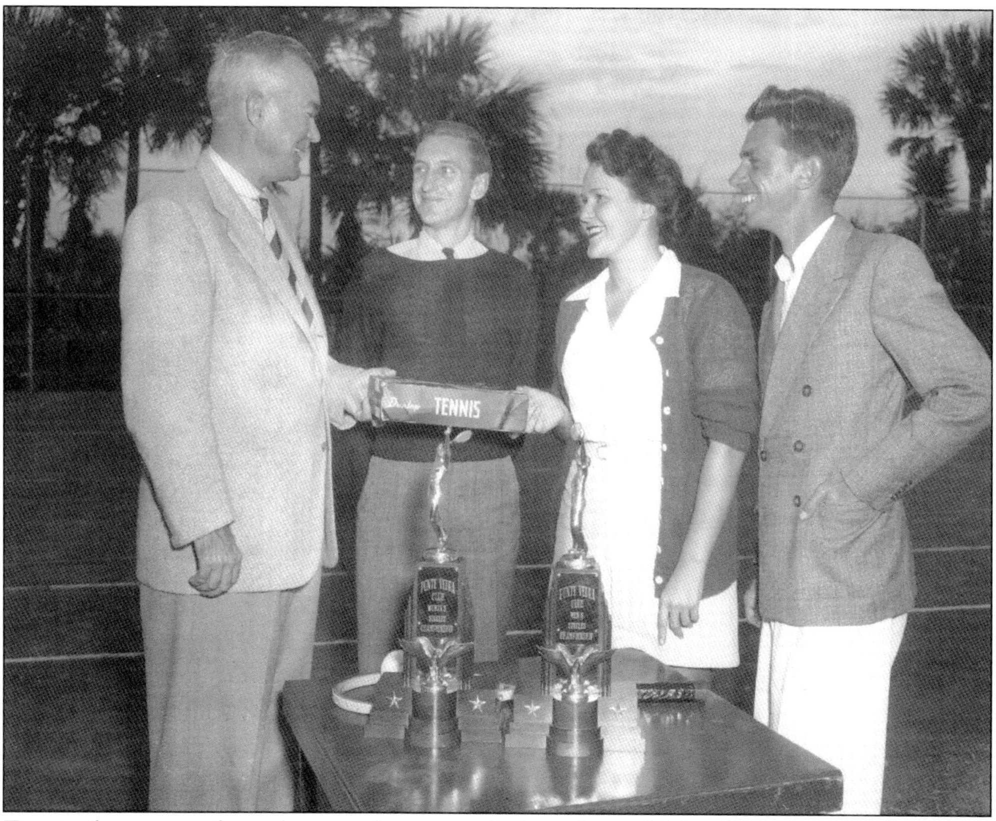


Tennis players pose for a photograph at a net during a Ponte Vedra Club championship in the 1940s. The sport drew a large number of players as well as spectators.

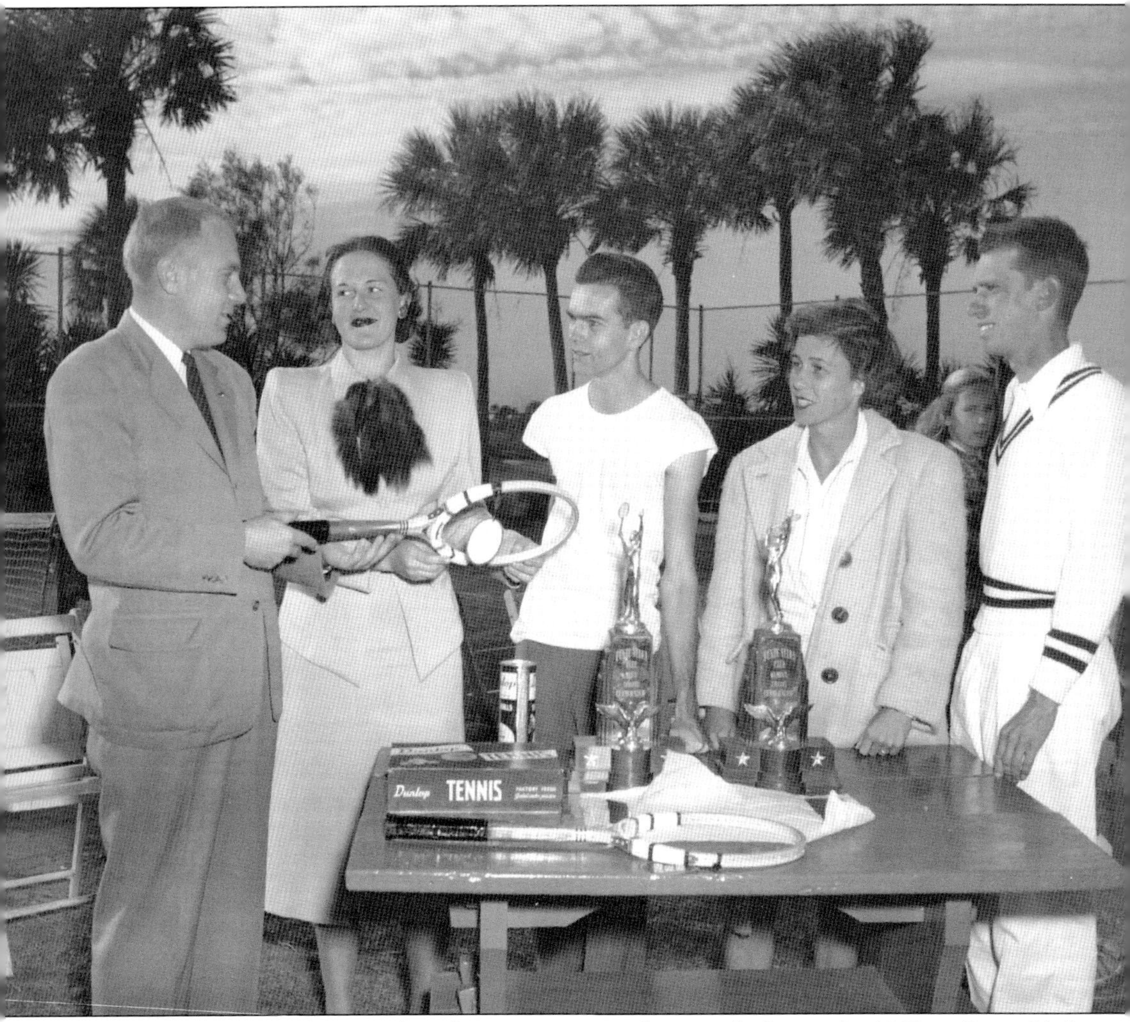


A group of tennis players gathers for a tournament photograph during the 1940s in Ponte Vedra Beach. It was an increasingly popular sport in town. The Ponte Vedra Club Racquet Club started as a single court next to the inn in 1937. By 1958, there were four courts. In 1964, there were nine courts. The club had 11 courts by 1969 and 15 by 1974. As the community of Ponte Vedra Beach grew, so did the number of tennis courts. More courts were built as new communities sprang up, and almost every community had its own courts.

Two male golfers pose for a photograph in 1950 in Ponte Vedra Beach. Golf attracted many people to the community, especially in the years after World War II, as it grew in popularity with young men.

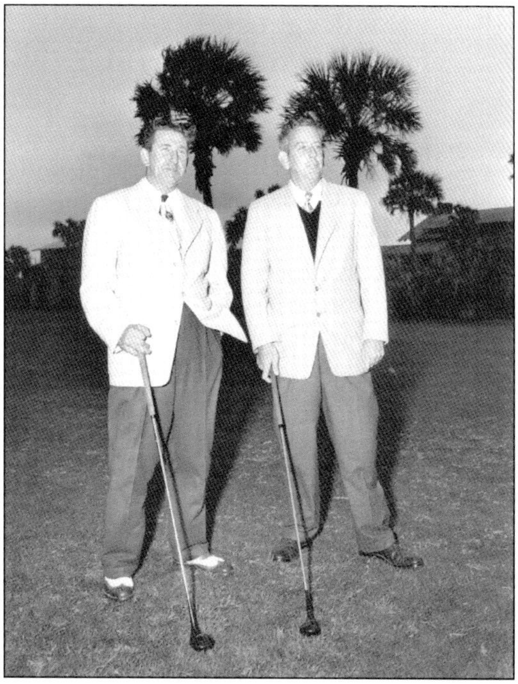

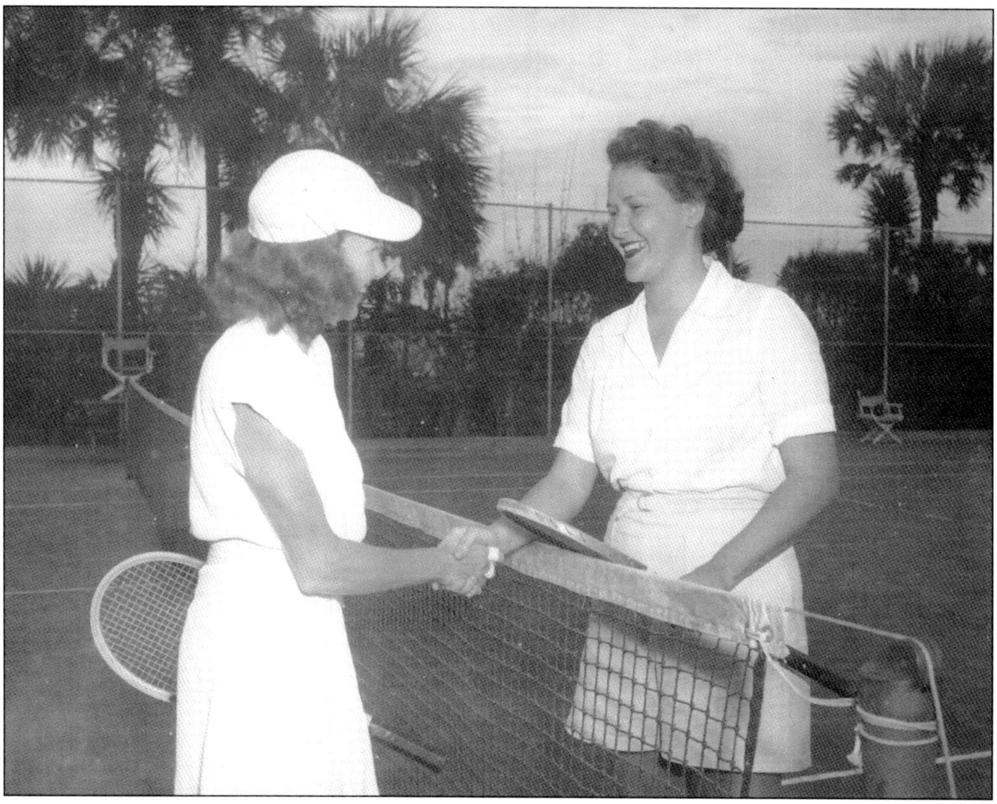

Young female tennis players shake hands at a Ponte Vedra Beach court in the mid-1900s. Throughout its history, tennis has been known as both a man's and a woman's game.

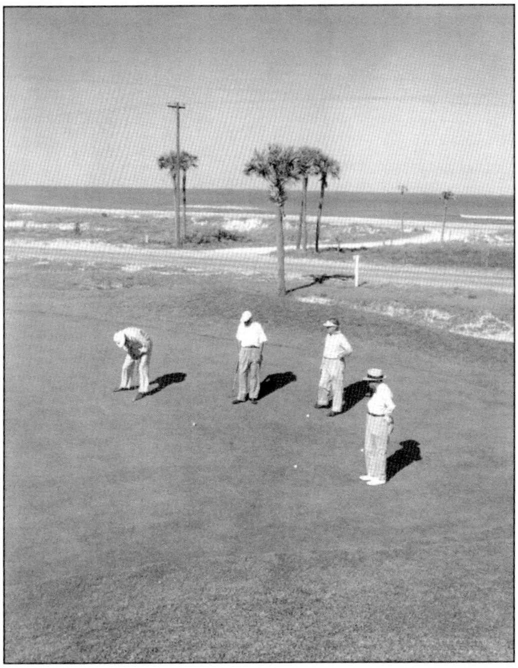

A foursome plays golf on a Ponte Vedra Beach golf course in the mid-1900s. Photographers provided players with images that they could take home and frame.

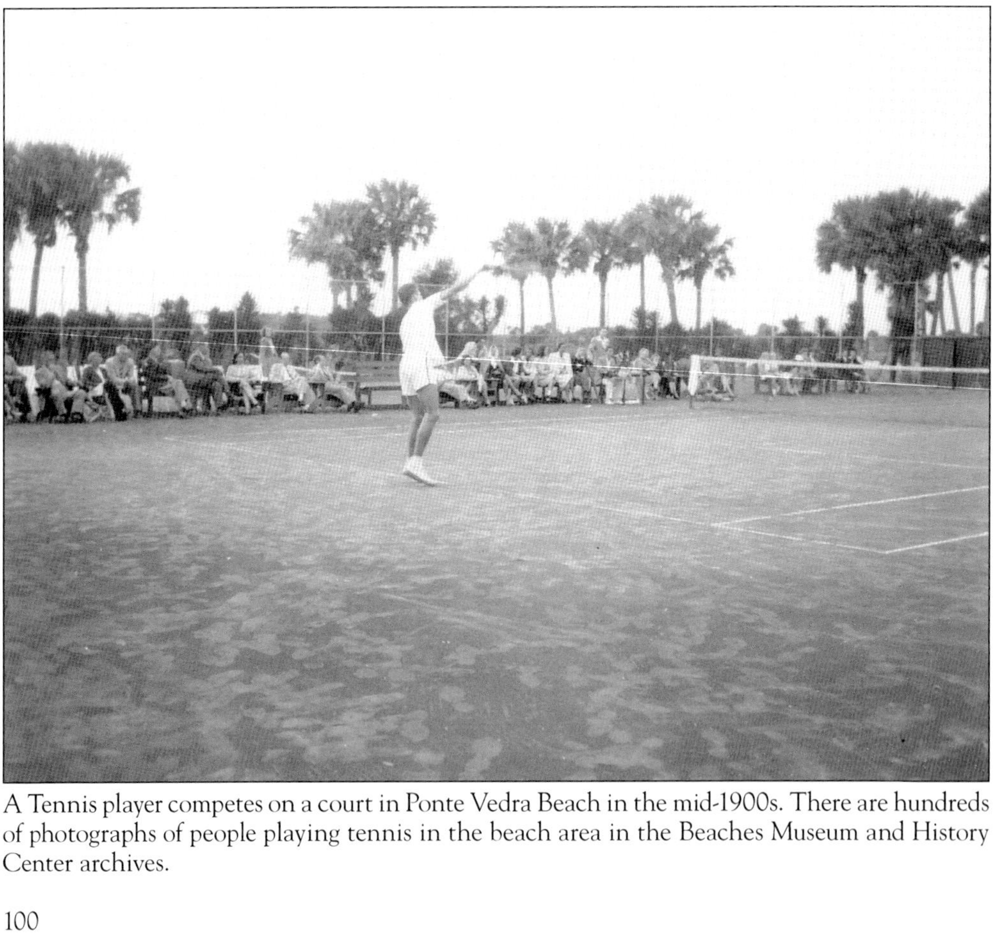

A Tennis player competes on a court in Ponte Vedra Beach in the mid-1900s. There are hundreds of photographs of people playing tennis in the beach area in the Beaches Museum and History Center archives.

A man is seen playing tennis in Ponte Vedra Beach in the mid-1900s. As the town developed, the sport was played by many residents and visitors.

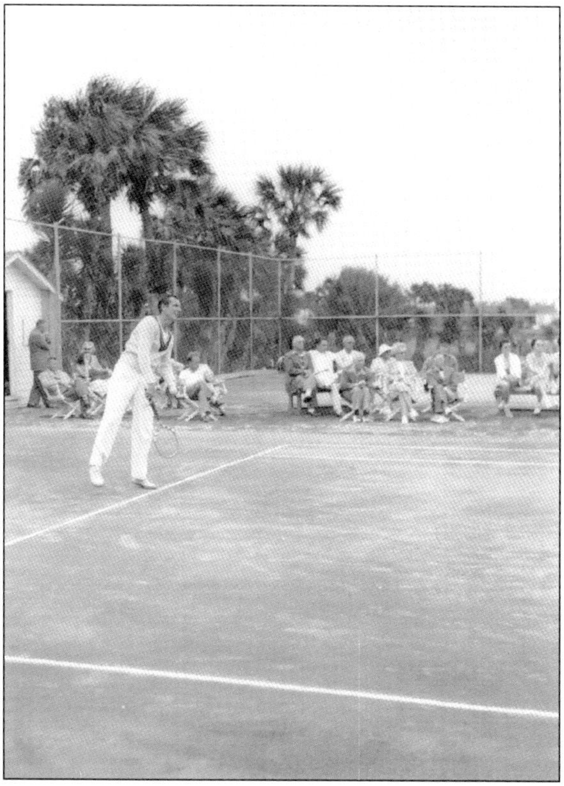

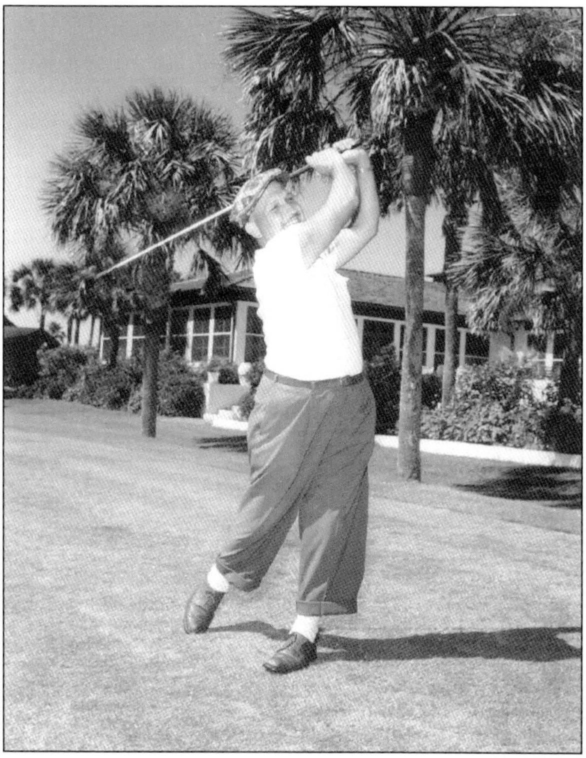

A man identified as Jim Federici, with the Prudential Life Insurance Company, plays golf on the Ponte Vedra Inn and Club Ocean Course.

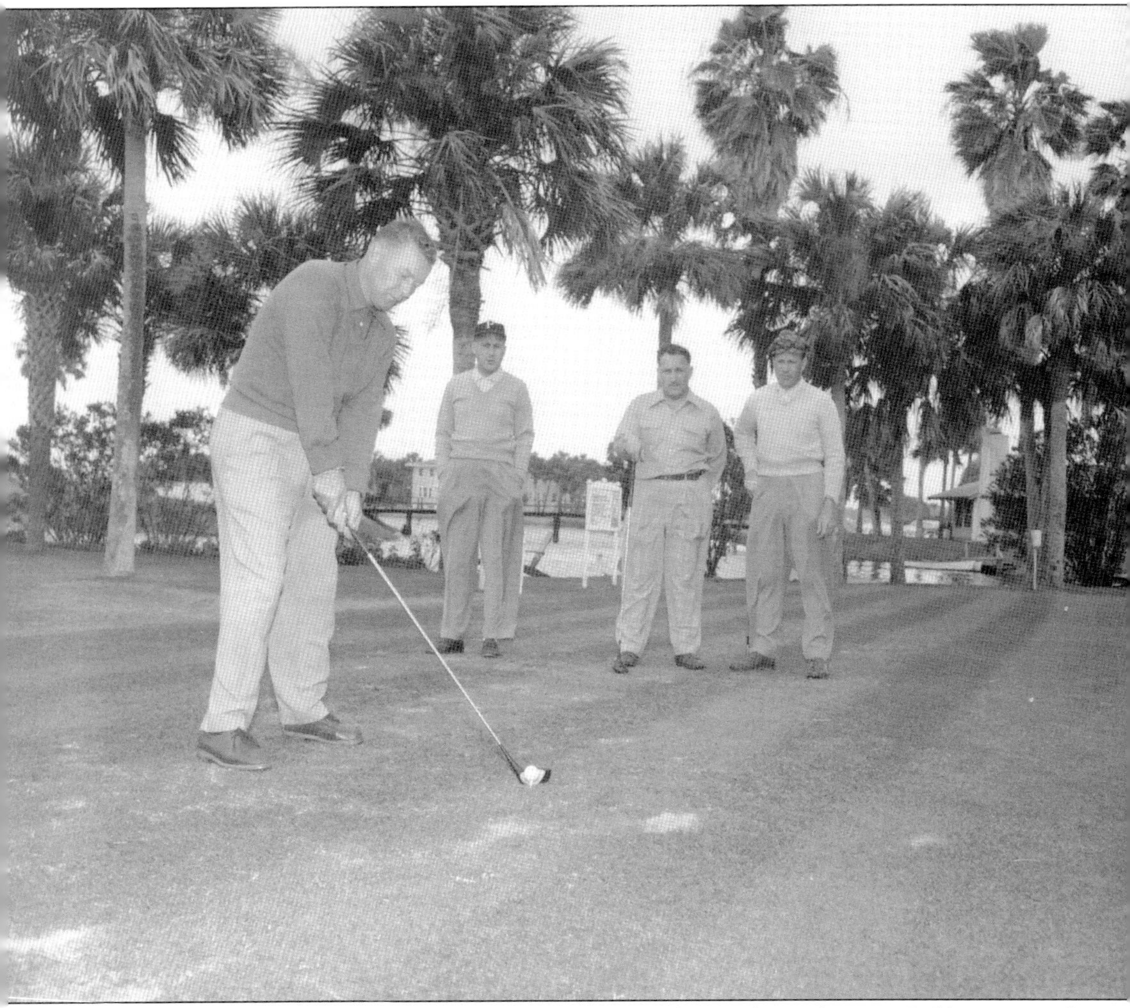

A foursome plays golf in Ponte Vedra Beach sometime during the mid-1900s. Golf was a popular sport for many in the town. The balmy climate and seaside course attracted golfers to the area.

An unidentified couple strikes a pose while attending a tennis tournament in 1954 at Ponte Vedra Beach. Tournaments were popular social events, with many spectators coming to watch and support their family and friends.

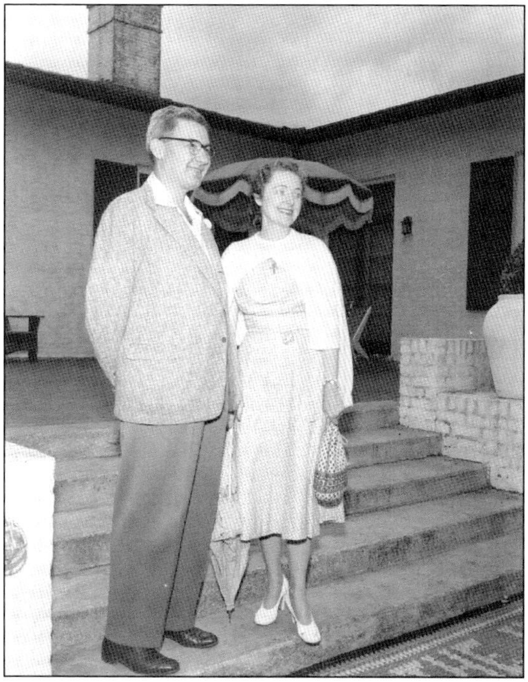

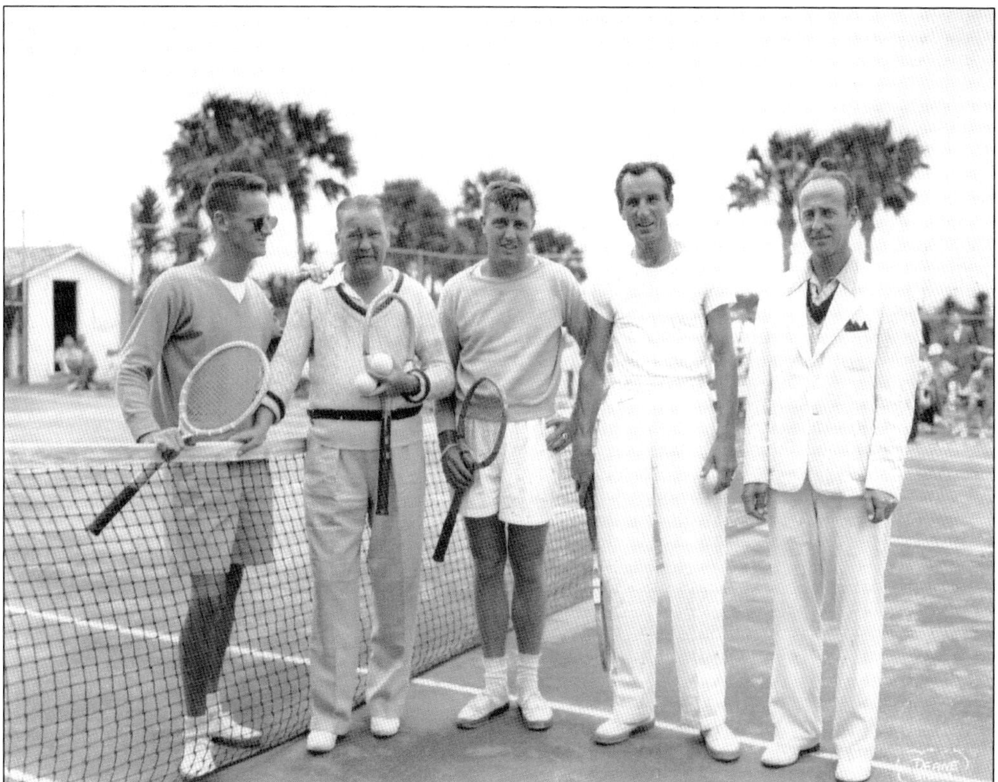

Five men pose for a group shot at a tennis court in Ponte Vedra Beach sometime in the mid-1900s. The weather is ideal for tennis much of the year, especially in the fall and spring.

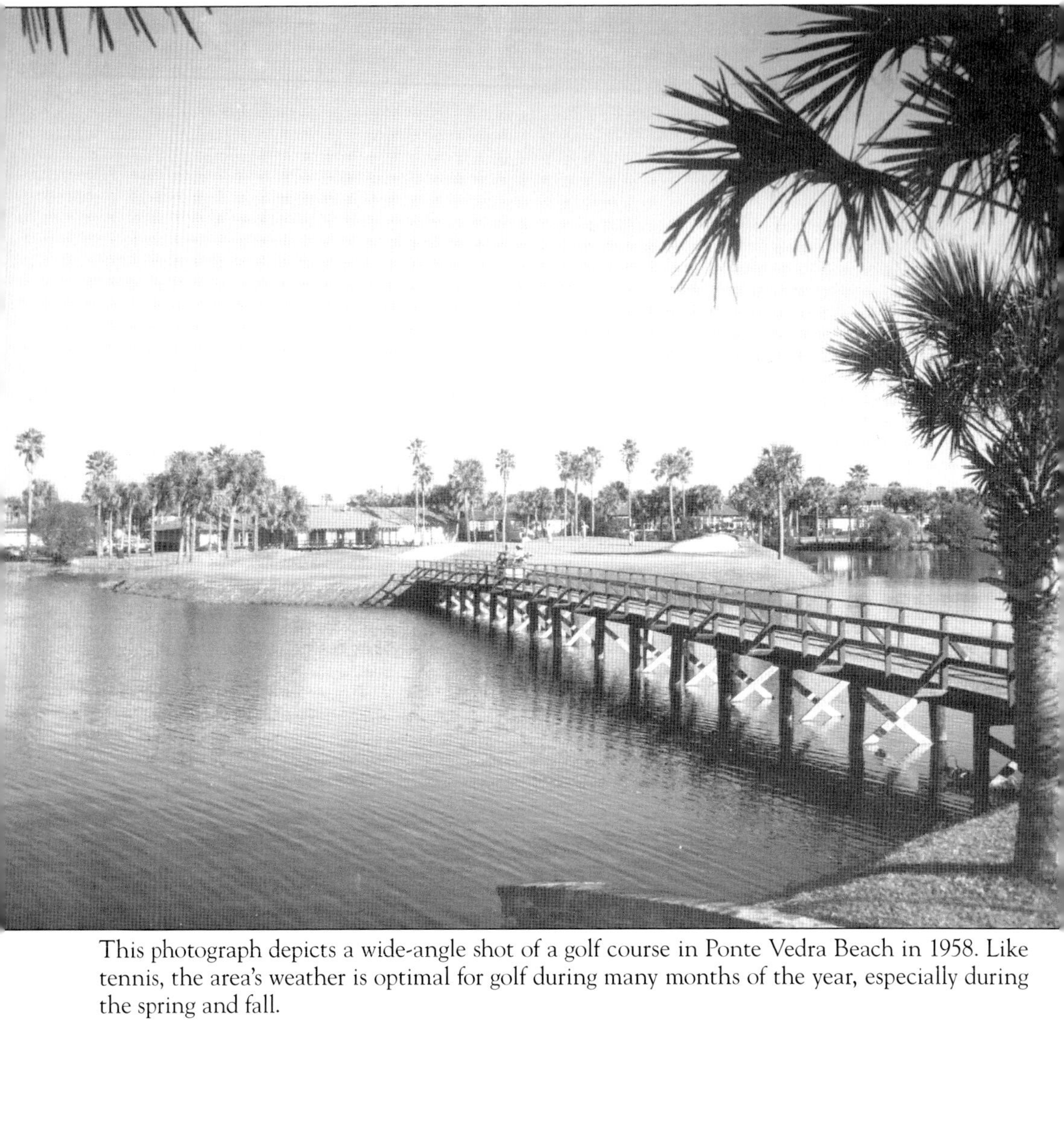

This photograph depicts a wide-angle shot of a golf course in Ponte Vedra Beach in 1958. Like tennis, the area's weather is optimal for golf during many months of the year, especially during the spring and fall.

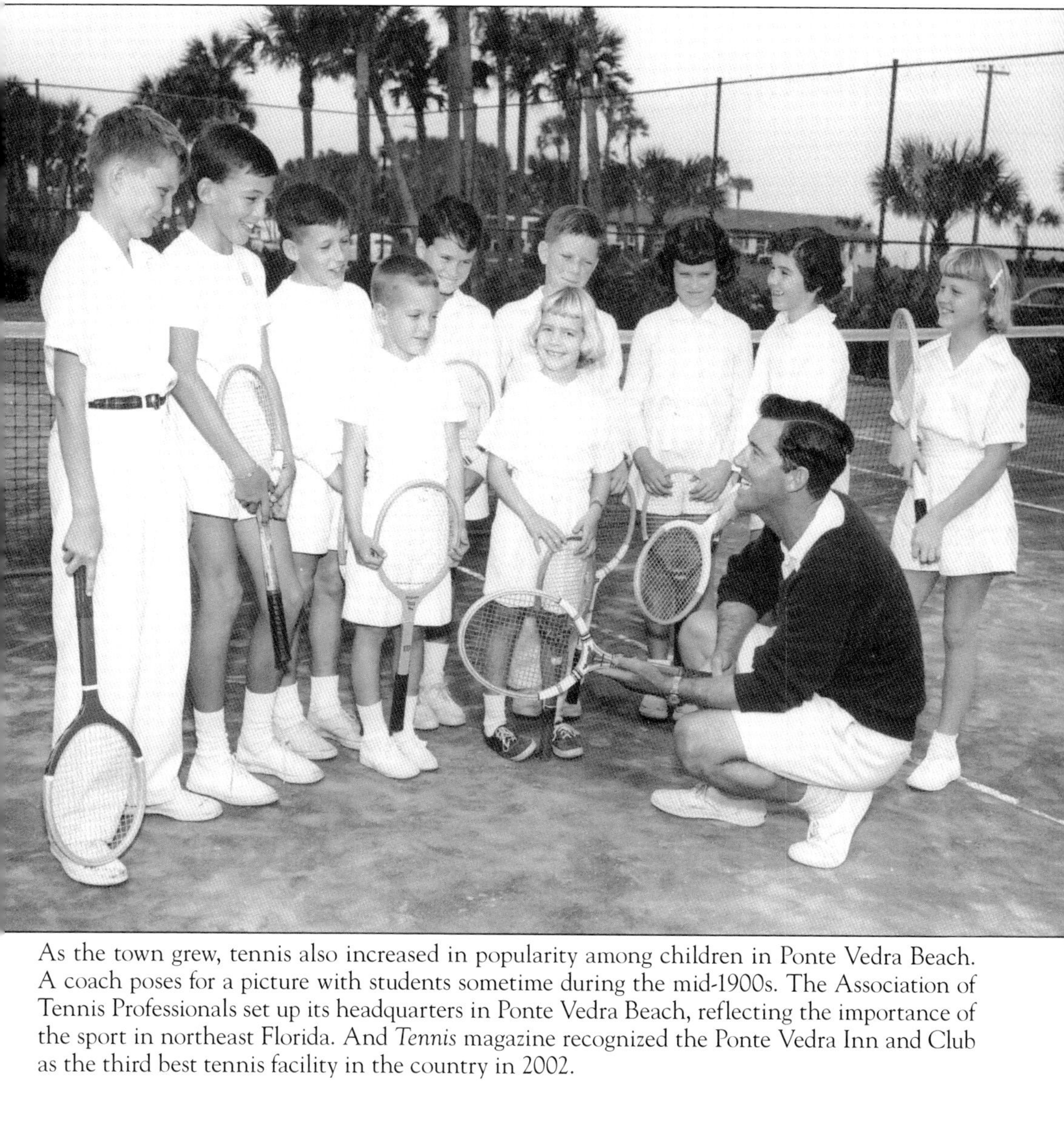

As the town grew, tennis also increased in popularity among children in Ponte Vedra Beach. A coach poses for a picture with students sometime during the mid-1900s. The Association of Tennis Professionals set up its headquarters in Ponte Vedra Beach, reflecting the importance of the sport in northeast Florida. And *Tennis* magazine recognized the Ponte Vedra Inn and Club as the third best tennis facility in the country in 2002.

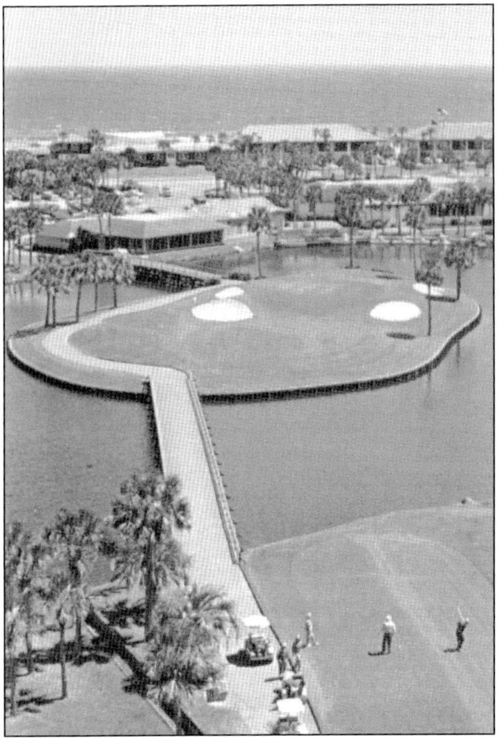

People play golf at the Ponte Vedra Club during the mid-20th century. The beautiful course is close to the Atlantic Ocean.

A woman watches a man play golf in Ponte Vedra Beach sometime during the 1970s. As the number of courses grew, more women also took up golf at that time.

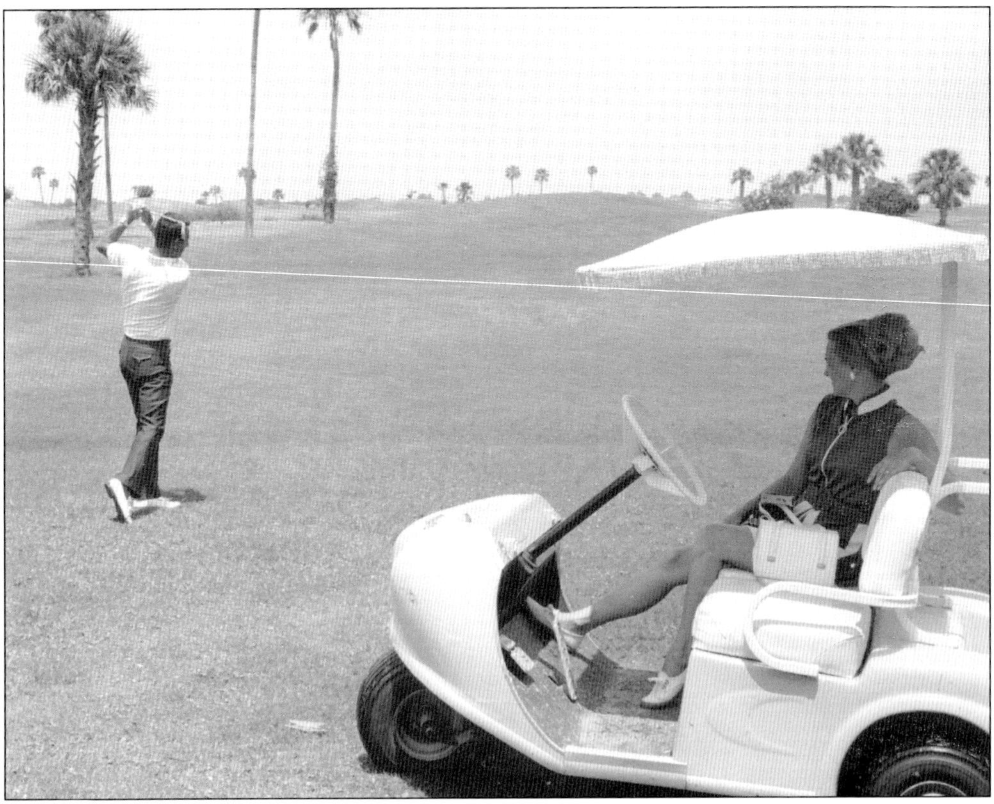

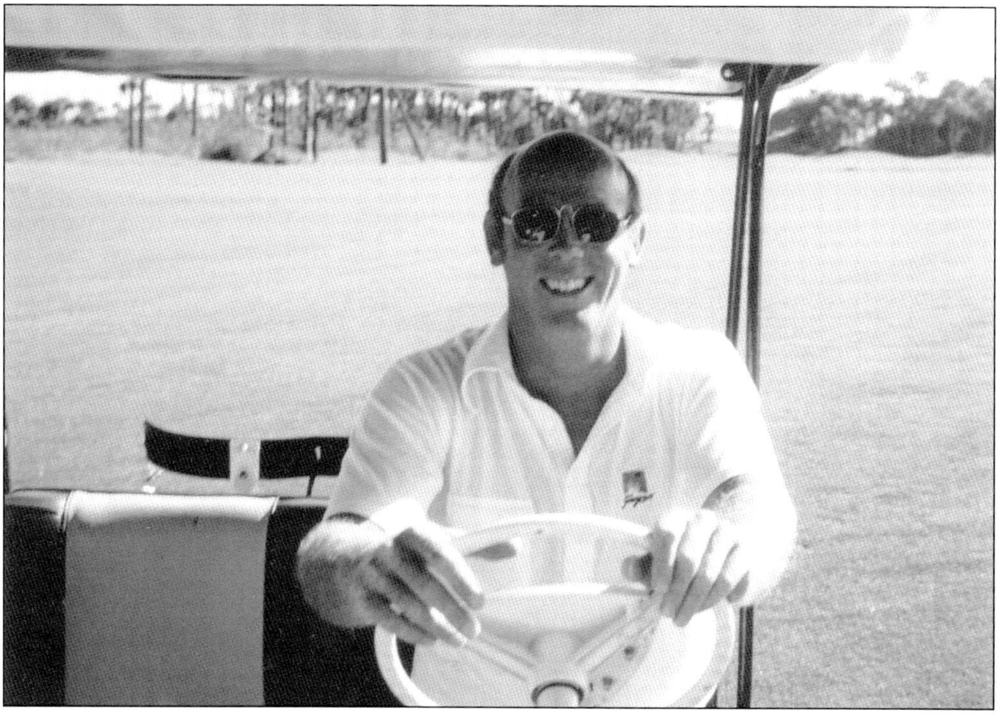

Ed Seay, the golf course architect for Sawgrass Country Club, drives a golf cart in Ponte Vedra Beach in August 1974.

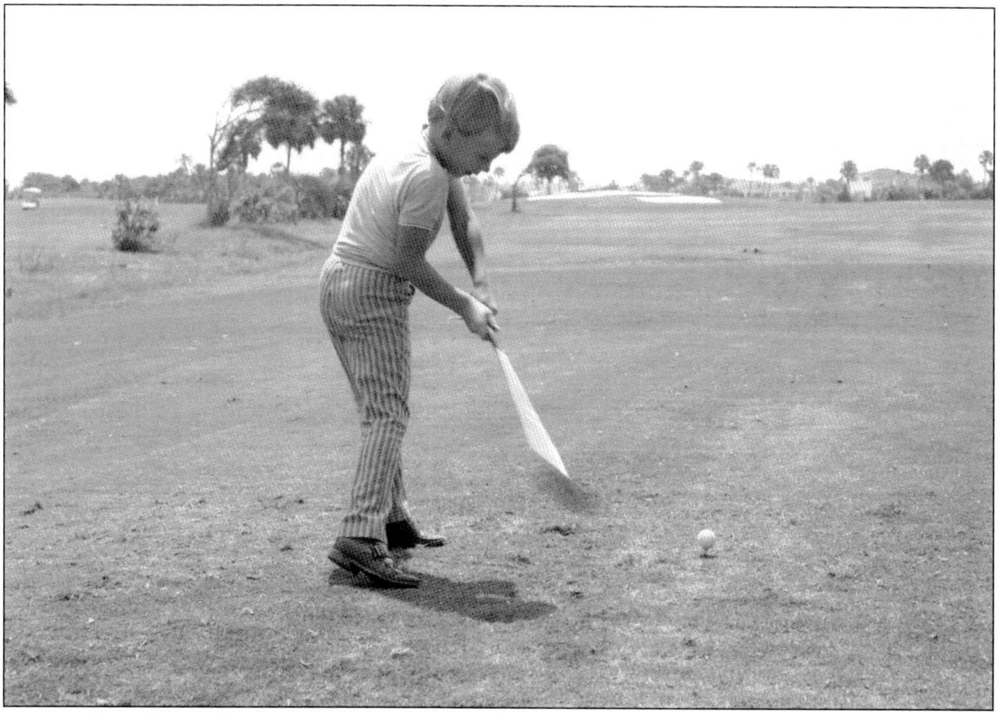

A young boy plays golf on a Ponte Vedra Beach course in the 1970s. As the sport grew in popularity with adults, they introduced it to their children.

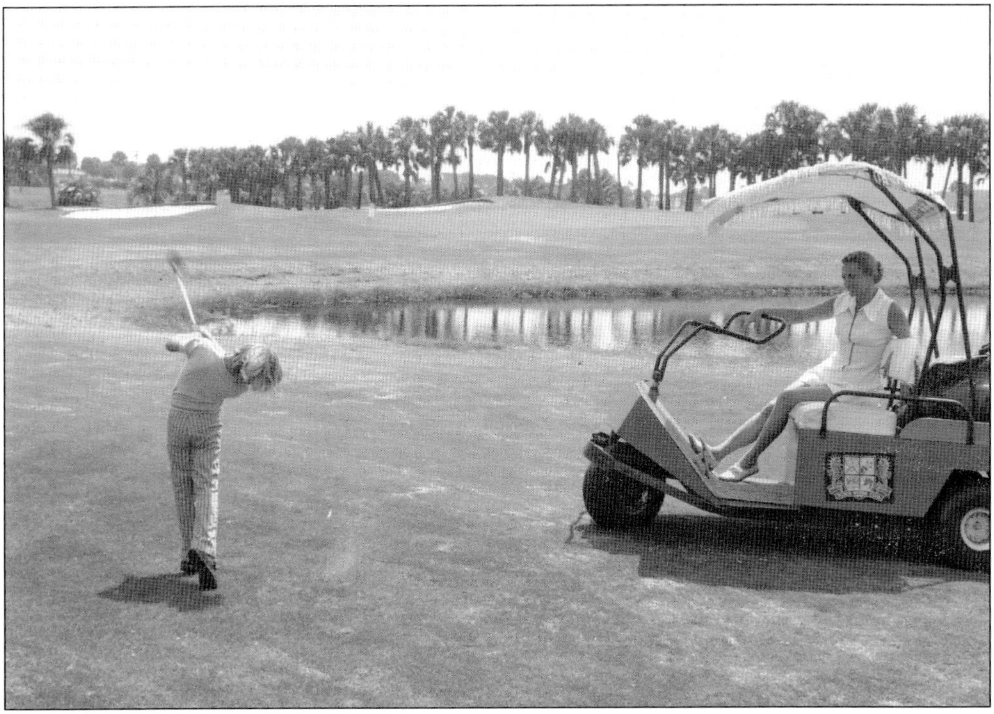

The young boy's mother watches her son play golf in Ponte Vedra Beach in the 1970s. As the number of golf courses grew, there were more opportunities for children to learn the sport.

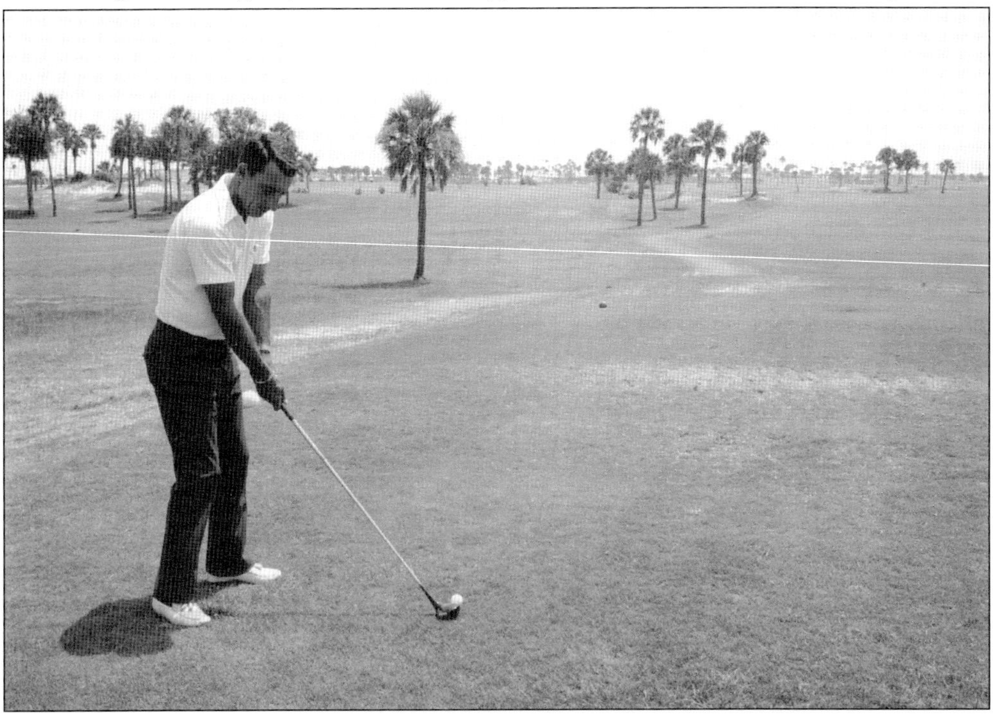

This photograph shows a wide view of a Ponte Vedra Beach golf course as the sport grew in popularity throughout the area. Today, there are many golf courses.

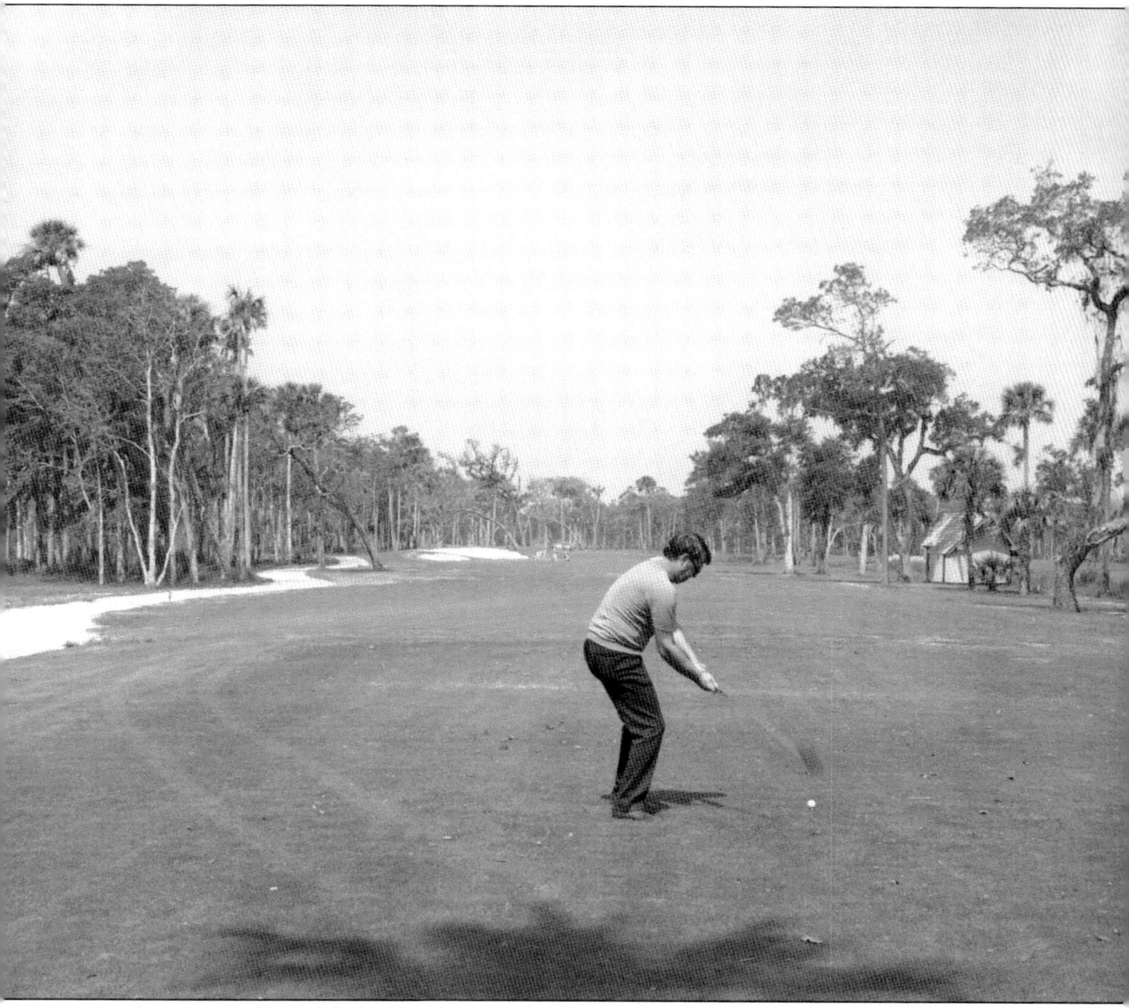

A man plays golf in Ponte Vedra Beach during the 1970s or 1980s, when new golf courses were being developed all around the town. Many new communities were established at that time, some with their own 18-hole courses.

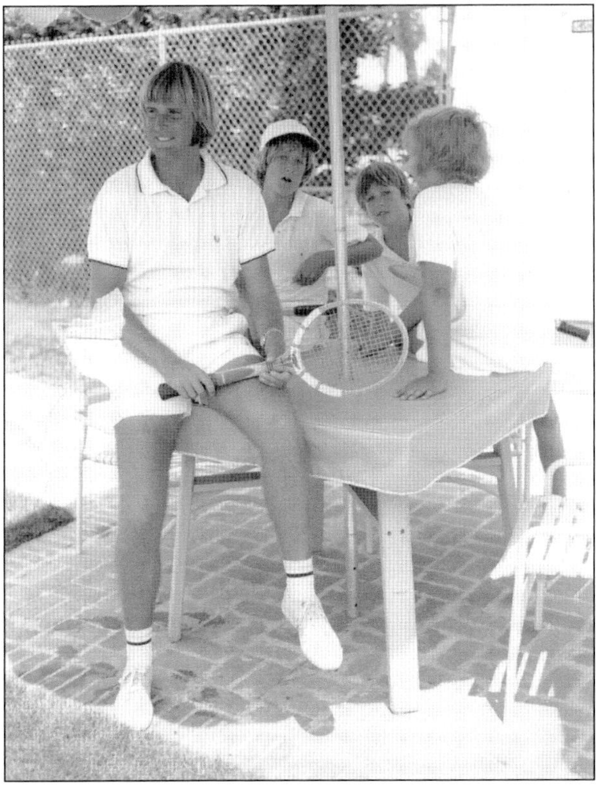

A group takes a break during a day of tennis in Ponte Vedra Beach. As Ponte Vedra Beach developed, the number of tennis courts grew, inspiring many children to take tennis lessons.

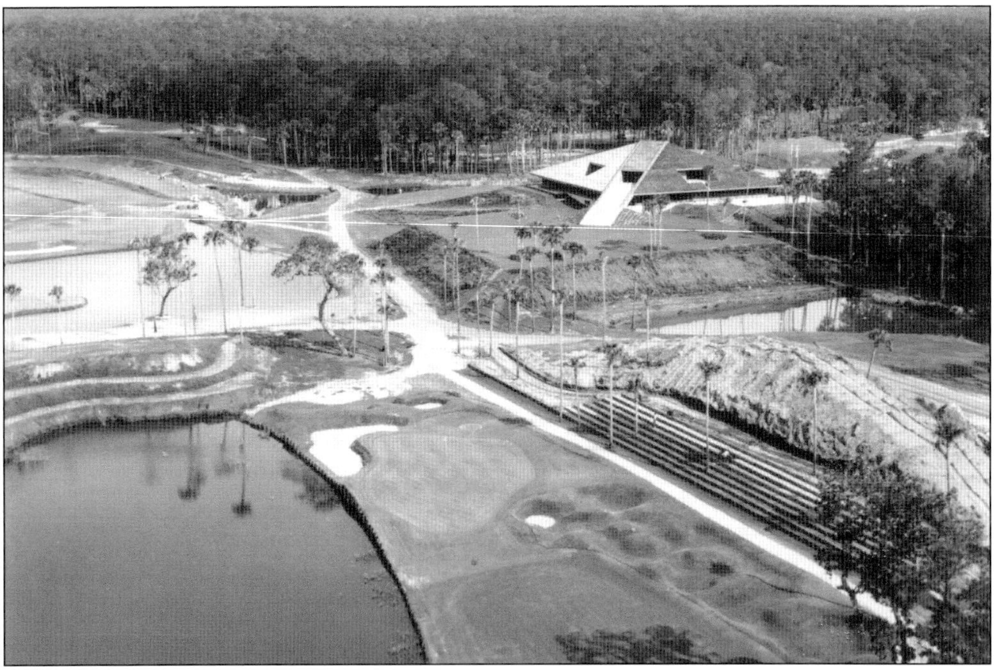

This photograph shows the TPC Sawgrass Stadium Course under construction. The PGA headquarters opened in Ponte Vedra Beach in the fall of 1980, a few months before the stadium course was completed. The Players Championship is played there every May.

# *Seven*

# Growth and Development

When Mineral City became Ponte Vedra Beach in 1928, developers asked the government to build Florida A1A along the oceanfront. B.B. McCormick and his construction team went to work, using mules to build the road that linked Ponte Vedra Beach to Jacksonville Beach to the north and Vilano Beach to the south. It was an important throughway that launched the town's expansion and development.

For almost four decades, A1A ran north and south near the ocean, the site of the current Ponte Vedra Boulevard. After A1A was rerouted west to its current location, new communities were built along it, and oceanfront homes were erected along Ponte Vedra Boulevard.

In the early 1970s, developer Jimmy Stockton Jr. built Sawgrass Country Club on the east side of the new A1A, facing the front entrance of the gated golf course community toward the road.

In the early 1980s, the Arvida corporation built the large gated Sawgrass Players Club community on the west side of A1A. The adjacent Sawgrass Village shopping center was also created during that time of rapid development.

Other shopping areas and communities went up along A1A, including L'Atrium, Ponte Vedra Lakes, Fairfield, and Seaside.

Ponte Vedra Beach also expanded westward as communities sprang up along Palm Valley Road toward the Palm Valley Bridge, through the area once known as Diego Plains.

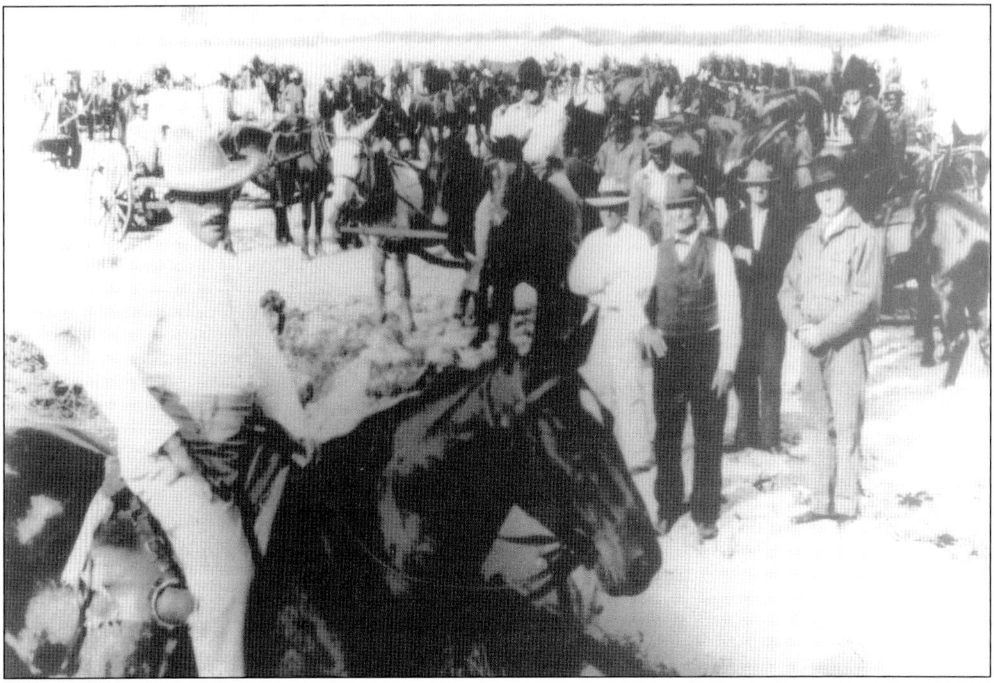

B.B. McCormick, on horseback, oversees the construction of Florida A1A through Mineral City in 1926. The building of that road was an important milestone in the town, soon to be renamed Ponte Vedra Beach.

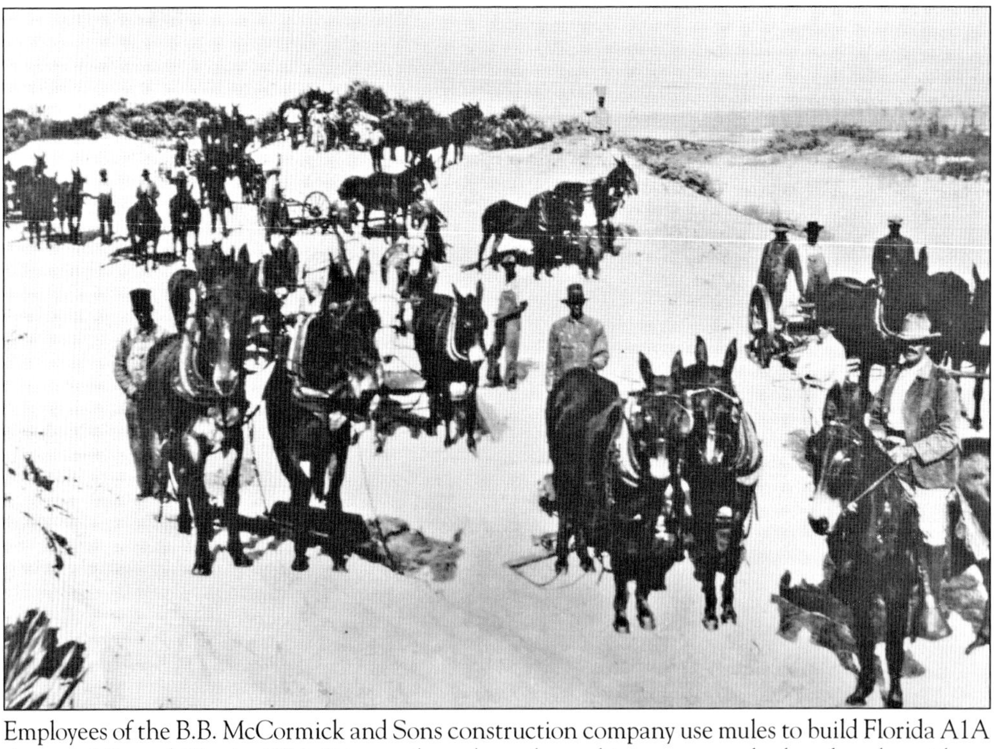

Employees of the B.B. McCormick and Sons construction company use mules to build Florida A1A through Mineral City in 1926. Prior to that, the only road in town was the beach at low tide.

By 1931, when this photograph was taken, some new families were moving to Ponte Vedra Beach. Here, Patti Stehlin is carried by her nurse at a beach house.

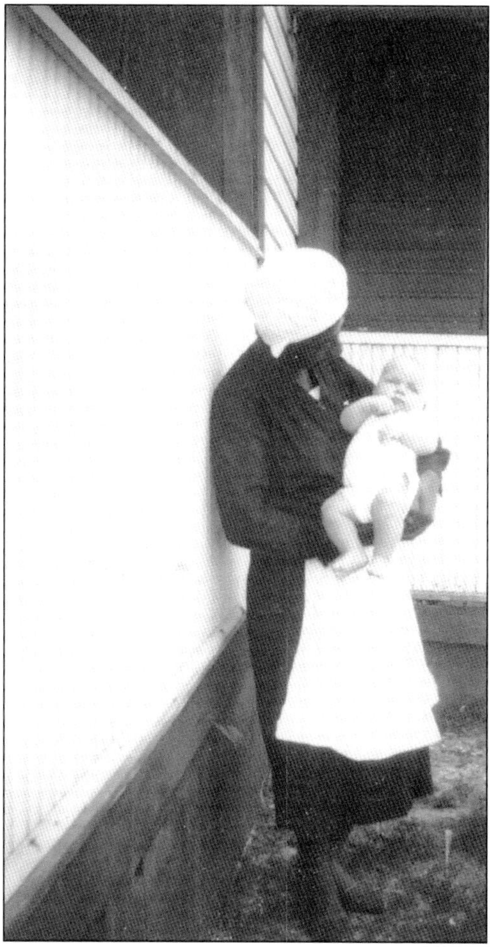

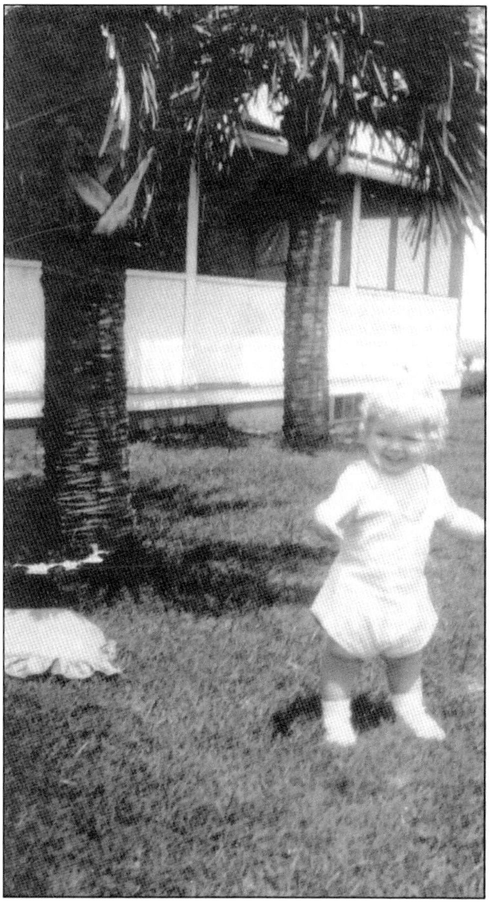

Toddler Patti Stehlin poses for a picture on a Ponte Vedra Beach lawn in 1932. There were few children in the early years of the town, and they attended school in Jacksonville Beach to the north.

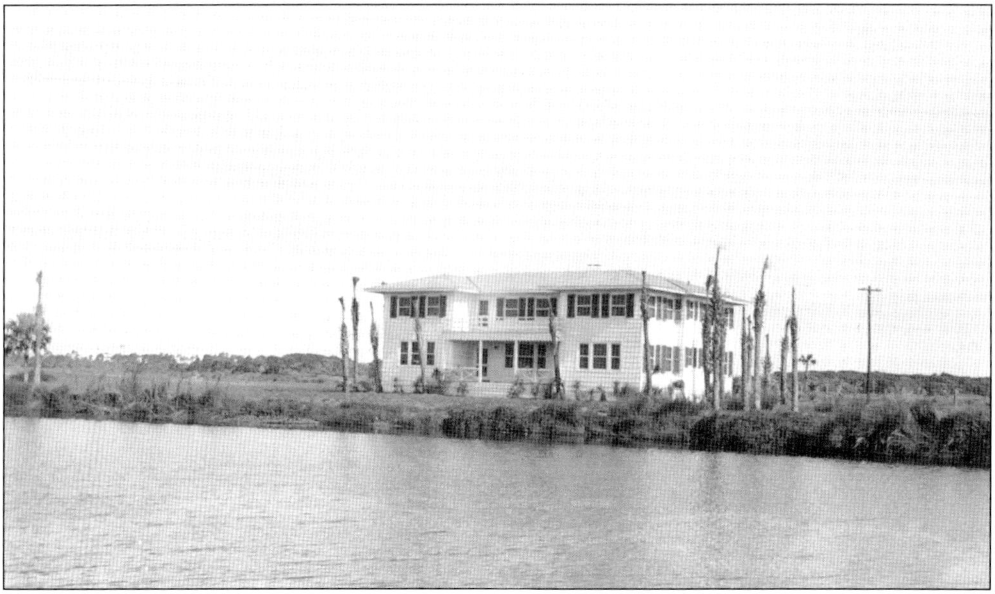

This 1935 photograph shows the Ponte Vedra Club Apartment House framed by a lagoon, proof of the town's development during that decade. The image also shows how much more land was available for development at that time.

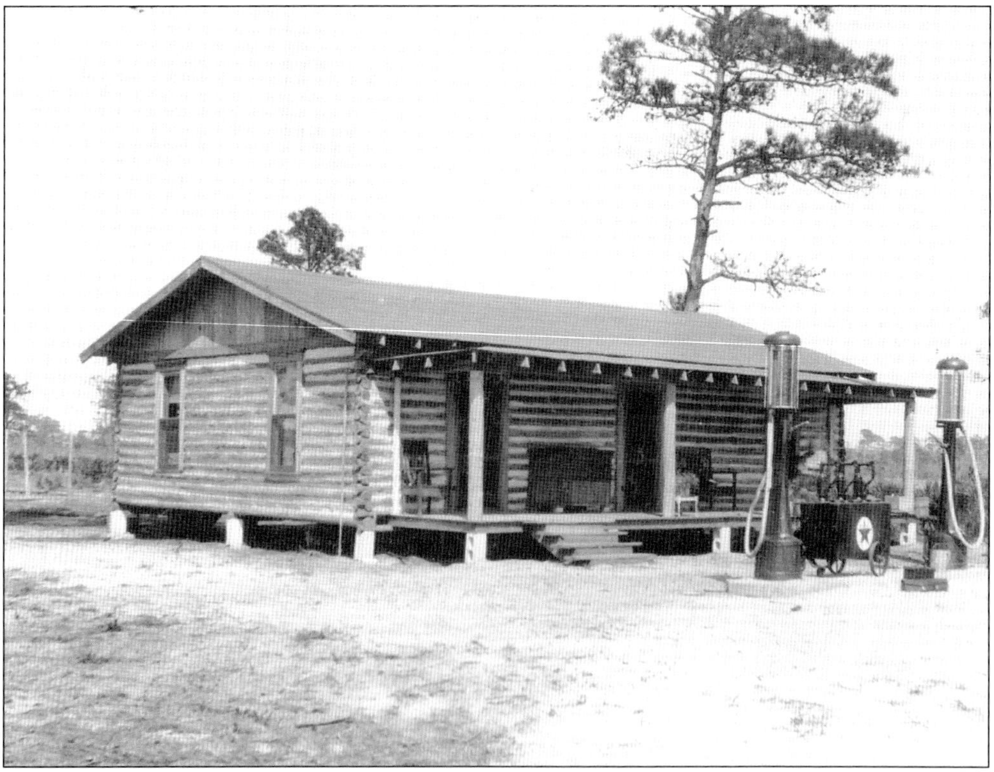

The Texaco gas station at Mickler's Landing was an important stop for automobiles in Ponte Vedra Beach in the 1940s. It had two gas pumps and an oil pump cart. Gas sold for 18¢ to 20¢ a gallon. The building, which had a porch, sat on cinder blocks.

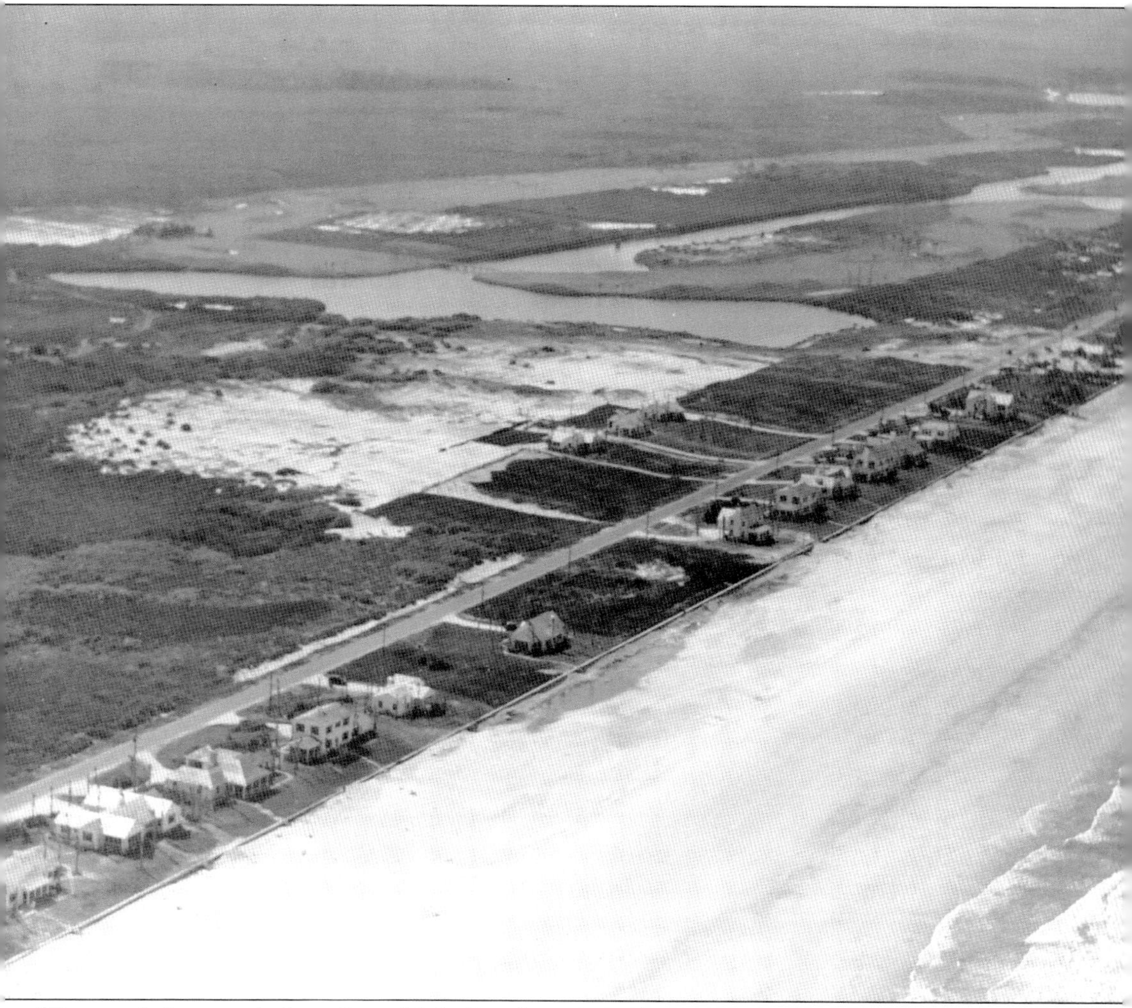

This aerial photograph shows Ponte Vedra Beach in 1940. The 500 block of Ponte Vedra Boulevard is seen framed by the Atlantic Ocean. At that time, there were beachfront homes, but much of the land west of the beach was undeveloped.

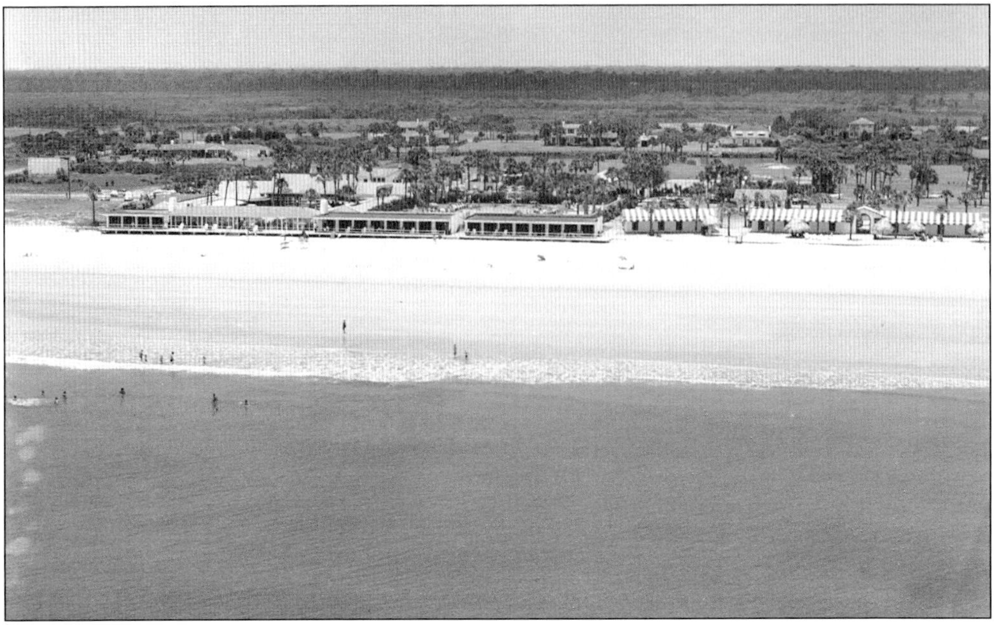

This is a wide-angle aerial shot of beachfront in Ponte Vedra Beach in the 1940s. Photographs such as this document the town's growth since its beginning and show how much it has grown since that time.

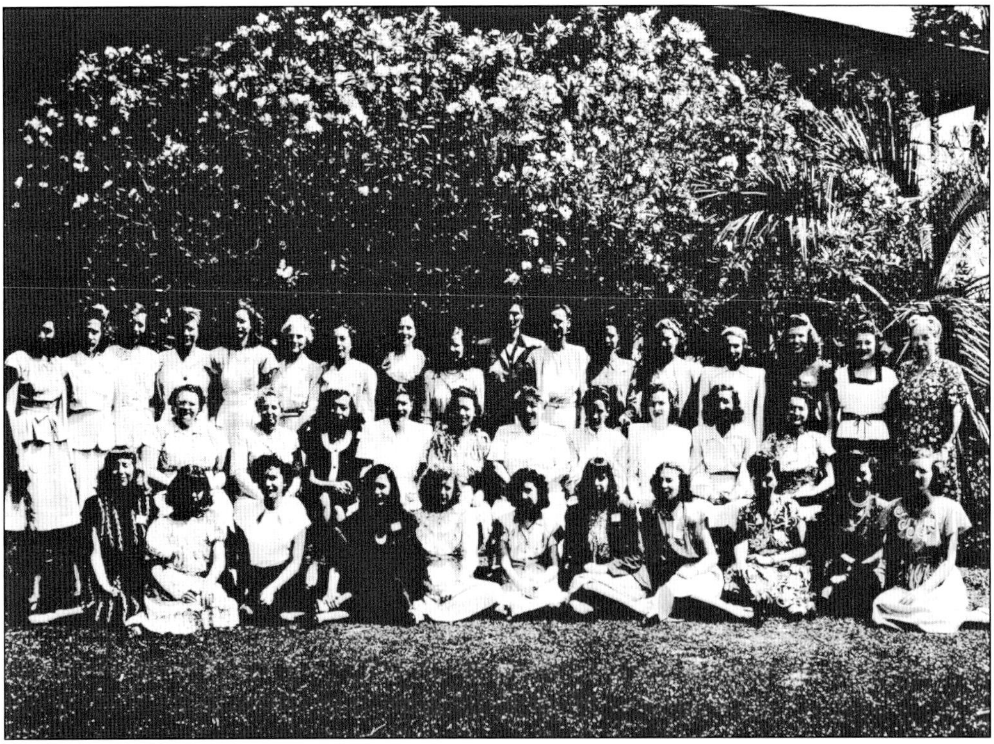

People gather for a group photograph in 1947 in the Ponte Vedra Beach area, which was growing rapidly during that decade. Vacationers were attracted to the area, but many people moved there to live.

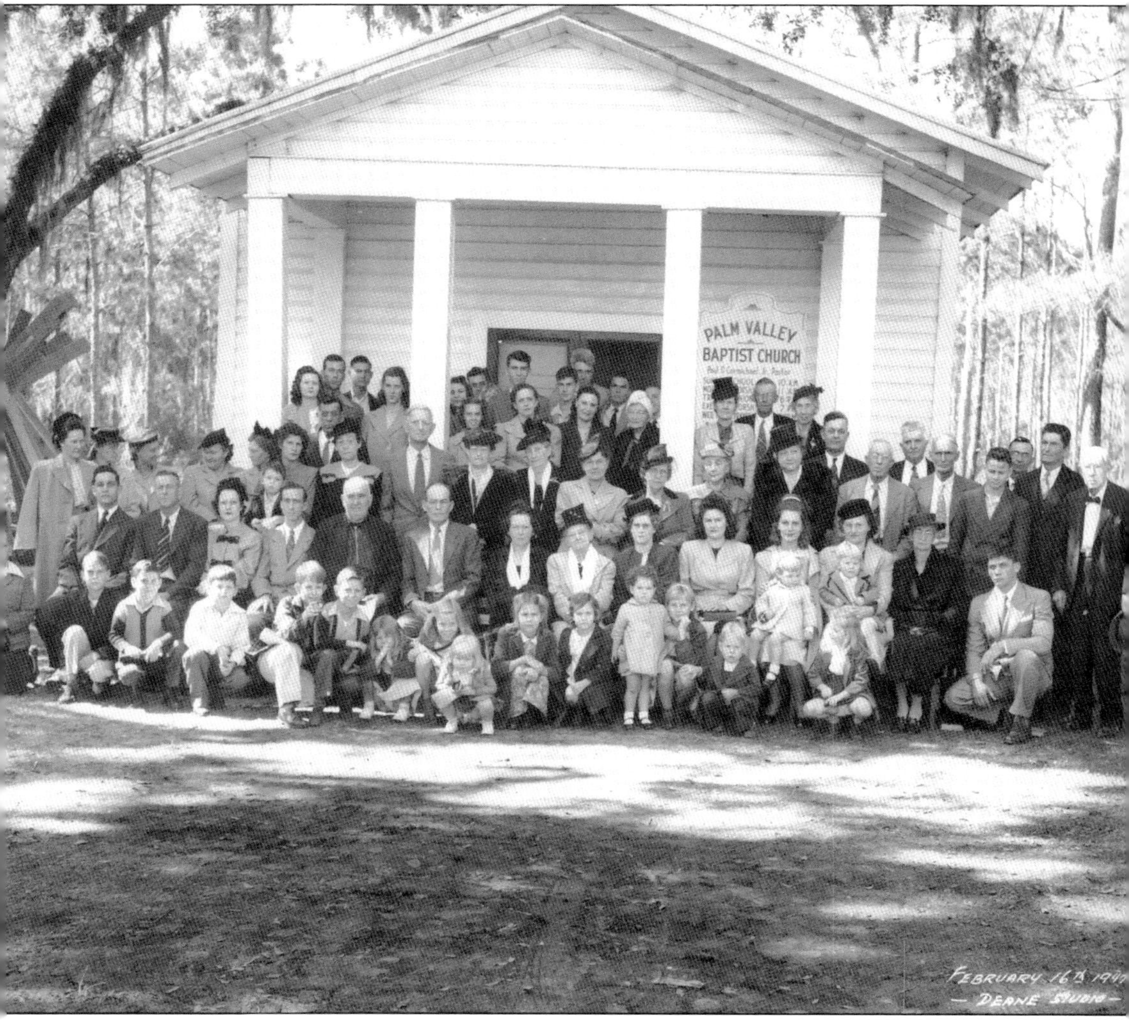


Members of the Palm Valley Baptist Church gather in their Sunday best for a group picture on February 16, 1947. It was one of the first churches in the area. As Palm Valley and Ponte Vedra Beach increased in population, more churches were created. Today, Roscoe Boulevard, a major road through Palm Valley, is lined with churches and a synagogue.

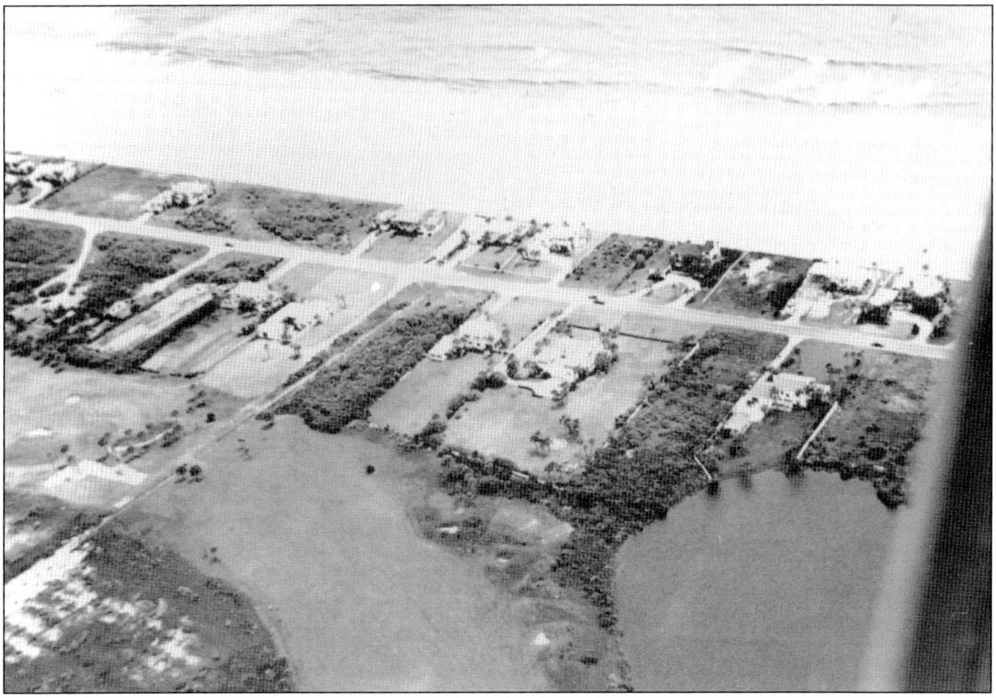

This 1948 aerial photograph shows the 400 block of Ponte Vedra Boulevard looking east. As the town developed, many people built oceanfront homes on the boulevard, the area's most valuable real estate.

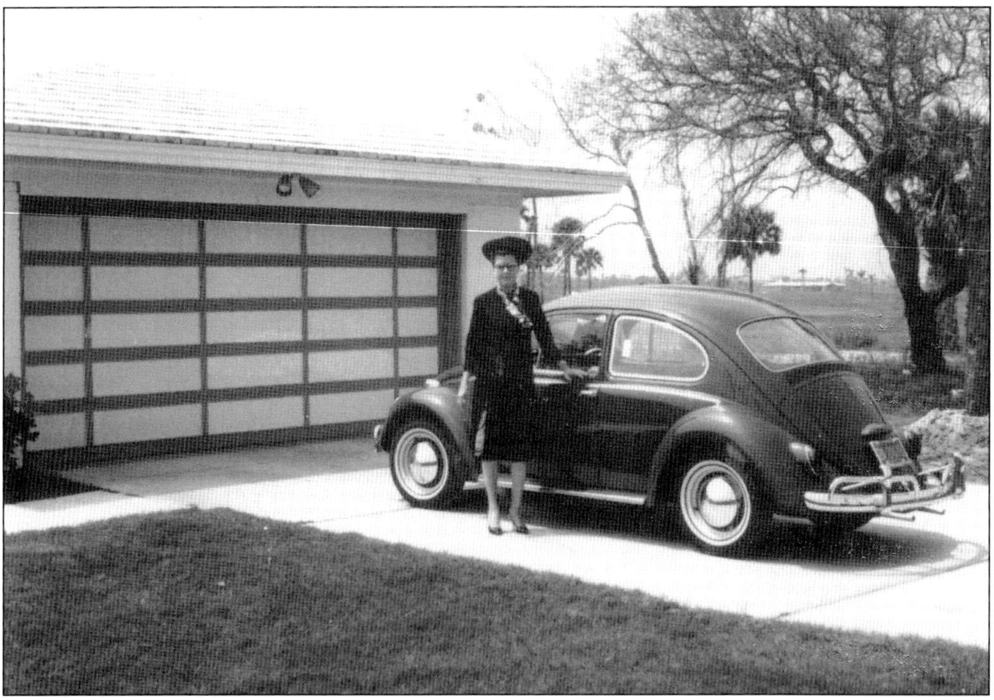

A woman stands by her new house in Ponte Vedra Beach in the mid-20th century. New houses sprang up during that time in many parts of town.

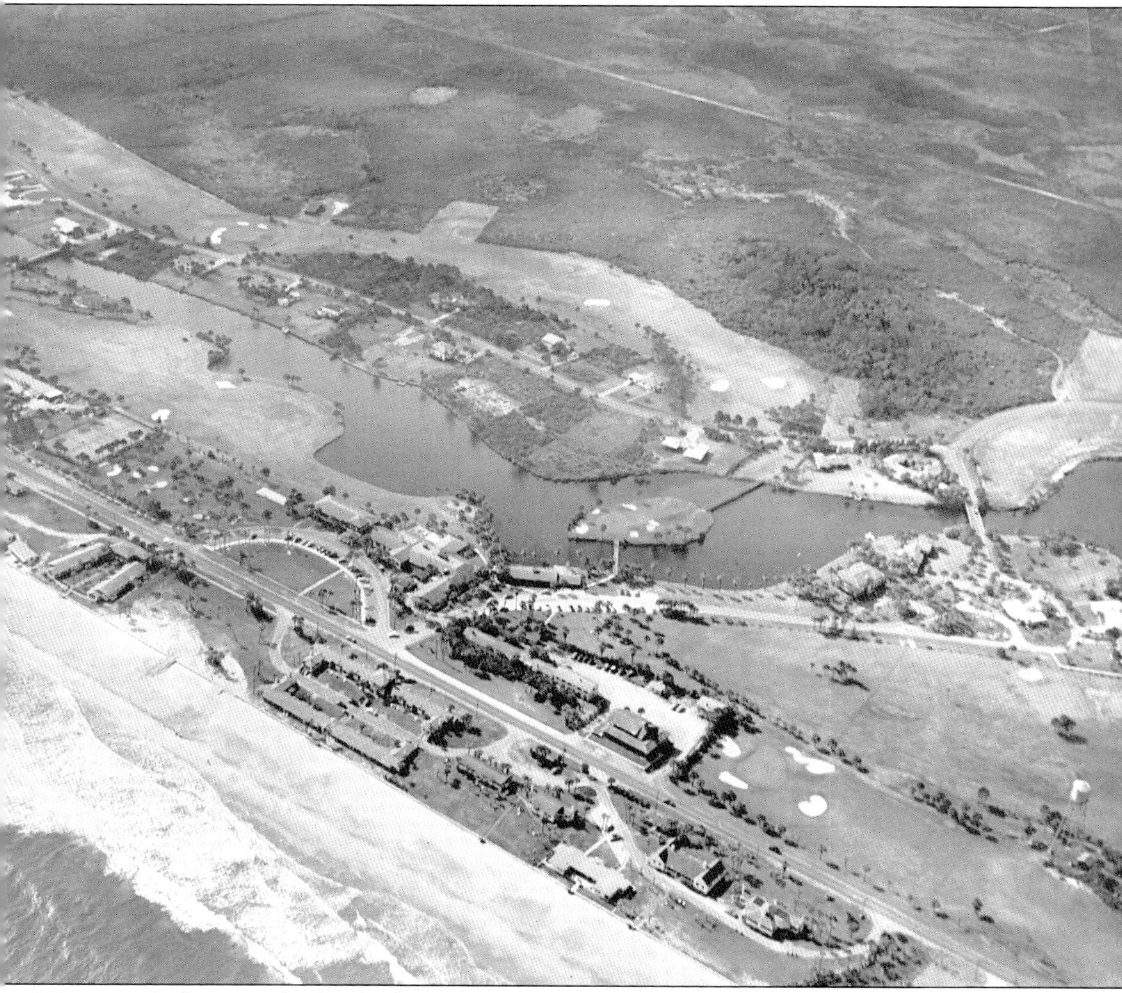

This aerial photograph clearly shows much of Ponte Vedra Beach in the mid-1900s. The year is not identified, but the image depicts the development of the town since it began as a mining operation.

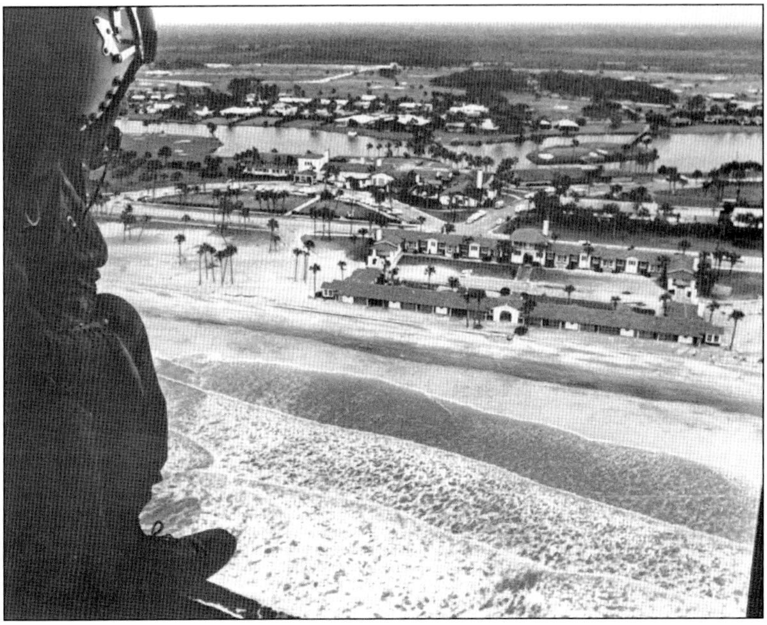

A helicopter pilot looks down on Ponte Vedra Boulevard in 1964. That was the year Hurricane Dora came ashore to the south, causing a lot of damage to oceanfront properties. The town soon recovered.

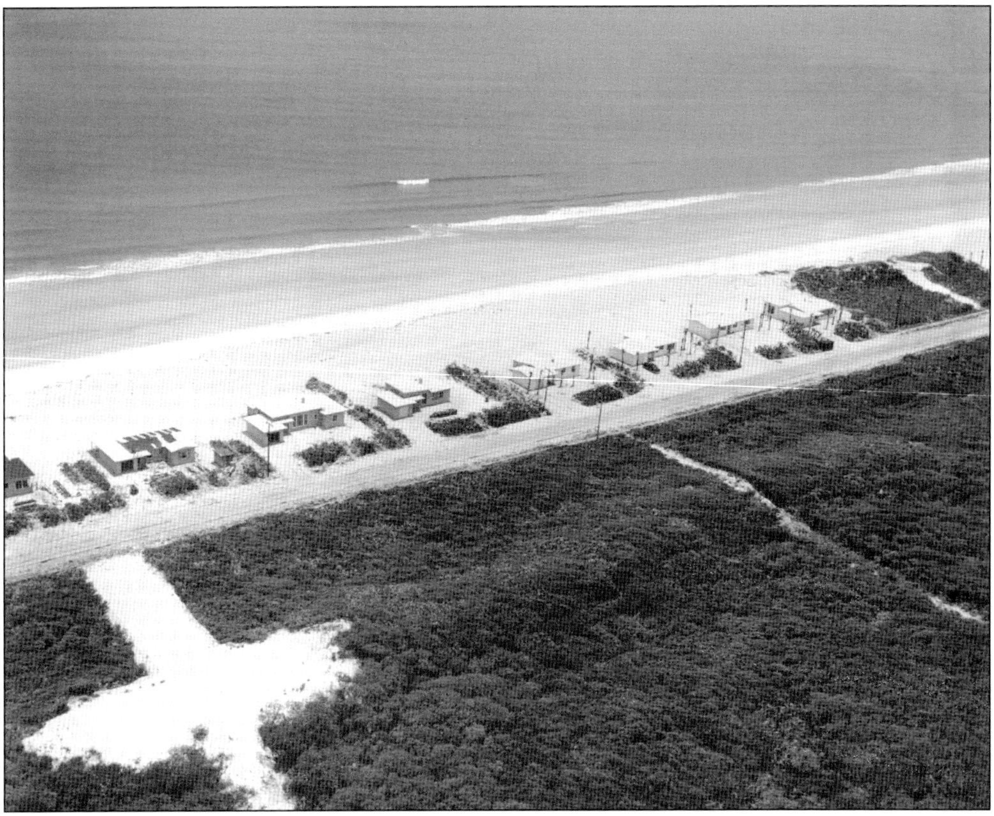

This aerial photograph shows how Ponte Vedra Beach was growing in the middle of the 20th century. Today, the town is famous for being the home of the PGA Tour and the site of The Players Championship, which many consider golf's fifth major.

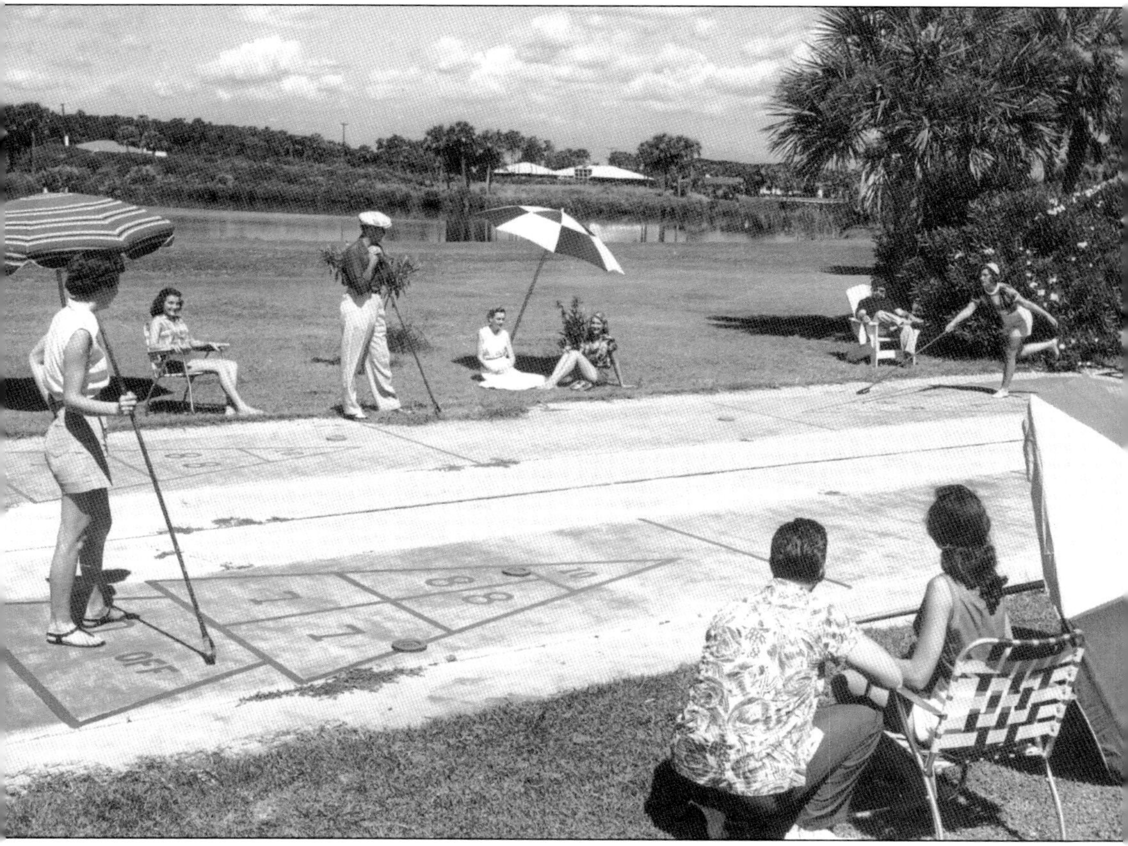

People play shuffleboard in Ponte Vedra Beach sometime during the mid-1900s. The image captures a slice of life in the growing northeast Florida seaside community.

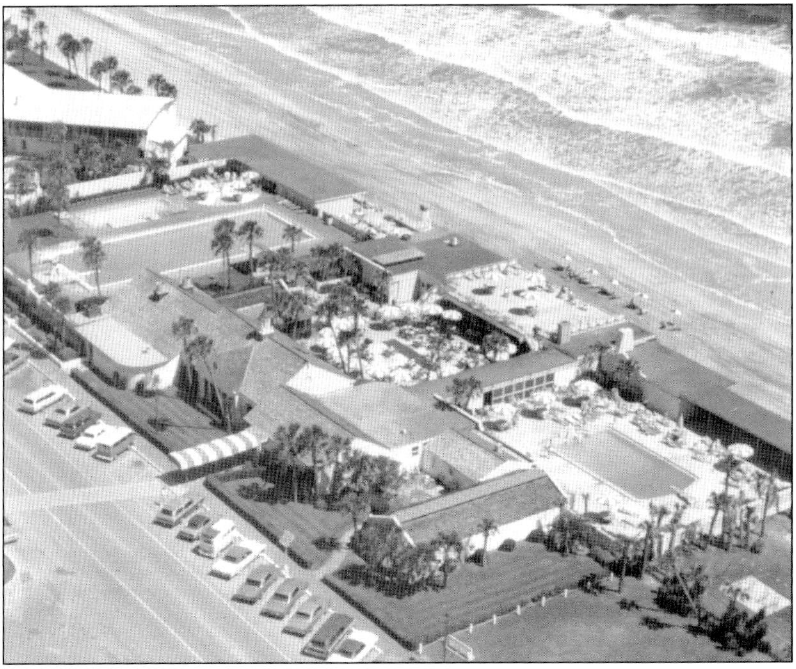

This is an aerial shot of the Ponte Vedra Club in the mid-1900s. The club drew people from nearby Jacksonville, 18 miles north and west, and other areas of the country.

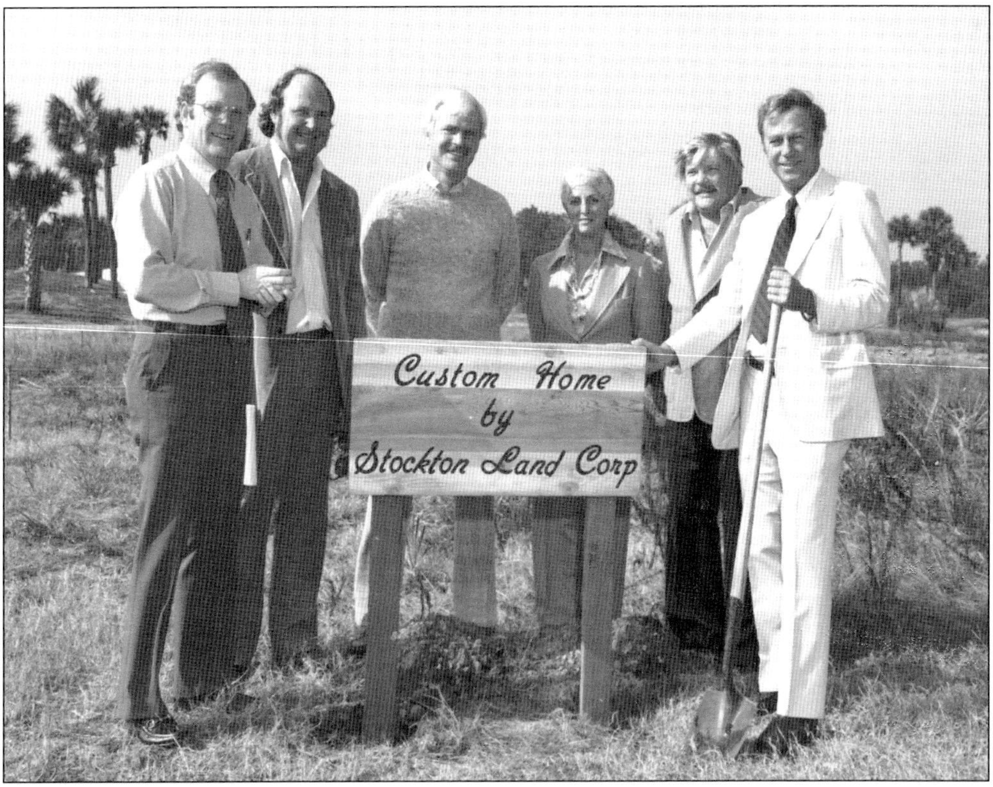


Developers stand by a sign for custom homes in the growing community of Ponte Vedra Beach. In the 1970s and 1980s, more people moved there from the North, attracted to the beautiful area and its balmy weather.

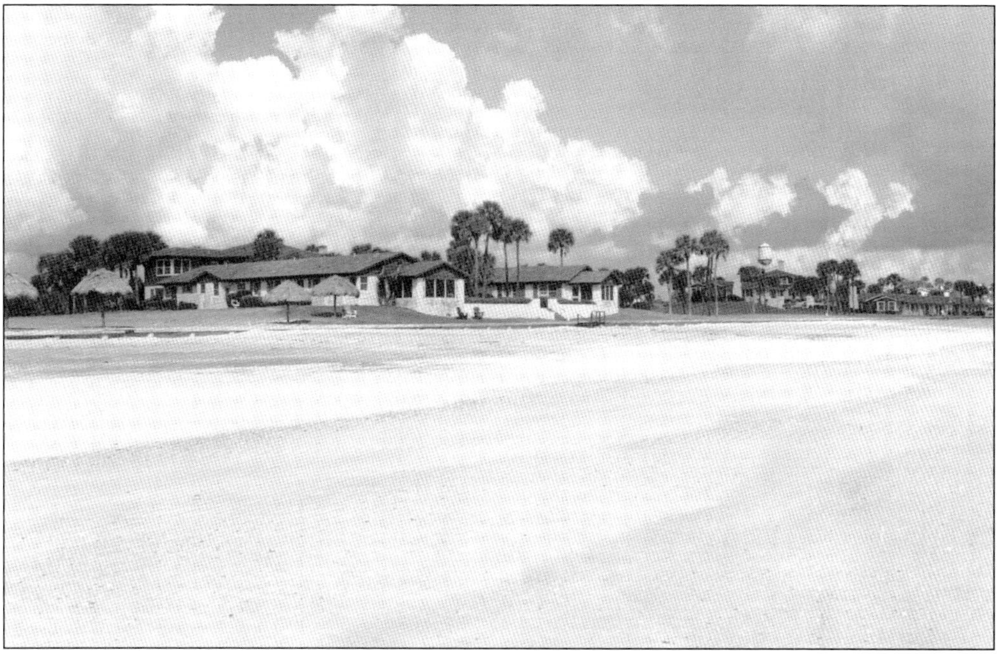

This wide-angle shot of Ponte Vedra Beach was taken by popular Jacksonville Beach–based photographer Virgil Deane in 1953. The thousands of photographs Deane took over several decades preserved the visual history of the town and the other beach towns east of Jacksonville.

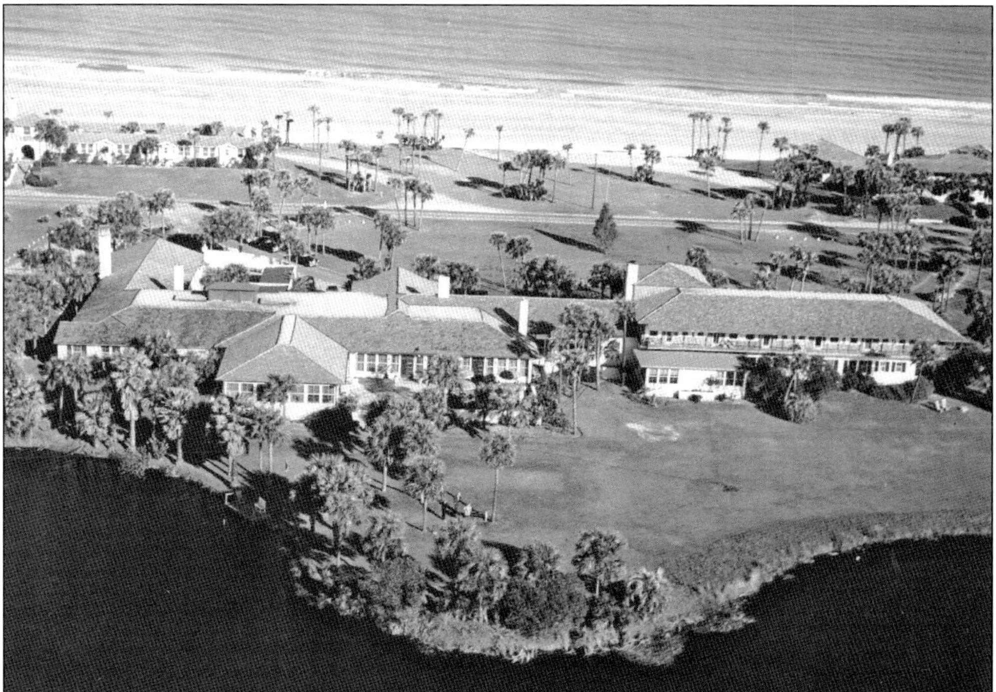

This is a mid-20th-century aerial image of the Ponte Vedra Club overlooking the Atlantic Ocean. The club had grown from its earlier years, when it started with a log cabin clubhouse and a nine-hole golf course.

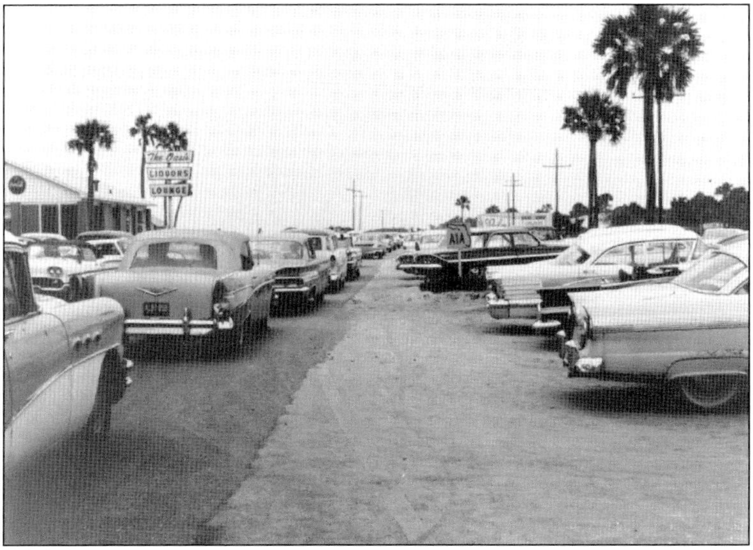


Cars fill the parking lot of Oasis Liquors and Lounge in 1962. The popular Ponte Vedra Beach establishment was owned by Barney Compton. Some regulars called it Barney's, and it was popular with people from Jacksonville Beach. Located near the site of the present-day lodge and club, it was torn down in 1968.

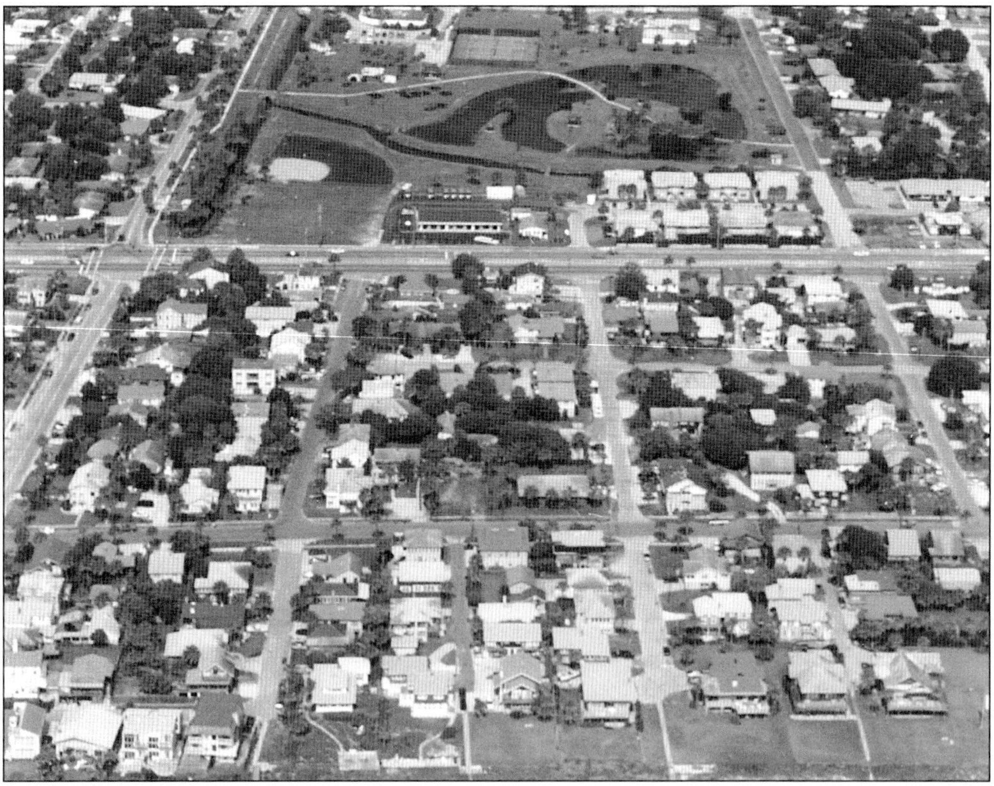

This aerial photograph shows Ponte Vedra Beach in the middle of the 20th century. More people were discovering that the unincorporated town located 26 miles north of St. Augustine was a great place to call home.

This is a 1969 aerial view of Ponte Vedra Beach. By that year, the town was growing rapidly, but the image also indicates how much land was still available for development at that time.

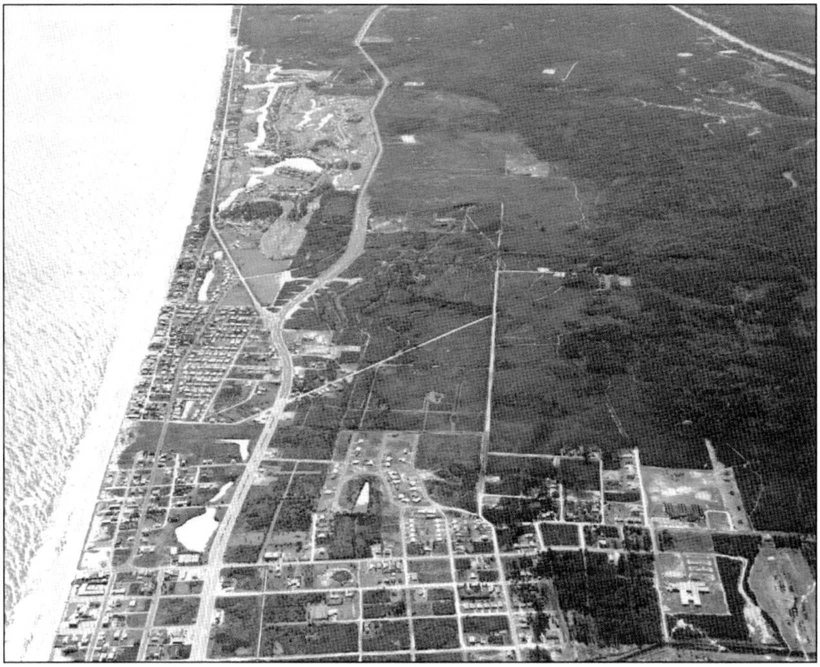

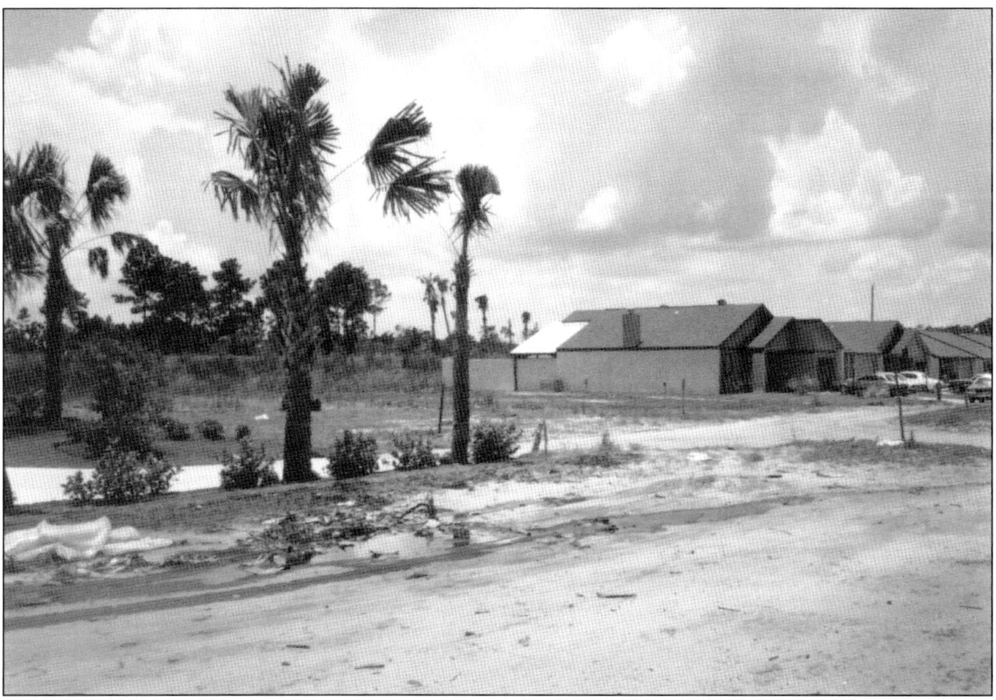

The community of L'Atrium was developed in the 1970s in Ponte Vedra Beach, east of Florida A1A. This photograph shows construction of the community's entrance. The community is located directly across A1A from Sawgrass Village shopping center in the heart of town.

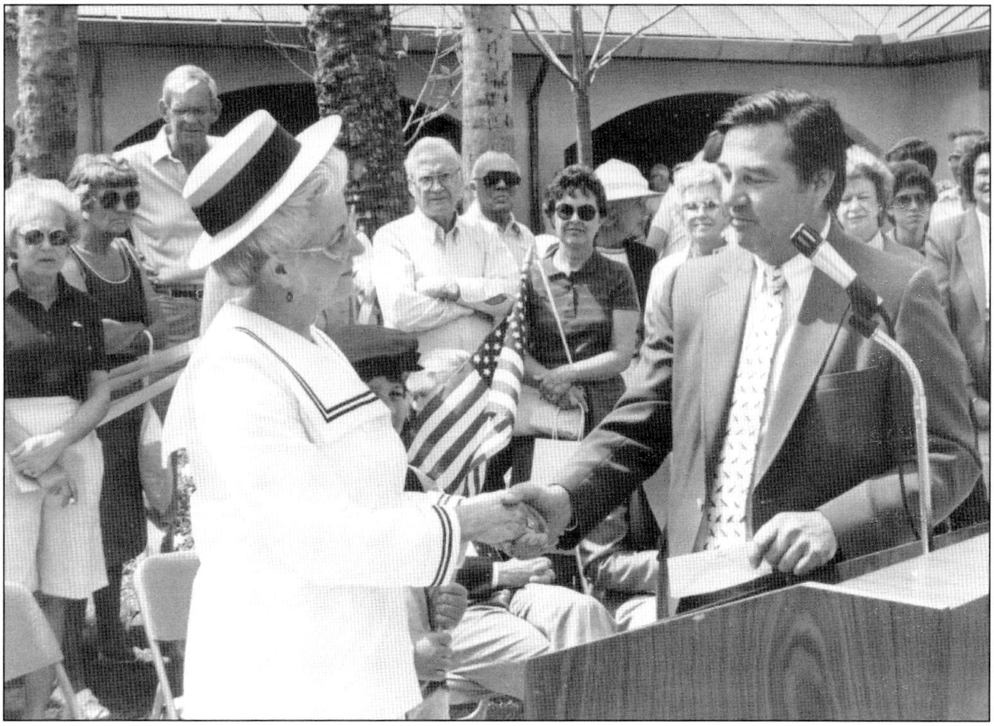

The Sawgrass Village shopping center on Florida A1A opened in 1984. Seen at the opening, celebrated on March 17, Jean McCormick, president of the Beaches Area Historical Society, accepts a donation check from Bill Shuben, president of the Arvida Commercial and Industrial Division.

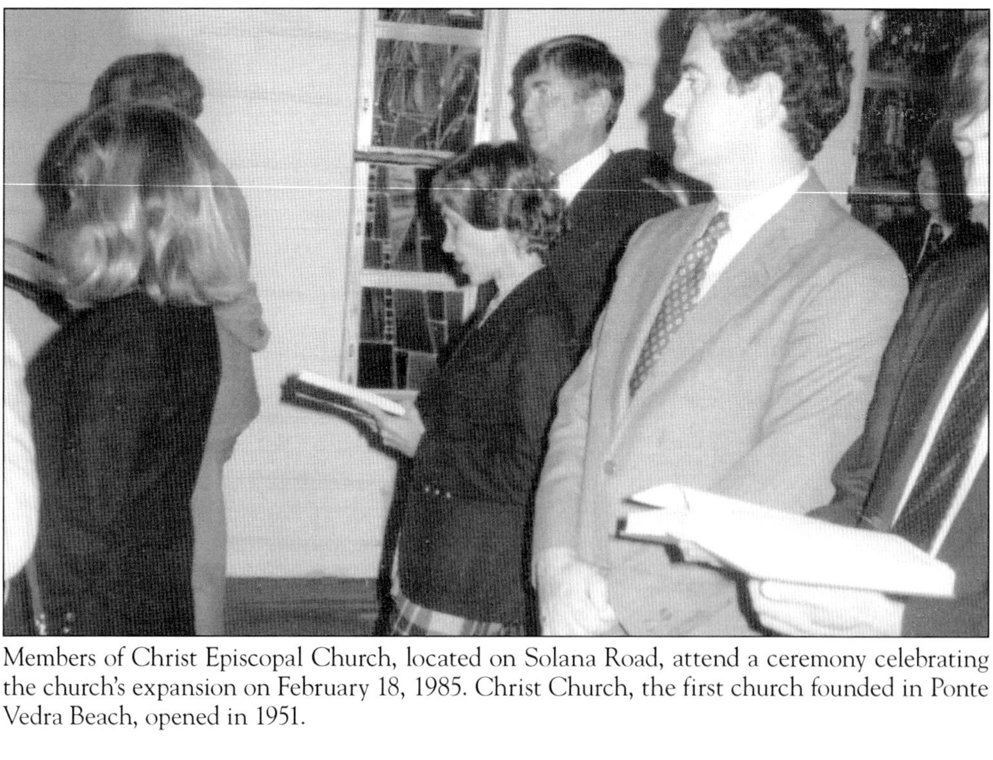

Members of Christ Episcopal Church, located on Solana Road, attend a ceremony celebrating the church's expansion on February 18, 1985. Christ Church, the first church founded in Ponte Vedra Beach, opened in 1951.

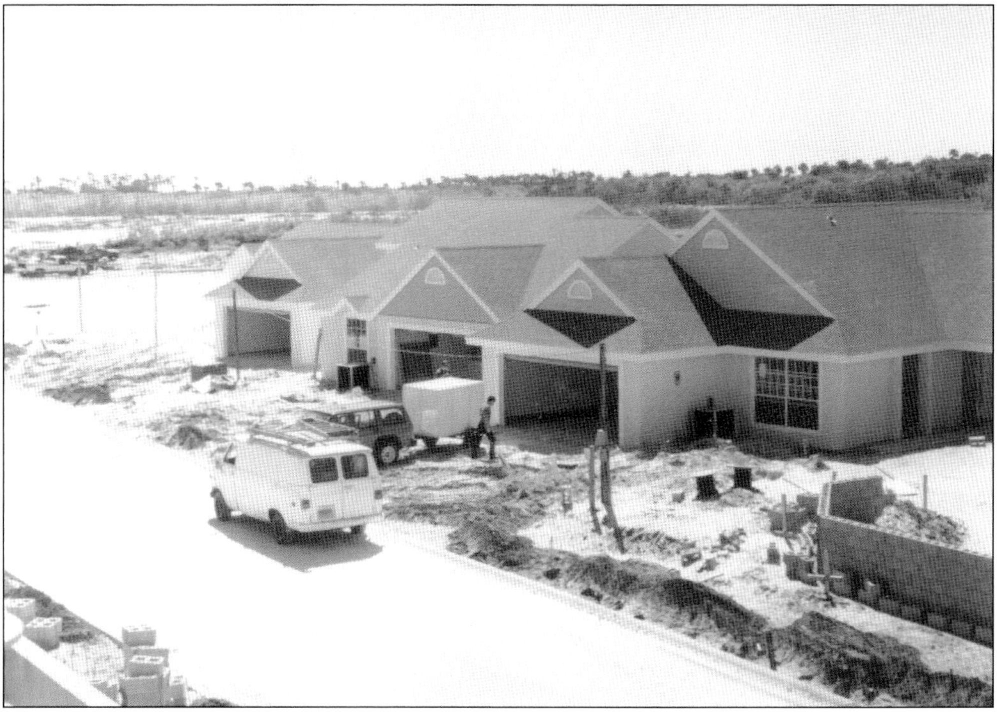

The Ponte Vedra Beach community of Fiddler's Marsh was built east of Florida A1A, behind L'Atrium, in the 1980s. This photograph shows construction of the entrance.

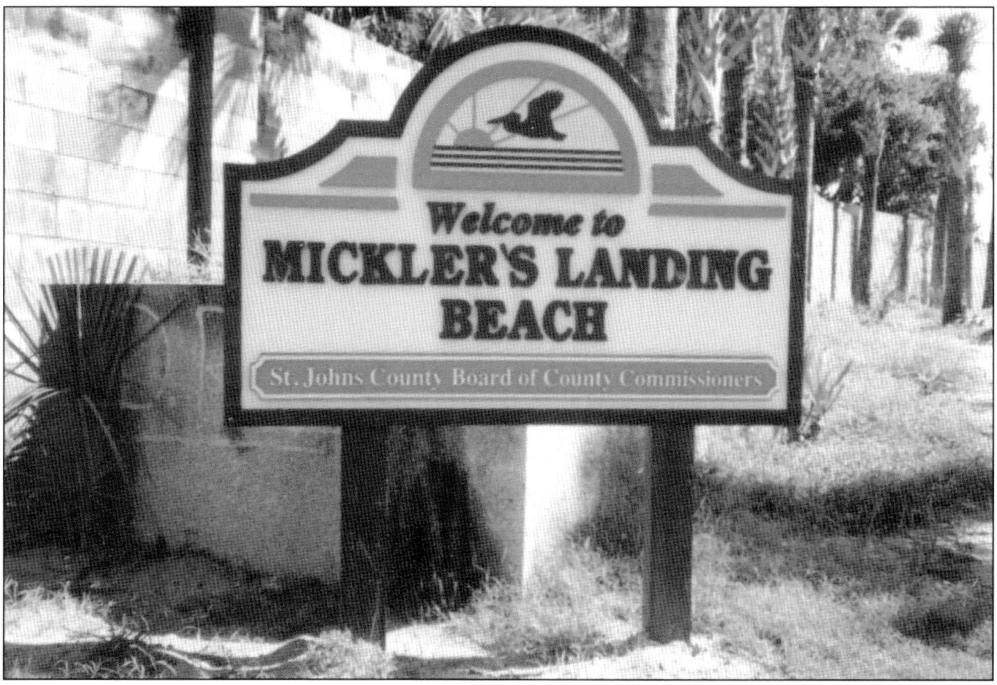


This picture shows the sign at Mickler's Landing Beach in 1999. Owned and managed by St. Johns County, the site is the only public beach access point in Ponte Vedra Beach. Manned by lifeguards, it is very popular in the summer.

# Discover Thousands of Local History Books Featuring Millions of Vintage Images

Arcadia Publishing, the leading local history publisher in the United States, is committed to making history accessible and meaningful through publishing books that celebrate and preserve the heritage of America's people and places.

Find more books like this at
**www.arcadiapublishing.com**

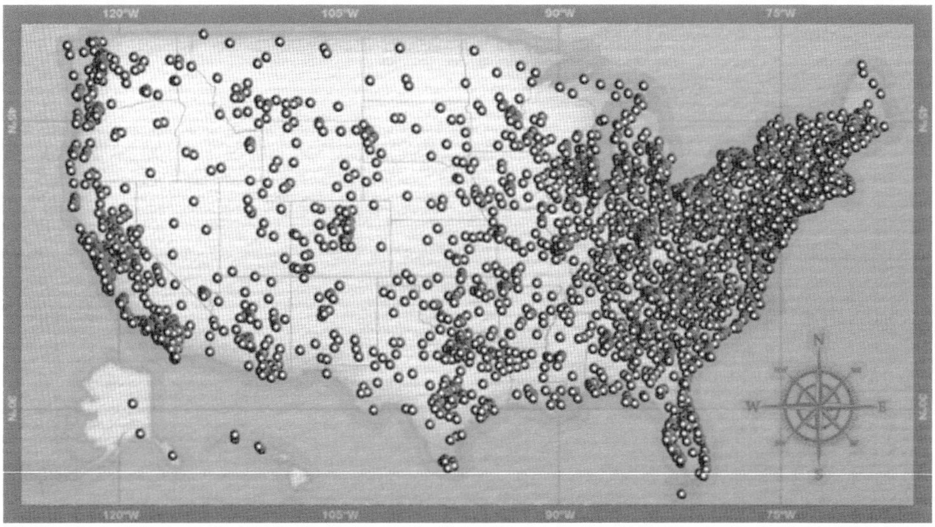


Search for your hometown history, your old stomping grounds, and even your favorite sports team.

Consistent with our mission to preserve history on a local level, this book was printed in South Carolina on American-made paper and manufactured entirely in the United States. Products carrying the accredited Forest Stewardship Council (FSC) label are printed on 100 percent FSC-certified paper.

MADE IN THE USA